Advance praise for
The Money-Making Guide to Bonds: Straightforward Strategies for Picking the Right Bonds and Bond Funds
by Hildy Richelson and Stan Richelson

"The Money-Making Guide to Bonds is a **clear and comprehensive** road map for the novice and professional investor alike. This book is **required reading** for those who want to take charge of their financial destiny."

> JOHN B. BRYNJOLFSSON
> Manager
> PIMCO Real Return Bond Fund

"In these times, when good information is more important than ever, we're pleased to see this volume about bonds. Our association is committed to making sure investors have access to timely, accurate information about bonds and the bond markets, and this book helps achieve that goal."

> MICAH S. GREEN
> President
> The Bond Market Association

"This excellent resource is designed for investors of all means and sophistication who want to take responsibility for their own financial lives. **It's one of the best books on bonds I've seen.**"

> GEORGE D. KINDER, CFP
> Author, *The Seven Stages of Money Maturity*

"From far away all bonds may look alike. The Richelsons hone in on the details to show the many differences among bonds and explain how investors can use these differences to their advantage. *The Money-Making Guide to Bonds* is **packed full of essential information presented in an understandable way.**"

> ROBERT L. FREEDMAN
> Senior Partner, Estate and Financial Planning
> Dechert

"A terrific primer for the investor who wants **an education on the basic principles of investing in bonds.**"

> BILL D'ALONZO
> CEO
> Friess Associates LLC, which manages the
> Brandywine Funds

THE
MONEY-
MAKING
GUIDE TO
BONDS

Other Titles from Bloomberg Press

Investing in REITs: Real Estate Investment Trusts
Revised and Updated Edition
by Ralph L. Block

Wall Street Secrets for Tax-Efficient Investing:
From Tax Pain to Investment Gain
by Robert N. Gordon with Jan M. Rosen

Investing 101
by Kathy Kristof

Investing in Hedge Funds: Strategies for the New Marketplace
by Joseph G. Nicholas

The New Commonsense Guide to Mutual Funds
by Mary Rowland

Investing in IPOs—Version 2.0: Revised and Updated Version
by Tom Taulli

A complete list of our titles is available at
www.Bloomberg.com/Books

BLOOMBERG PERSONAL FINANCE® magazine is for active sophisticated investors. Every issue brings you professional insights into making the best investments, building a solid portfolio, and keeping more of your wealth. See **Bloomberg.com** for subscription information or call 1-888-432-5820.

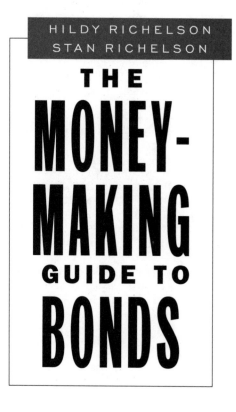

HILDY RICHELSON
STAN RICHELSON

THE
MONEY-
MAKING
GUIDE TO
BONDS

**Straightforward Strategies
for Picking the Right Bonds
and Bond Funds**

BLOOMBERG PRESS
PRINCETON

Books are available for bulk purchases at special discounts. Special editions or book excerpts can also be created to specifications. For information, please write: Special Markets Department, Bloomberg Press.

This publication contains the author's opinions and is designed to provide accurate and authoritative information. It is sold with the understanding that the author, publisher, and Bloomberg L.P. are not engaged in rendering legal, accounting, invest-ment-planning, or other professional advice. The reader should seek the services of a qualified professional for such advice; the author, publisher, and Bloomberg L.P. cannot be held responsible for any loss incurred as a result of specific investments or planning decisions made by the reader.

First edition published 2002
1 3 5 7 9 10 8 6 4 2

Library of Congress Cataloging-in-Publication Data

Richelson, Hildy.
    The money-making guide to bonds : straightforward strategies for picking the right bonds and bond funds / Hildy Richelson and Stan Richelson.
        p.   cm.
    Includes index.
    ISBN 1-57660-122-6 (alk. paper)
    1. Bonds.   I. Richelson, Stan.   II. Title.
HG4651 .528   2002
332.63'23 --dc21   2002006573

Acquired by Kathleen A. Peterson
Book design by Don Morris Design

To our mothers, Elsie and Bea, who give us hugs.

*To our children, Jolie and Evan Carpenter and Scott Richelson,
who nurture us.*

*To those special people in our lives, Carole Haas Gravagno,
Drs. Sam and Diana Kirschner, Judith and Milton Moskowitz,
George Robinson, and Dr. Abby Van Voorhees, who have
mentored us and provided intellectual and
emotional support to us over the years.*

CONTENTS

PART II: BOND CATEGORIES 39

PART III: BOND PURCHASE OPTIONS   165

CHAPTER 10

The Self-Directed Approach:
How to Buy Individual Bonds 167

CHAPTER 11

The Managed Approach:
How to Choose among Bond Funds 181

PART IV: BOND INVESTMENT STRATEGIES 211

CHAPTER 12

Asset Allocation: How to Fit Bonds
into a Portfolio That's Best for You 213

CHAPTER 13

The Maximization of Profits:
How to Make the Most Money from Investing in Bonds 229

Appendix: Useful Websites 255

Notes 259

Index 264

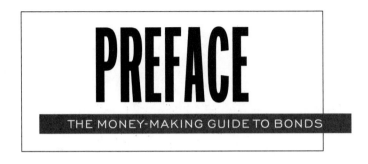

PREFACE

THE MONEY-MAKING GUIDE TO BONDS

INVESTING IN STOCKS was all the rage in the late 1990s. However, stocks tanked in 2000 and 2001, and investors were reacquainted with the old Wall Street adage: Trees do not grow to the sky. As stocks became scary, investors rediscovered the world of bonds and their benefits. Yet the reality is that bonds have always provided a secure place in the world of investments because of their enduring role in solving financial problems.

Investments in bonds have grown significantly since stocks peaked in March 2000. Investors now understand that they can make money with bonds, and that bonds, just like stocks, are an essential part of an investment program. In fact, for the investor who is risk averse or cannot afford to lose money, bonds are hugely important. While one can base a financial plan solely on stock appreciation, it is a risky strategy. Investing in bonds provides the income component that stocks used to provide.

The bond market may at first seem complicated. However, its principles are straightforward and can be mastered by everyone. This book provides you with the tools to understand and successfully master the bond market so that you can build and protect your capital and effectively realize your financial and life goals.

The world has changed drastically in the past twenty years. The economic safety net has become frayed. Job security has sharply declined, company-sponsored pension plans are becoming extinct, and many people worry about the health of the Social Security system. Given these concerns, we all benefit by taking responsibility for our own financial security. Many articles in the popular press describe bonds as the most misunderstood investment. This book answers the call for clarity and seeks to rectify misconceptions about bonds.

Who Should Read This Book?

THE MONEY-MAKING GUIDE TO BONDS is designed to educate novice and sophisticated investors alike and can serve as a useful tool for financial advisers as well. If you want to be able to take responsibility for your financial life, this book can be an indispensable guide to your decision making. We present a broad spectrum of bond investment options and advise how to use bonds to solve certain of your financial problems, how to purchase bonds at the best prices, and most important, how to make money with bonds.

The book offers a tool kit of straightforward bond strategies that are used by the wealthiest investors and financial advisers to maximize the return on their bond portfolios while providing security of principal. This information will enable you to successfully determine how bonds fit into your portfolio and investment program. Using these strategies can help you take control of your own financial destiny, by playing it smart while playing it safe.

We wrote this book to share our knowledge about bonds and the use of bonds in financial planning that we acquired over many years of practice. Stan Richelson practices as a fee-only financial adviser. Hildy Richelson limits her practice to advising on bonds and building bond portfolios on a fee-only basis.

The Case for Bonds

IN TODAY'S FINANCIAL MARKETS there are powerful reasons why you should include bonds as part of your investment strategy. Here are some of the advantages that bonds provide:

◆ **Preservation of principal.** Investing in highly rated bonds enables you to make money without significant risk to your principal. Joe Lewis once said that money quiets the nerves. The peace-of-mind factor is something the bond investor can come to know and appreciate. One of our simple investment rules is "Don't lose money." Although losing money is never pleasant, the older you are the more difficult it becomes to recoup losses with your future earned income. Investments in bonds can be essentially risk free if you learn about them, buy them in appropriate situations, and follow the advice that we provide in this book.

◆ **Predictable interest payments.** Bonds serve as a powerful vehicle to help you realize your financial and life objectives. The return on bonds is to a large degree predicable. You know what stream of income the bonds will produce and the date that the face amount will be returned to you. This stream of income provides a cushion if the cash flow from your paycheck dries up.

◆ **Price appreciation from trading.** Some bond investors trade bonds like stocks in order to increase their overall return. The hope is that interest rates will decline, thus boosting the value of bond holdings that can be sold to reap a profit. Likewise, some bond funds are dedicated to a total-return approach. They frequently turn over their portfolios more than 100 percent per year aiming to produce a higher return. Bond interest payments cushion the price fluctuations of the funds, making them less volatile.

Organization of the Book

THE MONEY-MAKING GUIDE TO BONDS is laid out in four parts, namely: bond basics, descriptions of the major categories of bonds, how to buy bonds, and using bond strategies to structure your portfolio.

Part I provides an overview of bond basics. In Chapter 1 we show how bond structures are rooted in history. Bond language, often arcane, is easier understood placed in its historical context. In Chapter 2 we explain how a bond is created, issued, priced, and traded. While other bond books describe basic concepts, we provide this information in an easy-to-grasp way, placing it within the context of a bond's life.

Part II introduces all the major categories of bonds and compares them in detail in a uniform and user-friendly format. There are descriptions of Treasuries, inflation-protected bonds, U.S. savings bonds, agency bonds, mortgage securities, municipal bonds, and corporate bonds (including junk bonds). In addition, there is a chapter describing certain bond look-alikes (CDs, fixed annuities, and preferred stock). The distinguishing feature of Part II is that each bond's advantages, disadvantages, tax implications, pricing, and special features are highlighted, allowing for easy comparison from one bond type to another.

Part III describes how an investor can buy bonds using a broker, online, or through mutual funds and similar vehicles. Included is thoroughly practical "real-world" advice on how to buy bonds without the use of an investment adviser, how to best use a broker, and how, through use of the Internet and other techniques, to evaluate the price of a bond. Hildy draws on her many years of experience representing clients in their purchase and sale of bonds. This chapter tells the secrets of the trade from the perspective of the experienced investor.

If you do not want to direct the purchase of bonds, you can rely on Chapter 11 to learn how to buy bonds through mutual funds, unit investment trusts, and exchange-traded funds. As an aid to our readers, we provide comprehensive treatment of all the different types of bond funds and indicate in what fund format they are available.

Part IV, dealing with bond strategies, is rich in detail and will enable you to determine how bonds can best fit into your portfolio. Chapter 12, on the vital subject of asset allocation, describes how to apportion your assets between stocks and bonds, and then how to choose among the bond categories to support your financial and life needs. Chapter 13 not only discusses techniques geared for the individual investor but also offers a complete checklist of strategies useful as well for investment advisers and other professionals. Specific strategies address the following topics: determining when to buy and sell, finding bargain bonds, keeping away from overvalued bonds, what to do when interest rates are rising or are falling, investing for tax advantages, investing by risk tolerance, and investing for income needs.

Finally, an Appendix of useful websites annotating those mentioned throughout the text serves as an invaluable reference for finding information on the Internet. You will discover sites for bond calculators, yield curves, and other practical tools.

How to Use the Book

THE MONEY-MAKING GUIDE TO BONDS may be used in a number of ways. If you are curious about the history of bonds, and especially if you are a novice bond investor, we recommend Chapter 1. Read Chapter 2 if you are unfamiliar with bond terms. A host of specialized vocabulary relating to bonds is defined in these two chapters.

If you already understand bond terminology, you might use the book more as a reference tool by skipping around the categories of bonds found in Part II. You can look up a particular kind of bond or a bond look-alike, for example, and readily compare one bond to another.

Once you decide to buy bonds, visit Part III to determine whether to buy individual bonds or bond funds. If you are interested in buying individual bonds, see Chapter 10 on how to choose and work with a broker and find pricing information online. Chapter 11 describes how bond funds are organized and all the different kinds available, including their advantages and disadvantages.

Visit Chapter 12 for guidance on the all-important topic of asset allocation in the context of financial planning. And keep in mind that at any and all points in your involvement with the bond world you will want to think strategically. If you are already generally knowledgeable about bond categories, you might want to read Chapter 13, the strategy chapter, first.

Surf the Internet using the sites listed throughout the book, or find them collected in the Appendix with an annotated summary. However you decide to approach this book you will find it has a wealth of practical information about bonds and bond funds.

Acknowledgments

THE MOST SIGNIFICANT CONTRIBUTION to *The Money-Making Guide to Bonds* was made by Patricia A. Taylor, the editor of this book and an author in her own right. Her fingerprints are everywhere, simplifying and clarifying very difficult concepts. She also made major contributions to the organization and style of the manuscript. We are grateful for her help.

We want to express our appreciation to the staff at Bloomberg L.P. for their expert and very professional help in producing this book. We wish to particularly acknowledge Bloomberg Press senior acquisitions editor Kathleen A. Peterson and associate editor Tracy Tait, as well as Joe Mysak of Bloomberg News and Christopher Graja of *Bloomberg Markets* magazine for their thoughtful editorial comments.

We would like to express our deep appreciation to the following individuals who reviewed portions of the book and shared their wisdom with us, with the understanding that all errors are ours. We particularly wish to thank and acknowledge Victor Keen, Esq., Chair of the Tax Practice Group at Duane Morris, who reviewed some of the tax aspects of bonds, and John B. Brynjolfsson, CFA, Executive Vice President, Pacific Investment Management Company (PIMCO), who provided significant help on the Treasuries chapter.

We also wish to thank the following people who read portions of the book and helped with our research: Jolie Carpenter, a teacher in Tarrytown, New York; Evan Carpenter, an analyst at Gabelli & Co.; George H. Connerat, a financial adviser for a private client group in New York City; Jeffrey J. Morse, an investment adviser in a private banking group in Chicago; and Roland Stoever, of Stoever Glass in New York City.

We would like to express our appreciation to the partners of the Visionary Venture Group, L.P.: Jerry Cooper, Esq.; Dr. Sam Kirschner; and Philip Wachs. We were inspired by our association with the Souls Network: Don Arnoudse, Peter Blake, Tom D'Aquanni, Vince DiBianca, Tony Freedley, Dr. Sam Kirschner, Jim Selman, and Gary Taylor. Both of these groups have provided us with love and encouragement.

We wish to acknowledge our friends in the investment community who teach us daily about bonds: Frank B. Ackerman, Joe Arena, Bill Burdick, Ben T. Eiler, Christopher Genovese, Lane Katz, Richard Kidd, Peter Mangin, Peter Mayo, Keith Basilo Papa, Daniel Quigley, Frederick C. Uhde, and Debra Weiner.

We learn about investments and the real world every day from our friends and fellow investors who provide the real-life context to our study and work. By asking questions and sharing aspects of their lives with us, they have helped us enhance and sharpen our skills. We wish to acknowledge and thank: Dr. Edward Adams; Dr. Marilee Goldberg Adams; Rebecca Bell; Dean Bress, Esq.; Dr. Jeffrey Chodakewitz; Douglas Crowley, Esq.; Christopher Doyle, Esq.; Dr. Linda Dresnick; Mark Dresnick, Esq.; Michael Druckman; Nancy Druckman; Jack Frank; Paul Frankel, Esq.; Dr. Robert Gibson; Ellen Greif; Lucien Greif; Carol Leimas; Irwin Leimas, Esq.; David Lihn, Esq.; Michael Nicita; Michael C. Phillips; Neeru Phillips; Dr. Sue Ann Prince; James Quigley; Susan Shane; David Siegel, Esq.; David Smyk; Juliet Spitzer; David L. Threlkeld; and Dr. Stanley Wulf.

PART
ONE

BOND
BASICS

POPULAR THINKING TODAY holds that you can never be too thin or too rich. We guarantee that this book will not make you thin. However, we do believe it will help you to increase your wealth. These pages present detailed information on all types of bonds and also offer investment advice that teaches you how to conservatively preserve your capital and make money with bonds.

This first part explains the history, language, and basics of bonds. Once you have read and digested this material, you will be better equipped to evaluate the information and strategies we present in the remainder of the book. You may think that this is too much work. Why should you be bothered learning all this stuff? You can take the easy way out and invest in stocks or diversify in bond funds without too much thought.

If you believe that the above investment approach affords safety, you may be missing out on an important, fundamental concept. Let us explain it to you this way: *Bonds come due.* You know when you get your principal back! You will get your principal back if you invest in high-grade bonds. Stocks and bond funds do not come due.

In addition, every moment of every day, whether you are awake or sleeping, the interest on your bond is compounding. When the bond pays interest, the money will flow into a money market account, if you so direct your broker, earning interest there until you are ready to reinvest it. If the great bugaboo of inflation raises its head, that should be of no concern of yours if you did not purchase long-term bonds. With each rising sun, your bond comes one day closer to maturity. The passing of each year brings it closer to redemption when it will repay at face value. When inflation lights a fire under the yields, driving the price of your bond down, this is not a reason to despair. You will reinvest your money at a higher rate. *Your bond will come due at face value. You will get your money back.*

In sum, when you make an investment in bonds, you get interest that compounds and grows with every beat of your heart. You have the opportunity for better yields if we have inflation, you are protected from the worst returns in a deflation, and you get your money back. Sounds like a pretty good deal to us!

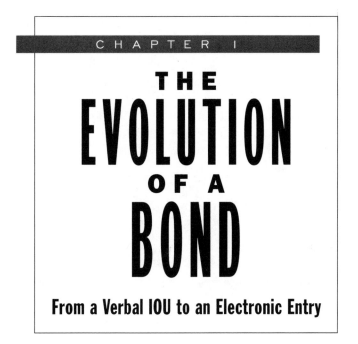

CHAPTER 1

THE
EVOLUTION
OF A
BOND

From a Verbal IOU to an Electronic Entry

BONDS ARE NEGOTIABLE or saleable loans, and what is special about them for investors is that there is a ready marketplace in which to trade them. Some three centuries ago, in 1704, England passed a law making loans negotiable. Today, bonds can be traded like wheat and pork in the commodity markets. The bond markets are called the credit markets, the place where governments and corporations come to gather money to create their dreams. Formerly the province of bankers and kings, these markets are open to us all.

To fully understand these markets, it helps to know why they exist as they do. And while it is true that bond brokers speak English, they use expressions that act as shorthand, creating a special language in the process. To make learning their lingo and the forms it describes interesting, we have traced the development of the words through bond history.

Financial language derives from a vocabulary created over the centuries. It is particularly puzzling to those new to marketable securities based on debt: namely, bonds, notes, bills, and other fixed income investments. Based on United States case law, a *bond*, according to *Black's Law Dictionary*, is "evidence of a debt wherein the bond issuer agrees to pay a certain sum of money to another person at a specified day."[1] This is the definition we will be using in this book. All the following terms can be subsumed under the general heading of debt:

A *bill*, as in dollar bill or Treasury bill, is also a promise to pay. Standing alone it "means a bank note, United States Treasury note, or other piece of paper circulating as money."[2] In financial usage, a bill is a short-term obligation of the U.S. Treasury.

A *note* is a "unilateral instrument containing an express and absolute promise of its signer to pay to a specified person or order, or bearer, a definite sum of money at a specified time."[3] In current usage, a note refers to intermediate corporate bonds that were issued with maturities of around twelve years or less, or issues of the U.S. Treasury with an issuance life between one and ten years.

Another term you might hear is *paper*. Paper is "a written or printed evidence of debt, particularly a promissory note or a bill of exchange, as in...commercial paper."[4] *Commercial paper* is short-term unsecured debt issued by a corporation. Although as an individual investor you probably will not buy commercial paper directly, you likely own it through your money market fund. When you call a broker and ask to purchase a bond, the broker might respond, "What kind of paper do you want?" As such, it could refer to any of the above financial instruments or others described later.

Evolving in Early History

MOST OF THE EARLIEST legal codes sought to prevent the use of credit or limit it altogether. The biblical Israelites did not permit lending at interest. Ancient South Indian literature reviled usurers and set interest limits. However, merchant activity requires the use of loans. The earliest use of loans in trade was in the form of bills of credit. Merchants financed their trade with written promissory notes entitling them to get money in distant ports. That way they did not have to carry hard currency with them.

During the Dark Ages merchant activity for all intents and purposes ceased. In addition, Charlemagne became the first ruler to prohibit all usury. If the result of lending was considered usury, the punishment was death. The Catholic Church effectively prevented all above-board acts of lending and borrowing, except as conducted by the Church itself.[5] The Church had liquid capital that was lent to nobles and secured with land. The loan was called a *land gage*. It was a *live gage* when the land's revenue repaid the debt, and a *mort gage* (mortgage) when it did not.

By the fifteenth century, the pressure to borrow was intense. With credit scarce and tax revenues falling short, as usual, kings and popes resorted to creative money-raising schemes to finance their armies, wars, luxuries, and political ambitions. Merchant banks were the entities that came into being to finance the monarchs' needs. In lieu of interest, the lenders were compensated by participating in the kings' monopolies and by franchises, special privileges granted to them[6]—much as with venture capitalists today in their role as financiers to emerging enterprises.

After the Protestant Reformation in 1517, interest became an acceptable form of payment in Europe, making lending and borrowing easier. Interest was then accepted as compensation for risking the loss of borrowed funds and the possibility that the funds could be put to better use elsewhere. Catholic countries resisted the acceptance of interest. It wasn't until the early nineteenth century that the Holy Office decreed that interest at rates defined by law could be taken by anyone. As recently as 1950 Pope Pius XII attempted to eradicate the stigma of the past in formally declaring that bankers "earn their livelihood honestly."[7]

Today negotiable loans pay interest. *Black's Law Dictionary* defines *interest* for money as "...the compensation allowed by law or fixed by the parties for the use or forbearance or detention of money."[8] From Roman times, a distinction was drawn between aforementioned *usury,* the price paid for borrowed capital, and interest. Usury was considered to be profit. It included being paid more than the legal limit and/or a purpose of mind to get more. Interest, on the other hand, was associated not with profit, but with loss. It was compensation for the loss of the use of money. At first, it was levied only if the loan was not repaid on time. Later there were other qualifying reasons. For example, if it were viewed as a wage, compensation for the time and effort in making the loan, then it became acceptable to levy interest from the beginning.

Today, the market defines what is an acceptable level of interest. You are compensated through the payment of interest when you lend money by buying a bond. You will be told at the time of purchase whether you will be paid interest monthly, semi-annually, or only when the bond comes due. In the United States, state law defines usury; however, the term is not used the same way in all states.

THUS, BY THE TIME Europe's Great Age of Exploration began in the sixteenth century, many of the concepts underlying today's bonds were already in place. The term *bond,* for example, is not used when a loan is made to an individual. Bonds are negotiable— they can be bought and sold. Bonds, in other words, are only issued by central governments and their agencies, supranational governmental agencies such as the World Bank, state and municipal governments, and corporations.

Our large-scale bond markets were based on patterns developed in Venice and the other merchant towns in Italy and later on the financial success of the Dutch cities of Antwerp and Amsterdam, where a popular government was able to pledge the resources of a town, province, or nation. In the eighteenth century the English made two improvements to the Dutch systems of finance. First, the English clearly stated on each issue how much money was being borrowed, when the bonds would come due, and if there were any special terms that were part of the loan. For example, a special feature might be the issuer having the right to call in the bonds before the redemption or due date. Second, they did not change the terms or features of the bonds from one issue to another. Once you understood the nature of the bond, you could buy any subsequent bond without having to consider the terms of the loan. Furthermore, the issues were for large amounts of money, enabling large-scale investors to purchase blocks of bonds to meet their investment needs instead of buying many little issues that each required analysis.[9] Today the Treasury and Euro markets most reflect these advances. Issues of bonds by large corporations can also approximate this ideal.

Debuting in Colonial Times

FROM COLONIAL TIMES ON, bonds have been part of American history. Although the colonists lived in relatively basic conditions, they had the heritage of English law and finance to help shape the nation. England, whose bonds were primarily issued to pay for wars, laid the debt for the Anglo-French war on the doorsteps of the colonies. Massachusetts was the first colony to offer bonds to cover its costs. In 1690 Massachusetts issued paper to help pay for its share of the debts incurred by all the colonies while helping the British fight a war with the French Canadians. The attitude of the English was that it was a war to protect the colonies, so the citizens of the New World should bear the responsibility of the debt.

Massachusetts's first issue was successfully repaid from tax payments. (Today we call municipal bonds backed by property and other tax receipts *general obligation bonds,* in that they are the obligation of everyone in the political entity issuing them.) Looking for other ways to raise revenue, in 1744 Massachusetts became the first colony to use a lottery to help pay off the war debt. The English Act of 1709 had prohibited the use of lotteries in England, but this law did not apply to the colonies. They passed their own laws limiting or prohibiting its use later on.[10] If the lottery had been a revenue stream guaranteed for the repayment of bonds, those bonds would be called *revenue bonds* today. However, the lottery was just a means for the government to raise more funds. Massachusetts had a successful lottery; the one in New York two years later failed.

In keeping with the informal character of business in the colonies, a group of savvy Boston merchants decided to issue their own paper money in 1733. This bond was backed by a set amount of silver that could be redeemed after ten years. When the price of silver increased by almost 50 percent above the redeemed price, these notes were hoarded. In this case the issuer bore the risk of inflation. Usually if there is inflation it is the lenders that suffer because they are repaid in depreciated currency.[11]

Between 1751 and 1764, England stamped out the issuance of paper money by the colonial governments. Unable to issue paper money, the colonial governments issued Treasury bills instead that were redeemable in gold and silver after two to three years. Like modern municipal bonds that are the general obligation of the state, the bills were backed by actual tax payments rather than lotteries. With the solid financial guarantee of the government, these Treasury bills did not depreciate.

Developing after the American Revolution

THE STATES STILL ISSUE BONDS today, but the term *Treasury bond* is restricted to bonds issued by the United States Treasury. After the American Revolution, one of the first acts of the U.S. Treasury in 1789 was the assumption of all war debts incurred by the states. Although the federal government agreed to pay, it did not have the money. In 1795 Alexander Hamilton, the Secretary of the Treasury, decided to adopt a method borrowed from the British using a so-called sinking fund. In essence, this consisted of money set aside and invested to pay off a debt through the accumulation of interest. Sinking funds are still a feature of some revenue bonds today, although the money might not actually be set aside for the periodic debt recall. Usually the funds kick in after fifteen years.

Hamilton's successor, Albert Gallatin, quickly figured out that the scheme was not working: interest on the debt was growing faster than the sinking fund interest that was supposed to pay off the debt. His solution was to reduce the debt by buying bonds in the marketplace if they were selling at or below face value. In so doing, he created the U.S. government's first open market operations. The Federal Reserve periodically engages in such activity today, buying and selling bonds in the open markets to expand or contract credit.

Gallatin also supported and planned the construction of roads and canals in the new republic. Direct federal funding for these plans ended, however, with the election of Andrew Jackson in 1830. The job of completing them fell to state and local governments that had little experience and money to complete the costly projects.

Lack of experience, however, did not deter state governments from freely issuing debt for railroads, turnpikes, and other public improvements. It was commonplace in the early 1800s for banks also to issue notes to finance such projects. There were soon so many notes in circulation that they did not retain their value.

In order to create some clarity as to the strength of the issuer, John Thompson started the Thompson Financial and Rating Agency in 1842. He rated bank notes by sending his sons to banks to redeem notes for gold. If the bank refused, Thompson would condemn the note to death by writing about it unfavorably. Out of this beginning came today's financial tabloid *American Banker*.

At the time Thompson was starting his agency, a depression had hit the U.S. economy, and state revenues had declined sharply. Payment of interest and principal was postponed in some cases for as long as seven years until all debts were repaid. Only two states repudiated their debt at that time, Mississippi and Florida. Lest anyone think that lenders have short memories when they have been stiffed, it is reported that when officials from Mississippi went to London to sell a taxable Euro bond issue in 1987, they were told, to the Mississippians' surprise, that "...the state's credit was no good. The state of Mississippi, the bankers explained, still owed London banks principal and interest on $7 million of defaulted state debt—sold 156 years earlier and repudiated in 1857."[12]

During the Civil War, the federal and confederate governments financed the war by selling bonds bought by the banks and sold to the general public. As the lines of credit evaporated, they issued *fiat money*, paper money not backed by gold or silver. The Yankees issued greenbacks, the predecessors of modern U.S. currency.

Following the Civil War, economic life was harsh for the southern states. This was aggravated by the nationwide Panic of 1873. Reeling under its impact and from the heavy load of bonds issued for railroads and so-called carpetbagger debt incurred after the Civil War, many states simply refused to pay a substantial portion of what was owed. The states relied on Section 4 of the Constitution's 14th Amendment prohibiting any state from paying debt incurred to fund a rebellion against the federal government. *The Bond Buyer,* a financial newspaper, reported that by 1873 a total of ten states repudiated $300 million of principal and interest, with Virginia leading the pack, owing $72,220,000.[13] The federal government refused to bail the states out.

Four outcomes of the profligacy of the states have served to define the bond markets today. First, as a result of these problems, state legislatures limited the amount of debt states could issue, although each did so in a different way. The controls placed on the issuance of state general obligation debt created strong state credits that are still respected in the marketplace. Second, local governments were encouraged to issue debt for their own developmental needs, and this they continue to do. Third, the troubled period established precedence for the repudiation of debt and the long-lasting consequences of doing so. Fourth, it established that the federal government would not always bail out state and local governments when they encountered problems.

It is important to note that in the present day as well, repudiation of debt is much more likely to occur when the populace does not specifically vote to incur the debt in the first place. Government officials always have visions of projects they wish to fund, some of which are basic improvements and others reflecting special interests. Tax-averse citizens try to limit their local government's ability to issue bonds. As you will later read, creative financing methods are developed to circumvent the restrictions the citizens vote upon. The state of California is at the forefront of these conflicting interests.

Entering the Twentieth Century

PERHAPS THE MOST SIGNIFICANT EVENT in the beginning of the twentieth century to affect bonds was the founding of the Federal Reserve in 1913. It established a central banking system long used in Europe to pool bank reserves and create a lender of last resort. The initial effect of the Federal Reserve was to smooth out the fluctuation of short-term interest rates by making short-term money nearly always available. With the advent of World War I, the Federal Reserve took on the additional responsibility to manage the issuance of Treasury bonds, which were absorbed by banks and the federal reserve system itself. Low interest rates soon became a government objective.[14]

Corporate bonds turned into a major factor in the U.S. economy with the advent of World War I. By law national banks were obligated to hold Treasury debt in order to issue bank notes. In 1917 Treasury bonds were yielding 2 percent and corporate bonds, under no restraining regulations, were yielding up to 5 percent. Not surprisingly, the general public preferred the more lucrative returns of the corporate debt.

The Treasury needed to entice the public to buy its bonds, so that the looming war could be financed. It came up with a creative solution, called Liberty Bonds, and sold them through banks. If patriotic Americans wished to buy bonds but did not have the money, the banks lent it to them, charging the interest that the bonds paid. The American public bought the bonds on what is called *margin,* borrowing money to finance the purchase of securities. The call to patriotism led people to purchase Liberty Bonds that in 1917 yielded 3.5 percent for 15-year bonds and 4 percent for the 10-year. Banks were permitted to use the bonds as collateral for loans, and credit flowed freely as the banks lent liberally for the time.

In 1920, fearful of inflation, the Federal Reserve used its powers to control this rapid expansion of credit by raising the discount rate. Subject to the vagaries of the market, the yield in 1920 on 12-month Treasury certificates rose to 7.75 percent. Corporate bonds declined in value by 11 percent as interest rates rose from 4.95 percent to 5.56 percent, rates not seen again until 1967.[15] Against such competition, Liberty Bonds issued in 1918, with a coupon rate of 4.5 percent, declined by 17 percent. Of Liberty Bonds' 18 million owners, an estimated 14 million liquidated their holdings due to rapid price fluctuations in their value.[16] However, if they had kept those bonds instead of selling them, they would have seen their value appreciate. The year 1920 marked the peak of prime bond yields for close to five decades prior to and after that date. The holders of noncallable 100-year railroad bonds issued in the late 1890s with interest rates between 4 and 4.5 percent likewise saw their value plummet in 1920, but by 1946 those same bonds were worth 25–50 percent more than face value.

Bonds backed by mortgages had not even been imagined in the 1920s, but the seeds were sown with the creation of Fannie Mae in 1938, a government agency dedicated to the refinancing of unpopular long, fixed-rate mortgages. The creators could not have possibly realized that they were inaugurating an exciting new debt form that would evolve into the multitrillion-dollar mortgage-backed securities market.

During World War II interest rates remained low for Treasury bonds, with fixed rates ranging from 2–2.5 percent for the 25- to 30-year bonds. Despite the low returns, when the highest federal income tax rate hit 94 percent in 1944–1945, the tax-exempt appeal of municipal bonds became magnetic.[17] With 1945 came the end of the war and of long-term Treasury bond issuance for eight years. The so-called long bonds were eagerly bought in 1945 and again in 1999 when the government announced that it was going to pay down the government debt and reduce the supply of these 30-year bonds. Traders expected to see rapid price appreciation as their supply diminished.

Changing Through the Latter Twentieth Century

THE YEAR 1946 marked instead the beginning of the bear market in bonds that ultimately ended in 1981 when interest rates peaked. The yield on prime corporate bonds rose from 2.46 percent in 1946 to a whopping 15.49 percent in 1981.[18] The yields were even higher on sectors deemed riskier. The bond market experienced seven major price declines interspersed with six price rallies until yields on Treasury bonds peaked at 14 percent in 1982.

In the 1960s Treasury bond sales to the general public were in the form of United States Savings Bonds, series E, F, and G. The Treasury was able to sell a 25-year bond at 4.25 percent interest, while the yield on a 25-month note brought 4 percent, a much better deal. The legal interest limit was 4.5 percent. By 1965 a wage-price spiral had begun, accompanied by ballooning inflation. Borrowers focused on the short-term markets because the Treasury could not sell long-term debt beyond the legal debt yield, and corporations did not want to borrow for high, long-term fixed costs.

By the late 1960s, holders of savings bonds began to cash them in at such a rapid rate that federal government bond sales netted less than the redemptions. The savings bonds had a fixed rate of 4.5 percent interest, while corporate and muni bonds yielded much more. To staunch the flow, the Treasury allowed the holders of low-yielding Victory Savings Bonds to exchange them for higher-interest H Bonds in January 1972. In 1980, still trying to stem the flow of funds, the Treasury introduced a new series of higher-yielding savings bonds with more limited liquidity. These are the well-known EE and HH Bonds.

Stand-alone mutual funds were beginning to attract investors' cash, and the money market funds competed with all the banks and savings and loans for ordinary deposits. The process, known as disintermediation, whereby assets are invested outside of the traditional financial institutions, was well underway. Another major change was the appearance in 1970 of the first mortgage-backed security in the United States that was guaranteed by Ginnie Mae, as the entity is colloquially known. (This topic is described in detail in Chapter 6.)

The 1970s also marked the first appearance of so-called junk bonds. Prior to their first issuance in 1977, bonds of low quality that provided high yields were called fallen angels. Such bonds were issued by viable corporations with investment-grade ratings that simply had fallen on hard times. Junk bonds, by contrast, were bonds of companies that had succumbed to hostile takeovers and were loaded with debt.

Trading in junk bonds was largely the work of Michael Milken, partner in the firm of Drexel Burnham Lambert Group. Milken figured that the savings and loans that had invested in mortgages were failing because they had locked in long-term debt in the face of rising interest rates. Their depositors were leaving for more lucrative returns elsewhere. The S & Ls needed the quick infusion of income that junk bonds could supply.

In addition, junk issues offered a lower-cost financing alternative for corporations than borrowing from banks. In the 1980s junk bonds were used as financing vehicles in leveraged buyouts and hostile takeover attempts. Milken found that large, cash-rich conglomerates like RJR Nabisco could be bought using high-yield debt and chopped into pieces that were then sold to pay off the debt.

Milken created unusual debt forms to achieve his objectives. One such innovation for short-term financing was called increasing rate notes, which were developed for the RJR deal. These are notes that increased in yield the longer they remained unpaid. Certificates of deposit and some corporate bonds now carry this feature. Another innovation, called step-up notes, are temporary notes that are issued to cover a bridge loan until more permanent financing can be arranged.

Milken and Drexel were implicated in the insider trading scandals of the late 1980s. Milken went to jail for ten years and paid a fine of $600 million, while Drexel paid a $650 million fine.[19] The high-yield market tumbled in 1989, and Drexel declared bankruptcy. The junk bond market nearly dried up. However, today there is again an active market of such debt that prefers the name *high-yield* to junk.

In the 1970s high inflation, soaring interest rates, and heavy investments in junk bonds resulted in the bankruptcy of many banks and savings and loan associations. The period 1979–1982 saw inflation reaching double digits in three of those years, and interest rates were in the teens. Thereafter, however, following their peak in 1982, interest rates began a twenty-year decline. In that same year the stock market began to rise with great price gyrations not seen before in the post–World War II world.

The peaking of inflation, in that unprecedented 1979–1982

period, with resulting high interest rates and declining bond prices, imprinted the riskiness of bonds in the minds of investors and financial advisers alike. Bonds now had to pay more to compensate for this market risk. They were avoided, and the declining interest rates that eventually followed provided a big boost to the stock market. Yet a lot of money could be made in the bond markets as well, because the dramatically falling interest rates that made stocks look attractive also created huge capital gains on bonds.

Had you bought bonds in the early 1980s, you would have made double-digit returns because as the high interest rates later declined, the prices of bonds bounded higher as investors sought to grab the yields before they sank further. According to a study by Salomon Brothers entitled "What a Difference a Decade Makes," bonds were the most profitable place to store wealth in the 1980s, averaging a return of 20.9 percent. Stocks were second best, averaging 16.5 percent. In the inflationary 1970s, real assets such as real estate, natural resources, and precious metals had been king, and both stocks and bonds had suffered negative returns.[20]

Metamorphosing in Recent Times

THE EMERGENCE OF the information age has profoundly affected the bond world. In 1969 the firm of Cantor Fitzgerald introduced the Telerate machine that later became the electronic marketplace for Treasury bonds. In 1981 Michael Bloomberg developed the Bloomberg electronic information service that enabled bond traders to have instant access to information about bonds and interest rates. That same year J. J. Kenny Company established the first bond index as a yield benchmark for variable rate bonds.

The information age also revolutionized the tracking of bond ownership. So-called *bearer bonds* were the equivalent of money. They had coupons attached for the payment of interest that was deposited in a bank account when the interest came due. The coupon rate was literally the value of the coupon when it was deposited in the bank.

After July 1983 all new issues of bonds had to be registered. This coincided with establishment of electronic clearing among banks in 1983. When you own a *registered bond,* you receive a paper certificate, called a bond, and a check in the mail on each interest payment date instead of clipping a coupon. (The rate of interest on a bond is still called the coupon even though they are no longer issued.) So-called *book entry bonds,* bonds that can be held only in the custody of a financial institution, soon crowded out the registered bonds as the clearinghouses were able to transfer rapidly the ownership of securities without actually transferring paper. Registered bonds are still sometimes available to humor those investors who must be dragged kicking and screaming into the electronic age.

New forms of bonds developed as well as techniques for risk management. From the junk bond arena and corporations with better resources came high-yield zero-coupon bonds, pay-in-kind securities, extendable reset notes, convertible bonds, and different forms of preferred stock. The federal government developed inflation-protecting TIPS for the broader market and I Bonds for the everyman who bought savings bonds. Federal agency paper in the form of Ginnie Maes and later forms of federally sponsored paper exploded as Fannie Mae and Freddie Mac created a secondary market in mortgages, thereby enabling you to invest in them. Staid, conservative municipal bonds looked for new sources of revenue to back their bond issues. They created moral obligation bonds, which were soon displaced first by lease-backed bonds and later by certificates of participation (COPs) to expand debt issuance.

More novel still, financial innovators at the major financial firms created new trading instruments that depend on the value of other assets such as stocks, bonds, or market indexes. These so-called derivative assets or contingent claims are classified in the categories of futures or options. Bonds that were understood to have a given life, or maturity, that paid a certain interest, and were of a certain quality, were now sliced and diced in myriad ways. Interest payments were stripped from a bond and sold separately as zero-coupon bonds. Bond portfolios were managed for their total return, and individual bonds were analyzed based on their various attributes in ways not done before.

This groundbreaking approach began around 1980 with the

idea of selling the principal and interest of a bond separately, a technique called stripping. The notion that existing illiquid assets could be transformed revolutionized the bond markets. For example, banks sitting on mortgage bonds realized that they could package them and sell them to the public, a process called securitization, and make them tradable. This spawned the synthetic mortgage market (collateralized mortgage obligations or CMOs), where mortgage principal payments were sold separate from the interest payments, and both those payments were sorted into tranches based on the likelihood that they would be repaid. Car loans, credit card loans, home equity loans, manufactured house loans, and loans based on the sale of recordings by your favorite rock star later appeared.[21]

Instead of buying and selling bonds, traders began selling options to streams of income as a way to manage interest rate risk. Salomon Brothers engineered the first such swap between the World Bank and IBM in 1981. An *interest rate swap* involves an exchange between two parties of interest rate exposures from floating to fixed rate or vice versa.

In one example of a swap, one party sells the flow of fixed-rate interest payments on the bonds they hold in exchange for payments tied to a short-term variable rate of interest payments. Each party to the exchange is protecting a different financial position. Instead of buying and selling the physical security, traders are now selling options and futures they created based on, or derived from, holdings of bonds, stocks, or commodities. From nothing in 1980 this has become a trillion-dollar leveraged market that trades over-the-counter. In time of financial crisis, derivative trading can roil the bond markets in ways never seen before.

In the late 1990s, the Internet took off, opening up even more new possibilities affecting bonds. Although best known for all the new companies and stock that it spawned, the online revolution created possibilities for price transparency that did not exist before. Brokers started posting their offerings on websites; issuers began auctioning bonds directly, bypassing brokers. In 2002, issuers were able to electronically transmit offering statements for newly issued bonds to national depositories; many also posted the statements on the Web for information transparency to support bond sales. Mutual funds took advantage of the medium by posting their prospectuses on their websites to provide easy access to buyers and to reduce distribution costs. Information was available immediately in a quantity hitherto unimaginable. The effect was to make the sale and purchase of bonds quicker, easier, and simpler.

Inflation-indexed bonds, zero-coupon bonds, and many other bond types noted above are described in detail in the rest of this book. So traumatic was the inflation of the 70s that it led to the creation of these all-new bond types and ways to manage the risks associated with them. This book is going to tell you not only how to understand but also how to profit from all this creative turmoil. First, however, it is necessary to understand the basics of a bond—how it is created, issued, priced, and traded—and that is what the next chapter describes.

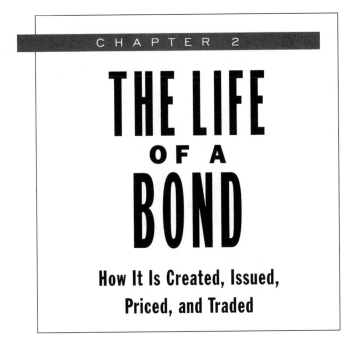

CHAPTER 2

THE LIFE
OF A
BOND

How It Is Created, Issued,
Priced, and Traded

THIS CHAPTER PROVIDES the information you need to

become an educated bond buyer. While it may be tempt-

ing just to skip this material and flip to the chapter on

buying bonds, consider this: It will be much harder to

profit from the money-making strategies we outline if

you don't understand bond basics. Read this chapter to

get an overview and refer back to it when you need a

refresher to help you understand a particular investment. When we first identify a word or term, we have highlighted it in boldface to make it easier for you to relocate it.

As a further reading inducement, remember that bond returns can be quite lucrative. Consider that when stocks collectively took a hit during the market downturn that began in March 2000 and continued into 2001, the 10-year Treasury bond gained 22 percent in value between May 15 and November 7, 2001.[1] At the same time, tax-exempt municipal bonds provided yields of 5 percent for bonds maturing between fifteen and nineteen years, and 30-year Treasuries were yielding 5.35 percent. That 5 percent return on municipal bonds is a taxable equivalent yield of better than 8 percent for someone in the highest tax bracket, a return that comes with little risk. Trust us, the more you know about bonds, the better off you'll be.

By Way of Background

LET'S START AT THE VERY BEGINNING. Every bond has two specified components: (1) a time span and (2) a face value. The latter is the term used to describe the amount of money or principal you will receive at the end of the specified time span when the bond comes due.

There are two basic ways to earn income from this arrangement. In the first, you receive regular interest payments over the life of the bond. As briefly noted in Chapter 1, people who received such income were once known as coupon clippers. That is because interest payments were printed on coupons that were attached to the bond. When they clipped the coupon and turned it in, they received their payment. The practice gradually phased out to one of automatic, direct payment and officially ended in July 1983 when municipal bond issuers finally did away with the paper coupons.

In today's more technologically sophisticated society, interest payments are automatically sent to whatever address you designate—be it a brokerage account or your home—and there is no need to physically present a coupon to get your income. The idea of a coupon lingers in bond terminology, however, as a bond's interest rate is referred to as its **coupon rate**, or just plain **coupon**.

The coupon rate is set as a percentage of the face value when the bond is issued. Thus, a $10,000 10-year bond with a coupon rate of 5 percent will annually pay $500, which is 5 percent of $10,000.

The second way of earning bond income involves buying a bond at less than, or at a discount to, its face value. For example, you may pay only $5,000 for a $10,000 10-year bond. This does not necessarily mean that you are getting a bargain. Sometimes the discount reflects the fact that the bond is out of favor, and investors feel it not worthwhile to hold the instrument until they can redeem it at full value. At other times, the discount is deliberate and includes no interest payments whatsoever. This kind of bond is called a **zero-coupon bond** (which makes sense because it has no coupons). The difference between your purchase price and the face value represents the income you receive.

These two basic bond structures provide financial peace of mind to many people because it means they will either enjoy a steady stream of income until, or receive a lump sum at, the time when the face value of the bond is returned to them. (This is called **redemption at maturity**.) People can also receive a mix of money now and money later.

In other words, you buy a bond; get regular income over a period of time, a lump sum all at once, or some mix of the two; and then get all your money back when the bond comes due. For this reason, bonds are frequently regarded as stodgy investments by countless investors, particularly by those who like to triple and quadruple their money by playing around in the exciting stratospheres of high-flying stocks. Of course, in times when the price of those stocks have sunk out of sight, the so-called stodginess of bonds becomes a little more appealing.

In truth, bonds are neither simple nor stodgy. They are, rather, very rewarding. In contrast to stocks, which represent part ownership of an entity, bonds are debt, pure but not always simple. As described in Chapter 1, companies, municipalities, states, and the federal government issue bonds for either short-term or long-term funding needs. The following describes the roles of various individuals and entities in creating and bringing a bond to market and how they shape its ultimate form.

Preparing a Bond

A FINANCIAL ADVISER is called in at the very beginning of the bond issuance process. The adviser is a consultant who helps the issuer decide if bond debt is the best and most appropriate means of dealing with a project or need. The federal government and its agencies have internal financial advisers that perform these services. Corporations often rely on their investment banks to act as financial advisers. With regard to municipal bonds, an outside consultant frequently works with the municipality's finance director and lawyers to organize, collect, and represent the financial data to prospective buyers of the debt, including the underwriters. Most municipalities come to market infrequently and do not have an in-house staff.

After the need for bond debt has been established and a preliminary draft completed, a bond counsel reviews the contract, called the **bond indenture**, and gives a legal opinion that the debt is being appropriately issued. In the early twentieth century, many bonds did not have legal opinions. As investors discovered that bonds with legal opinions were less likely to default, they began to demand opinions on all issues. Bond counsel also determines where in the receiving line the bondholders stand when cash is being handed out in troubled times. With regard to tax-free municipal bonds, bond counsel provides a legal opinion certifying that the bonds are in fact tax-exempt for federal income tax purposes.

Next, underwriters appear on the scene. They are necessary because bonds are generally not bought directly from the issuing entity. (Those issued by the U.S. government, as described in Chapters 3 and 4, are conspicuous exceptions to this practice.) An underwriter is the bank or brokerage house that initially buys the bonds from the issuer and then resells them to investors. Since buying a large block of debt and then reselling it into a constantly shifting market can be financially hazardous, underwriters spread their risk by having similar organizations share the bond's introduction. The resulting grouping is called an **underwriting syndicate**.

Lawyers are constantly involved in creating and issuing bonds. They next appear in the form of underwriters' counsel. In this position, they represent the brokerage house that will buy the bonds from the issuer. In today's marketplace, issuers may bypass the underwriter and sell the issue for the highest price to brokers, pension funds, bond funds, banks, or insurance companies.

At some point in this process, the decision is made as to whether or not the bond will be callable. A **call** is a kind of option that gives an issuer the right to redeem a bond issue prior to its maturity. Many bond issues have a fixed call prior to maturity. Municipal bonds may also have extraordinary calls that are triggered under certain situations. Bonds are called when it is advantageous to the issuer, leaving you to scratch around to find another bond investment, often at a lower yield. If you are worried about the possibility of early redemption, the most desirable bonds for you would provide at least seven years of call protection.

In the event of a bankruptcy, not all of an issuer's bondholders are treated equally. Some bonds have senior liens, meaning that they come first in line before other creditors if there is a problem. Other bond issues from the same company may only have subordinated or junior lien positions.

When a single issue consists of bonds with different redemption dates, the bonds are called **serial bonds**. These types of bonds give the issuer the flexibility of not having to pay everything off in one lump sum. Many municipal bond issues are commonly offered this way. A **term bond** is a longer-term bond with a final maturity date. Many corporate and U.S. government bonds are issued this way.

Once the issuer has assembled all the necessary information, writers specializing in obscure prose prepare an **offering statement (OS)**, or **prospectus**. As a friend of ours once described it, only half facetiously, "It is written about matters that few understand for people that will never read it." This document, produced under the issuer's aegis, sums up all the work of the professionals who created the bond and details its type, structure, special features (if any), and the strength and weaknesses of the issuer. It also describes any liabilities that might exist and the participants in the deal. If you take time to peruse it, you will learn a great deal.

It appears that the municipalities and corporations that produce offering statements feel they are not necessary to read prior to purchase since sometimes the OS is sent only after you have purchased a new issue bond. This situation is changing, however, as websites such as www.emuni.com, www.directnotes.com, and www.inter notes.com are beginning to post offering statements in advance of new bond issues. Individual issuers, such as the state of Utah, at www.finance.state.ut.us, are also posting prospectuses on their websites. We hope this trend will continue.

Rating a Bond

HAVING BEEN PRIMED and primped through many legal hands, the now dressed-up bond is ready to meet the rating analysts. These are the people who evaluate the riskiness of bonds as evidenced by the probability of buyers being repaid in a timely manner. As described in Chapter 1, rating agencies came into being as a service to describe any risk associated with a bond. Because there is a chance that an investor could suffer substantial losses if a bond defaults, bond issuers have to pay more to induce buyers to assume any extra risk.

Credit analysts do ratings work for bond insurers, underwriters and other large institutions, and rating agencies. Each organization relies on its analysts to review a bond's structure and its issuer's financial strength. Rating agency analysts are best known because their ratings are widely publicized and provide a recognized guide to bond purchasers. With this recognition, these analysts have become powerful players in the bond markets because their ratings strongly influence how much an issuer will have to pay to borrow money. If a bond, for example, receives the highest rating, it is deemed as having almost no risk of default. Thus, under similar time spans, an issuer with a bond boasting the highest triple-A rating might have to pay only 60 percent of the interest offered by an issuer with a bond rated double-B. All things being equal, bonds of the same rating and maturity are sold with similar yields. When there are sharp yield disparities among similarly rated bonds, you should investigate why this is so.

Bonds may be placed on **credit watch** if the financial conditions of the issuer deteriorate. Usually the adjustments in ratings are minor. Downgrades that bring the bond rating below the investment grade of triple-B are more serious. Institutions holding those bonds may be forced to sell them, depending on the covenants under which they operate, resulting in a general decline in the bond's price and value. Alternatively, going from double-B to triple-B can result in a nice pop-up in price.

When the changes in a bond rating are gradual and the issuer comes to market frequently, the ratings are more apt to be up to date and currently accurate than when an issuer only infrequently comes to market. When you purchase bonds that are not newly issued, the rating attached to the bond might not be current, and in that sense is less reliable.

Rating agencies are in a delicate position because they are paid by issuers to rate their bonds. Such a situation implies that an agency would give the most positive possible rating. On the other hand, if the public does not trust an agency's judgment, the value of its rating is useless, and issuers will no longer hire the firm. Rating agencies protect themselves by continually pointing out that their ratings are not meant to advise you to buy or sell. They also monitor the performance of their major clients, those whose bonds are actively traded in the market, and, often without being specifically paid to do so, will either downgrade or upgrade the debt of an issuer when financial conditions markedly change. This type of unsolicited rating also may occur on occasion when an issuer elects not to request a rating from one agency because they expect a different agency might be more generous.

As evident in recent precipitous defaults, such as Kmart, the rating agencies often play catch-up. Conseco, Xerox, and the Finova Group are other formerly blue-chip companies that have watched the sun quickly set on their company's prospects.[2] Rating agencies constantly ponder how they can provide better public notice without pulling the rug out from under an ailing company. "How volatile does the marketplace want ratings to be?" they ask. Market sentiment always precedes any downgrade. Thus, ratings are broadly viewed as lagging indicators, especially in the high-yield market.

With regard to the publicity surrounding the bankruptcy of Enron, it should be noted that rating agencies are not responsible for uncovering fraud. While cooked books ultimately make rotten financial stews resulting in precipitous downgrades, they are

The Rating Agencies

Credit Quality	Moody's	S&P	Fitch
Solid as a rock	Aaa	AAA	AAA
Very fine quality	Aa1	AA+	AA+
	Aa2	AA	AA
	Aa3	AA-	AA-
Strong capacity to pay	A1	A+	A+
	A2	A	A
	A3	A-	A-
	A	A	A
Adequate ability to pay;	Baa1	BBB+	BBB+
lowest investment grade	Baa2	BBB	BBB
for banks	Baa3	BBB-	BBB-
Somewhat speculative;	Ba1	BB+	BB+
risk exposure	Ba2	BB	BB
	Ba3	BB-	BB-
More speculative;	B1	B+	B+
risk exposure	B2	B	B
	B3	B-	B-
Major risk exposure;	Caa1	CCC+	CCC+
on verge of default	Caa2	CCC	CCC
	Caa3	CCC-	CCC-
Crucial risk exposure;	Ca1	CC+	CC+
may have defaulted	Ca2	CC	CC
on interest payments	Ca3	CC-	CC-
Default or Imminent Default	C	C	C
General default	D	D	D
No rating requested	NR	NR	NR

supposed to be part of accounting firms' oversight.

The three primary bond-rating agencies and their websites are Moody's Investors Service (Moody's) at www.Moodys.com, Standard & Poor's (S&P) at www.standardandpoors.com, and Fitch Ratings at www.fitchratings.com. All three agree that financial statistics are only a reflection of past performance, and not necessarily an indicator of future success. They feel, however, that while the future cannot be foretold, the prospects of an industry or geographic region can be carefully considered and evaluated.

The agencies readily admit that their ratings contain subjective judgments. All of life's experiences cannot be boiled down into numbers, and the value of "hard numbers" is often questionable. This, plus the fact that the agencies also can disagree on exactly how new circumstances will affect cash flow for particular loan payments, sometimes leads to dissimilar conclusions. When agencies do not agree on a rating, the result is known as a **split rating**. The split rating may vary by an entire category (e.g., double-A to a high single-A) or only reflect variations within a category (e.g., high single-A to a lower grade single-A).

While information that might affect the ratings can be found on the Internet, you have to search a bit to find relevant data. For example, you can obtain a free prospectus but no material event information on corporate issues by going to www.sec.gov/edgar/quickedgar.htm. The opposite is true with regard to municipal bonds. You can get free material event information from www.nrmsir.org or www.bloomberg.com but you will have to pay to obtain a prospectus. The latter websites are two of four approved by the Municipal Securities Rulemaking Board (MSRB) as private repositories for offering statements. Since they are private, the sites look to make money from the sale of bond information.

Setting a Coupon Rate

THE NEXT STEP in the bond debut process is setting the **coupon rate**, or the stated amount of interest. At all times, the issuer seeks to set a rate at which the largest buyers, mutual fund companies, banks, and insurance companies are eager to buy the bond.

Sometimes issuers sell zero-coupon bonds. As explained at the beginning of this chapter, these bonds do not pay interest. However, the issuers have to determine the extent of the discount to full value at which the bond will be offered. These bonds are also called **accrual bonds** because the interest accumulates and is not paid out. It is deferred until the bond comes due.

Most bonds have a **fixed rate**. That means that the coupon rate is set at the time of issuance and will remain the same for the life of the bonds. That is why they are called fixed-income securities. Once the bond is issued, its selling price may rise or fall, but its stream of interest payments, at the agreed upon coupon rate, continues unabated.

Other bonds are known as **floaters** or **variable-rate bonds**. As the names of these bonds indicate, their rates float, or are variable, and are reset periodically, generally in relation to some measure of current market rates on specified dates. Some of these bonds may have their interest rate fluctuation limited by a cap (maximum rate) and/or a floor (minimum rate). The floaters may move in the same direction as the rate to which they are tied (**reference rate**), or in the opposite direction, when they are then called **inverse-floaters**.

The kind of coupon rate attached to a bond is important because the value of the interest you receive is affected by inflation. The question is: Would the $100 you earned in interest purchase the same amount of goods this year as last year? The interest rate you receive is called the **nominal rate**. In theory, to find out what it is really worth to you, deduct the rate of inflation from the interest rate. If you are earning 5 percent on your bonds and reported inflation is at 1.5 percent, your **real rate of return** is 3.5 percent.

Launching a Bond

HAVING BEEN STRUCTURED, described, and rated, a bond then makes its market debut, where it is bought and frequently resold in what is known as the **over-the-counter market**. That means there is no organized exchange where buyers and sellers meet. There is no bond ticker showing the changes in prices for bonds, except for certain Treasury issues that are used as benchmarks for the entire bond industry.

Bonds are sold to the highest bidder in a competitive new issue, or sales prices may be predetermined through negotiation between the issuer and a selected brokerage syndicate. In a competitive deal, there may be three or four underwriting syndicates competing for the bonds. The bonds are then remarketed to institutional and retail buyers at the set prices. Once the order period is over, the bonds are free to trade at market rates.

At its first appearance, a bond is said to be in the **primary**, or new, **bond market**. Within the primary market, Treasury bonds are sold by auction at announced times. Some large corporate bond issuers have so-called shelf registrations and allow brokers to sell bonds over time. In this case the offering rate adjusts with the fluctuation of interest rates. Other corporate issuers, federal agencies, or municipal issuers arrange for the sale of their bonds all at once.

When a new issue bond is bought and remains in a purchaser's portfolio until the day it comes due, it never reenters the marketplace. It is simply redeemed by the issuer without cost. If, however, a purchaser resells a bond before its redemption date, the bond automatically enters the **secondary**, or previously owned, **bond market**. There powerful forces come into play and determine what the actual yield will be.

Understanding Risk

FOUR KEY FORCES affecting a bond's yield are the credit quality of the issuer; market supply of the bond and similar issues; market demand; and overall economic conditions, including inflation. These forces either drive up or push down the amount of money buyers are willing to shell out to purchase a bond. They are all associated with risk, and, thus, it is important to differentiate among the kinds of risk.

There are nine types of risks commonly associated with buying and holding bonds:

◆ **Default risk.** The risk that the issuer is unable to meet the interest and principal payments when due.

◆ **Market risk.** The risk that interest rates will rise, reducing the value of bonds. We know for certain that interest rates fluctuate and that there are long-term trends. What cannot be predicted is whether a shift in interest rates is only short-term volatility or whether it is reflective of a longer-term trend.

◆ **Liquidity risk.** The risk that bonds cannot be sold quickly at an attractive price.

◆ **Early call risk.** The risk that high-yielding bonds will be called away early, with the result that the proceeds will have to be reinvested at a lower interest rate.

◆ **Reinvestment risk.** The risk that the interest payments and principal you receive may have to be reinvested at a lower rate. Only zero-coupon bonds do not have interest payment reinvestment risk.

◆ **Event risk.** The uncertainty created by the unfolding of unexpected events.

◆ **Tax risk.** The possibility that changes in the tax code or in an individual's tax position might adversely affect the tax advantages of bonds.

◆ **Political risk.** The likelihood that an issuer will exercise its legal right to terminate appropriations for municipal issues and that changes in the law will adversely affect the credit quality of existing issues.

◆ **Inflation risk.** The possibility that the fixed value might be eroded with an increased cost of living. In the United States, this is a long-term risk that is best judged in hindsight.

Where appropriate, the implications of these risks are discussed under each individual bond's description in the next section of this book.

That amorphous creature called the market is at all times seeking to create equilibrium, a state in which all yields are in an approximately equal state, once risk and maturity have been factored in. Since the market cannot change the fixed-coupon rate, which is set in stone when the bond is issued, it affects the yield, which reflects the market's perception of risk associated with a bond and which also determines the price at which the bond is sold.

This connection between yield and market perception of risk is important to grasp. For example, when a bond carries a 5 percent coupon rate and the prevailing interest rates are 3 percent, buyers will pay more than the face value of the bond to receive the benefit of a higher coupon rate (the bond is then said to sell at a **premium** to face value). On the other hand, when that same 5 percent bond is selling at a time when prevailing interest rates are 10 percent, buyers can be tempted to purchase only at a price much lower than the bond's face value (thus buying at a **discount** to face value). Occasionally a bond will sell at its face value and at such times it is said to be at **par**. These price changes reflect changes in the bond's yield.

Determining a Bond's Yield

THE CONCEPT OF YIELD creates the equilibrium between bonds sold at different prices. This concept is so important that we are highlighting it: *bonds are bought and sold based on yield, not on price.* This represents a key distinction between these financial instruments and stocks, which are always bought and sold in terms of price. **Yield** is the general term for the percentage return on a security investment. It is often called the rate of return. In bond language, it is very different from the stated coupon rate. It is imperative to understand these concepts in order to understand how bonds are valued.

Sellers of individual bonds as well as bond funds use a variety of yield terms. Understanding them will enable you to buy bonds and invest wisely in bond funds. While many of the yields require a financial calculator to be computed accurately, the following discussion of six fundamental terms gives a general description of their use and value. Brokers will calculate bond yields for you, and funds are required to post the yields in their prospectuses. Sites that offer yield calculators include www.bloomberg.com and www.kiplinger.com.

As a general term, *yield* can and does mean many things to many people. Bond professionals in particular have come up with a bewildering array of meanings. Here are just a few: current yield, yield-to-maturity, yield-to-call, yield-to-worst, and yield-to-average-life. Each, in its own way, seeks to create equivalency among bonds with different characteristics.

CURRENT YIELD

CURRENT YIELD (CY) is the only simple calculation among the lot and is used for comparing cash flows.

$$\text{Current yield} = \frac{\text{Annual interest from the bond}}{\text{Amount paid for the bond}}$$

Simply speaking, the more money you pay for a bond above its face value, the lower the current yield. Conversely, the bigger the discount from par, the higher the current yield.

SIMPLE AND COMPOUND INTEREST

WITH THE EXCEPTION of current yield, all bond yield calculations take compound interest into account. Thus, this is as good a place as any to review the differences between simple and compound interest.

It is reported that when someone asked Albert Einstein what he considered mankind's greatest invention, he replied without hesitation, "compound interest."[3] Compound interest is called the eighth wonder of the world. Compound interest can work for you by creating wealth when you buy bonds, or it can work against you if you pay interest on your debts. It has great impartial power.

Simple interest is simple because it is calculated only on your initial investment or principal. Compound interest is complex—and rewarding—because it adds the interest to your principal and then compounds the new total; in effect, interest earns interest. The example below, in which we compare a $1,000 bond that pays an

Year	Principal + Simple Interest	Principal + Compound Interest
1	$1,050	$1,050
5	$1,250	$1,276
10	$1,500	$1,629
20	$2,000	$2,653
30	$2,500	$4,322

annual 5 percent interest once a year, illustrates the different returns from the two kinds of interest.

Compounding, the fact that interest earns interest, makes a dramatic difference over many years. Unlike bank certificates of deposit, which are sold with simple interest, bond interest is compound interest and thus grows at a much faster rate over the long term. The more frequently interest is compounded on the total amount, the more dramatic the difference. If you need to compare two investments, ask how much you will receive at the end of the investment. No matter what the calculation, it still boils down to your final dollars and cents.

The Rule of 72 tells you approximately how many years it takes money to double when it compounds at a particular rate of annual interest. For example, if the rate of return is 10 percent, you divide 72 by 10 and learn that it takes approximately 7.2 years for the money to double at the 10 percent compounded rate. Similarly, if the rate of return were 5 percent, it would take 14.4 years to double your money (72 ÷ 5 = 14.4 years).

YIELD-TO-MATURITY

YIELD-TO-MATURITY, popularly known as YTM, is the benchmark upon which individual bonds are traded and quoted. It and the following two yield calculations all utilize the concept of compound interest. In the bond world, calculations assume that money never lies fallow or hidden away in a mattress. Rather, it is constantly being reinvested to generate further income. While YTM is not a perfect calculation, it is widely used because it is the unifying standard for all bond pricing.

YTM is based on the following assumptions: (1) You retain ownership for the remaining life of the bond, and (2) All interest payments are reinvested at the same prevailing rate. However, as interest rates change over time, your actual return on a bond does, too, unless you own a zero-coupon bond. If rates rise, for example, and you are able to reinvest the semi-annual interest payments at a better rate, your actual return will be better than quoted. If interest rates decline over the life of the bond, and you reinvest the interest at a lower rate, your actual return will be lower. Note that the key concept underpinning all of this is compound interest. The YTM calculation assumes reinvestment of every interest payment, whether monthly or semiannually, at the YTM rate.

Whether or not you understand the dense calculations involved in determining YTM and assumptions upon which these calculations are based is irrelevant. For better or for worse, YTM is the calculation used in the bond market as the great leveler, the calculation that helps you to determine the value of one bond compared with another.

Keep in mind that the value of bonds declines when interest rates rise, and the value increases when interest rates decline. In short, we say that yield moves inversely to price.

Your monthly brokerage statement reflects the market valuation of your bond. The concurrent changes in yield are not shown. This is called **marking-to-market**. This is of interest to you if you plan to sell your bonds. Otherwise, sit back and relax, because if we know nothing else, we know that interest rates, and therefore the price of your bonds, will fluctuate. We also know that bonds come due, and you will get your money back.

YIELD-TO-CALL AND YIELD-TO-WORST

SOMETIMES BONDS ARE PRICED to the call date instead of to the maturity date, and as a result the yields are calculated in terms of **yield-to-call** (YTC) instead of YTM. This occurs when interest rates have been falling and there is a good likelihood that the issuer may decide to exercise its right to redeem or repurchase the bonds early. This is especially likely if the coupon rate of the bond is higher than the prevailing rate of interest. If there is more than one call, the bond price is set by the **yield-to-worst** (YTW), the worst possible yield that you could receive for the bond. Request a YTC and a YTW calculation from your broker, since you don't know what direction interest rates will take.

YIELD-TO-AVERAGE LIFE

THE TERM **YIELD-TO-AVERAGE LIFE** is used in a number of different ways. It comes into play in situations in which the actual maturity is not known but, rather, is estimated.

For example, when an individual bond has a **sinking fund**, a lottery determines where bonds are called, with a rising proportion of bonds called each year. Even though these bonds have a call feature, it doesn't necessarily mean they will be called. Since you can't tell if your particular bonds will be called away, your broker will provide you with the yield-to-average life (also called the yield to the intermediate point), the point when half the bonds can be called away.

Municipal bonds often have sinking funds. Mortgage-backed securities also use this term. In both instances, yield-to-average life uses the anticipated compound rate of return and presumes the reinvestment of the cash flows as received. For muni bonds, the cash flow consists of the interest payments; for the mortgage-backed securities, it includes both principal and interest.

DURATION

INTRODUCED AS A CONCEPT in 1938, **duration** has become an increasingly popular analytical tool for evaluating the attractiveness of bonds. In effect, the duration measure tells you how much the selling price of your bond will change with a corresponding change in interest rates. It is influenced by three factors: time to maturity, coupon rate, and yield-to-maturity.

Individual bonds are evaluated based on their duration in addition to their maturity. Portfolios of bonds are given a composite duration to estimate the likelihood of bonds being called away. Duration is an oft-quoted measure of a bond fund.

All you really need to know—and what your broker or financial adviser should be able to tell you—is how a change in interest rates, whether up or down, will affect the value of your intended purchase. Think of it as a measure to explain any interest risk. In and of itself, duration is neither bad nor good—it is how you interpret the interest risk that is most important.

The longer the duration of the portfolio of bonds, the greater the volatility in price as interest rates fluctuate. For zero-coupon bonds the maturity of the bond matches its duration; these bonds are the most volatile of all.

Pricing a Secondary Market Bond

PRICING BECOMES TRICKY within the secondary market. Corporate and agency bonds change in relation to Treasuries, although the actual spreads over Treasuries vary because they are based on the market's view of the particular bond being sold. In this case the **spread** is the difference between the yield of the Treasury and the other securities. This kind of spread is sometimes called a **credit spread**, thus distinguishing it from the spread that refers to the difference between the broker buy and sell price. A broker asks a customer to buy a bond (**ask price**) and offers to buy bonds by placing a bid in to purchase bonds (**bid price**). The spread between the bid and the ask is generally tiny for Treasury bonds, while widening out for less frequently traded securities. If you want to have an idea as to the spread on the bond you are considering purchasing, you can ask the broker to give you a hypothetical bid as well as his selling price. If you ask him to drop the jargon, you are less likely to be confused.

The spread is measured in **basis points (bp)**. One basis point is equivalent to one hundredth of 1 percent (.01 percent). The difference between a yield of 5 percent and 6 percent, for example, is 100 basis points. If a Treasury bond was yielding 5 percent and the spread over Treasuries was 125 basis points, the yield on a corporate bond would be 6.25 percent.

The yields on Treasury bonds are benchmarks for all bonds, although as noted above, they are particularly useful for corporate and agency securities. They are in constant flux. The latest, most liquid 5-year and the 10-year Treasury bonds are the benchmarks for evaluating other taxable bonds with similar maturities. These are called **on-the-run** Treasuries, compared to other **off-the-run** Treasuries, or those that are not actively traded.

To illustrate how spreads are used in pricing corporate bonds that are not in alignment with their ratings, we present their value quoted in basis points compared to the 10-year Treasury on February 13, 2002:

◆ triple-A rated General Electric Corporation 7.375 percent of January 19, 2010, was priced +85 basis points to the 10-year Treasury

◆ A2/A+ Target Corporation, the retail department store, 6.35 percent of January 15, 2011, was only +80
◆ WorldCom Inc., the telecommunications company, 7.5 percent coupon due May 15, 2011, still rated A3/BBB+, was +320

The numbers above reflect the marketplace's estimation of risk despite the ratings. The marketplace determined that General Electric's balance sheet was, in effect, guilty until proven innocent, while lower-rated Target's reputation was not in jeopardy. World Com had already been judged risky, and the spread over Treasuries reflected that. The market's evaluation of WorldCom was prescient because the accounting scandal announced in June 2002 sent the value of WorldCom bonds to the deep sea.

Municipal traders in the secondary market use price matrixes to determine what a bond is worth, since most munis trade infrequently. Traders see where other similar bonds are trading and price the bonds accordingly. This is like pricing a used car. In an unstable market, those prices can be very misleading.

The scale for muni bonds will be different than the scale for corporate bonds or Treasury bonds. Each is a separate though related market. Muni prices are not adjusted as quickly as Treasuries, although they also move in relation to Treasuries. This difference exists because munis serve a different market, namely, buyers interested in a tax-exempt product. Demand and supply differences skew the prices.

Why bother with the concept of basis points and yield? Why not just look at the cash you have invested and the cash return you are getting on your money—so-called cash on cash? Or simply consider the following questions: What is the cash flow? How much money will be paid to you in interest every month? How much money will you get when the bonds mature? How much call protection is being offered to protect your cash flow? These are all pertinent questions. However, to compare one bond to another, brokers use yield and basis points, and you should, too.

PART
TWO

BOND
CATEGORIES

IN THIS PART, we describe what may seem a dizzying array of bond choices. We are your guide through this maze so that you can increase your capital. We want your money to work as hard as you do, to put in over-time chugging out interest while you sleep. We want you to be able to rest easy, knowing that you have invested wisely and that your funds will be there to take care of you and the people you love.

The United States has the largest debt market in the world, with more than $15 trillion in outstanding debt. Through the credit markets, loans are sold in the form of Treasury debt and inflation-protected securities, while government agencies package housing loans into bite-sized securities. The agencies add liquidity to those markets and finance themselves as well by selling bonds. They can also add liquidity to your portfolio.

Sold directly to you by the federal government are savings bonds: EE, HH, and I Bonds. These bonds are purchased through bank branches in small denominations and are accessible to every person, enabling even those with small sums of money to put their dollars to work earning interest. These bonds are complex, however, and we show how you can use them to your advantage.

Combined with anticipated federal revenue, or solely using their own sources, municipalities sell bonds to finance sewers, transportation, health care, education, energy, economic development, and other projects. This borrowing ability of state and local governments enables them to build an infrastructure so that businesses and individuals may grow and prosper. Most of these bonds are superb investments, though some are hazardous to your financial health. You'll understand why when you read Chapter 7.

Corporations sell bonds to provide liquidity for the development of new ideas and projects and for refurbishing the old ones. Banks, brokerage firms, airlines, chemical companies, retail clothing chains, computer companies—you name it—access the credit markets to build factories and offices and to explore new markets. Corporations also borrow using medium-term notes and convertible bonds. We describe how these bonds may start out as high-yield bonds or be transformed along the way.

Finally, there are bond look-alikes that use banks, brokers, and insurance companies to tap your funds for income-producing investments. Included in this category are the ubiquitous certificates of deposit issued by banks, preferred stock sold by corporations, and fixed annuities sold by insurance companies. We warn you of some of the pitfalls associated with these financial instruments and highlight their usefulness.

For the sake of clarity, we have used the same format to describe all the bonds in this part of our book. For each one, you will find information on its advantages, risks, and tax implications as well as any special features. This format should make it easy for you to compare one bond with another and to see which ones will best suit your needs and enrich your portfolio.

CHAPTER 3

U.S. TREASURY SECURITIES

THIS CHAPTER DESCRIBES the marketable bonds and

other securities issued by the U.S. Department of the

Treasury. Popularly known as Treasuries, these are all

backed by the full faith and credit of the U.S. govern-

ment. With the U.S. rise to world economic dominance,

such backing represents the strongest safety guarantee

to be found. Accordingly, these securities have less

default, event, liquidity, and political risk than just about any other investment. This does not mean that they are completely without risk. Most Treasuries still have substantial market risk.

Marketable securities, as the name implies, can be sold to other individuals or entities. Thus, if you buy a 5-year Treasury note on a Monday morning, you can sell it that Monday afternoon. Oddly enough, you can never have physical ownership of a marketable Treasury. In other words, you never receive a certificate from the government with your name on it. Rather, all Treasuries are available in what is known as book-entry form. These entries, with your name, are recorded in the books (or, in today's more modern terms, the accounting records) of commercial firms such as banks or brokerage houses or in the records of the U.S. government itself. However, you do receive a statement confirming your ownership of a Treasury.

Before 1985, the government issued 30-year bonds that it could call—that is, buy back—should it choose to do so. The Treasury could demand redemption of these bonds five years prior to their maturity date. In 2000 and 2001, when the government was running budget surpluses, many of these older bonds were called and thus retired from public circulation. Needless to say, owners of 30-year Treasuries that were bought in 1981 with an annual 14 percent interest rate were not happy in 2001 when they were told by the government that the party was over and that they had to part with those bonds at a time when other bonds were yielding about 4.5 percent.

All Treasuries issued since 1985, however, are noncallable prior to their maturity date. The last callable bonds to be issued were the 30-year bonds that came to market in November 1984. These bonds have a guaranteed coupon of 11.75 percent, and the government can recall them on November 15, 2009 rather than waiting until November 15, 2014 to do so.

The interest rate on Treasury securities is initially set at public auction. Since 1998, the Treasury has utilized a method known as a *single-yield auction.* In this process, the lowest yield that will allow the Treasury to sell all the bonds offered becomes the selling yield. Everyone who bids this yield or below gets to buy them at this single clearing yield (hence, the term single-yield auction). The Treasury has found this approach to be very advantageous: it is a win-win. The Treasury gets to pay the lowest possible yield (while encouraging investors to be extra aggressive), and the most aggressive investors need not fear overbidding and getting too low a yield.

All Treasuries are issued with a minimum face value of $1,000 and in increments of $1,000 above that. They can be purchased (except for cash management bills and 4-week bills) at auction by using the TreasuryDirect system. TreasuryDirect is a book-entry securities system, operated by the U.S. Bureau of the Public Debt, that allows you to maintain accounts directly with the U.S. Treasury. Alternatively, all Treasury securities can be purchased from a bank or a brokerage firm, either in the open market or at the Treasury auction. With the exception of Treasury STRIPS, you can transfer most types of Treasury securities that you buy from your bank or broker to your TreasuryDirect account.

There are two principal advantages of using TreasuryDirect. First, you pay no fee and no spread (the difference between the broker buy and sell price) to purchase Treasuries. Second, the custodian of your Treasury securities is the federal government. Thus, the possible risks associated with a failed brokerage firm holding your securities do not exist. The two principal disadvantages of using TreasuryDirect are that you can purchase only Treasury securities at the time of an auction and that TreasuryDirect will not make a margin loan. A more detailed discussion regarding TreasuryDirect and the purchase of bonds is found in Chapter 10.

The Bureau of Public Debt provides a superb information source on all U.S. Treasuries at its website, www.publicdebt. treas.gov.

With this general background as a prelude, the remainder of this chapter describes in detail the various Treasury securities.

U.S. Treasury Notes and Bonds

TREASURY NOTES AND BONDS are quite similar in that they pay interest every six months and are initially sold at auction. Although both Treasury notes and bonds are issued to finance the longer-term needs of the U.S. government, they are distinguished by the terms of their maturities. The maturity of Treasury notes is set at a minimum of one year and does not exceed ten years. In general, the government sells notes with only three different maturities. Auctions for 2-year notes are held at the end of each month and those for 5- and 10-year notes are conducted on a quarterly basis. Treasury bonds have maturities of more than ten years from their issue date and have traditionally been auctioned semiannually.

Although the maturity time frame makes it easy to distinguish between Treasury notes and bonds when they are first issued, it can be confusing when they are sold in what is known as the secondary market or aftermarket. As noted above, these issues can be freely traded much as stocks are. You can buy Treasuries that are currently outstanding that will come due in any year. For example, a Treasury bond that was originally issued as a 30-year bond in 1993 would in effect be a 20-year bond in 2003 because it had been outstanding for ten years. It would still be known as the 1993 30-year bond.

All fixed-income investors should at least consider ownership of Treasury notes or bonds because of their safety and liquidity. Their rates are widely quoted in the financial pages and on television as an indicator of the rate and direction of all interest rates. Until recently, only the rate on 30-year bonds was closely watched. When the U.S. budget went into surplus in the late 1990s, however, the government began to buy back large quantities of these bonds, causing their value to rise and distorting their yield. The 10-year Treasury bond then became viewed as a better interest rate benchmark. With the disappearance of surpluses in 2001, the 30-year bond emerged again as an indicator, and both it and the 10-year bond are now quoted as benchmarks.

>>ADVANTAGES
Treasury notes and bonds are the most liquid securities in the world. This means that you can easily buy or sell them, and the cost to purchase or sell is extremely low. When you sell, you receive cash the next day; often it takes longer to receive cash when you sell other types of securities.

>>RISKS

Treasury notes and bonds are not immune to the market risks that affect all bonds. The interest rate volatility in the period from August 11, 2001, to January 10, 2002 (a period which included the tragic events of September 11), provides a clear example of how Treasuries can be affected by such swings. On August 11, 2001, the 10-year, 5 percent Treasury sold at par; on October 31, this Treasury sold at 103.5, reducing its yield to 4.25 percent; and on January 10, it again sold at par, to yield 5 percent. Those buying this Treasury in October and selling it in January suffered a capital loss that wiped out all the interest income. While the September 11 tragedy added to the market's volatility, severe interest rate swings on long-term bonds are not unusual.

>>TAX IMPLICATIONS

Interest income from Treasury notes and bonds is subject to federal income tax, but not to state and local taxes. The interest paid at six-month intervals is taxable in the year received. In addition, if a Treasury bond is purchased for less than its face amount, the difference between the amount paid and its face value is taxable as interest income over the period between the date of acquisition and the earlier of the maturity date or the date you sell the bond. If you pay more than the face amount for the bond, you are entitled to deduct the difference between the amount paid and the face amount over the same period.

The fact that Treasury bonds are not taxable for state and local purposes can provide significant after-tax advantages for those living in high tax states such as California or New York. For example, assume that you buy a $1,000 bank certificate of deposit (CD) and a $1,000 Treasury that both pay 5 percent interest and that your state income tax rate is 10 percent. You would receive $50 in interest, pretax, on both investments. However, with a state income tax of 10 percent, you would have to pay $5 in state taxes on the CD and only net $45 on an after-tax basis. Since you would pay no state tax on the Treasury, you would net the full $50 and quickly appreciate the tax advantages of Treasury notes and bonds.

Remember, sellers of Treasury notes and bonds must report the interest accrued to the date of sale on their federal income tax return.

>>PRICING INFORMATION

Unlike stocks, which are priced in decimals, Treasury notes and bonds are priced in fractions as low as $\frac{1}{32}$. Thus, a Treasury might be quoted as selling at $99^{20}/_{32}$.

Although Treasury notes and bonds are issued with face values at or in multiples of $1,000, the price you pay is subject to market conditions at the time. Thus, a $10,000 5-year note that was issued two years ago with a 7 percent coupon would be worth more than a $10,000 5-year note issued two months ago with a 3 percent coupon. Both bonds have the same face value, but investors will pay more than face value for the bond with the higher coupon rate.

>>SPECIAL FEATURES AND TIPS

Investors love the fact that Treasuries can be so quickly converted to cash. In addition, there is *always* a market in which to sell them and at a good price, no matter what disasters are going on in the world. This cannot be said for many other securities. Treasuries can be sold as one lot or sold and transferred in part only. For example, if you own a $10,000 bond, you can sell only $5,000 if you choose. You must, however, always sell in $1,000 multiples.

Treasuries can be used as collateral (i.e., security) for a loan from your broker. You can borrow up to 96 percent of the value at your broker's loan rate. For example, assume you have $10,000 of Treasuries in your brokerage account and need cash either for another investment or for a personal expense. Your brokerage firm would lend you up to $9,600 and use the Treasuries as collateral (security) for the loan. The interest rate charged on the loan would be a floating rate that would be much lower than a credit card loan because marketable Treasuries are considered such good security.

U.S. Treasury Bills

UNLIKE TREASURY NOTES and bonds, Treasury bills, popularly known as T-bills, are used to finance the short-term needs of the U.S. government. They are auctioned with original maturities of 28, 91, 182, or 364 days and are, respectively, known as 4-week, 3-month, 6-month, or 1-year T-bills.

The U.S. Department of Treasury usually auctions 3- and 6-month T-bills every Monday and 4-week T-bills on Tuesdays. One-year T-bills are generally auctioned on a monthly basis. From time to time, the government will also issue what are called cash management bills for periods as short as one day. These tend to be bought and sold by large institutions rather than by individual investors.

T-bills further differ from Treasury notes and bonds in that they do *not* pay interest every six months. Rather, they are sold at a discount to their face value. The difference between the discounted price you pay and the face value you receive at maturity is treated as interest income, rather than as a capital gain. Thus, T-bills pay interest only at maturity. In addition, while all T-bills can be sold at any time without penalty and are available in commercial markets, only those with maturities greater than four weeks are sold through TreasuryDirect. T-bills with four-week maturities are only available through financial institutions, brokers, and dealers.

>>ADVANTAGES
T-bills are considered a cash equivalent. As with Treasury notes and bonds, they are easily bought and sold at extremely low transaction costs.

>>RISKS
Of all Treasuries, T-bills have the least market risk because of their short-term maturities. The 4-week T-bills, which the government first started selling on July 23, 2001, are the safest investment that we know of.

>>TAX IMPLICATIONS

As with Treasury notes and bonds, income from T-bills is subject to federal income tax but not to state and local income taxes. As discussed previously under "Treasury Notes and Bonds," this feature can provide significant advantages for those living in high tax states. The interest income from T-bills is taxable when the T-Bill is redeemed or sold.

Unlike Treasury notes and bonds, T-bill purchases can be used as a short-term tax planning strategy. This is done by taking advantage of the fact that interest income from T-bills is only reported in the year in which the bill comes due. To move interest income from one year to the next, buy a T-bill that has a maturity date next year. For example, if you bought a 1-year T-bill on March 5, 2002, you would not report your interest income until March 4, 2003. That interest income would not be subject to tax in your 2002 federal income tax return, but would be subject to tax in your 2003 return.

>>PRICING INFORMATION

T-bills further differ from Treasury notes and bonds in that the prices are quoted in decimals rather than in fractions.

STRIPS

STRIPS IS THE POPULARLY USED acronym for the U.S. Treasury's Separate Trade of Registered Interest and Principal of Securities program. In many ways, the approach is similar to that of T-bills in that STRIPS are zero-coupon securities that are sold at a discount to their face value, with interest payments made only at maturity. As with T-bills, the difference between the purchase price of STRIPS and their face value provides the return.

The STRIPS program represents a unique partnership between the government and the private sector. In August 1982, Merrill Lynch became the first government dealer to create its own brand of zero-coupon government bond and gave it the catchy acronym of TIGRs, which stands for Treasury Investment Growth Receipts. Salomon Brothers produced CATS (Certificates of Accrual on Treasury Securities). LIONS and other acronyms soon jumped into the fray. There were two major drawbacks to these financial instruments: (1) Even though they were based on U.S. Treasury securities, they were not guaranteed by the U.S. government; and (2) their trades were limited to their sponsoring firm, thus curtailing their liquidity.

In 1985, the U.S. Treasury announced its Separate Trading of Registered Interest and Principal of Securities program. In addition to more accurately describing the different types of zero coupons offered, the Treasury program also registered each one traded. With this registration, all STRIPS securities are the direct obligation of the U.S. government even though brokerage firms and other financial institutions create them.

STRIPS are constructed by taking a Treasury note or bond and stripping off the interest coupons. Two different kinds of zeros are created in this process: coupon strips, consisting of the interest coupons, and a principal payment strip, consisting of the principal payment. These are then sold separately. The number of interest payments determines the number of coupon strips created from any one Treasury security.

For example, assume that a brokerage firm buys a $1 million Treasury note with a 6 percent coupon rate that comes due in ten years. Over the lifetime of that bond it will annually yield $60,000, which is 6 percent of $1 million. Since interest payments are made semiannually, each coupon will be a strip that is worth $30,000. When the coupons are stripped off, there will be twenty interest strips and one principal strip. Each $30,000 interest strip then becomes a separate $30,000 zero-coupon security, and the one principal strip becomes a separate 10-year zero-coupon security in the amount of $1 million. These strips may all be sold separately, with the price of each interest strip being dependent on the time remaining to its maturity and the market interest rates at the date of sale.

>>ADVANTAGES

Although STRIPS have the same backing of the U.S. government as other Treasuries, they may yield somewhat more than a note or bond with the same due date because the STRIPS are more thinly traded and, thus, harder to sell. You can check your local paper to compare yields. This, of course, is an advantage for those who like to buy and hold their bonds.

Another advantage is that the total return on STRIPS is known precisely at the date of purchase if you hold the STRIPS to their due date. In interest-paying bonds, such as Treasury bonds, the total return depends in part on how you reinvest your interest payments every six months. In addition, you can buy STRIPS to come due in any year that would be desirable for your retirement or college education program.

Since STRIPS are more volatile (they move up or down more) than other Treasuries, you can use STRIPS to speculate on interest rate movements. For example, if you want to place a bet that interest rates will go down, you might buy long-term STRIPS. Since STRIPS are more volatile than Treasury bonds, you would have a larger gain if you guessed correctly.

>>RISKS

STRIPS have market risk. The longer the maturity of the STRIPS, the greater the risk of market volatility compared to equivalent interest-paying Treasuries. In addition, since STRIPS are less frequently traded than Treasuries, STRIPS will be slightly more expensive to buy and sell because the broker has a larger risk of a price decline.

>>TAX IMPLICATIONS

Even though interest from STRIPS is exempt from state and local taxes, you should still consider the advantages of holding these bonds in a tax-sheltered retirement account such as an IRA as opposed to outside of such an account. Interest on STRIPS held in a tax-sheltered retirement account is not subject to federal income tax until there is a distribution of cash from the account. However, if you hold the STRIPS outside of a tax-sheltered account, interest on STRIPS must be reported annually in your federal income tax return as ordinary interest income, even though it is not received until the STRIPS is redeemed or sold by you. Such interest is referred to as *imputed interest* or *phantom income.* As a result, STRIPS are most often purchased in tax-sheltered retirement accounts.

>>PRICING INFORMATION

STRIPS are sold at discounts to their face value and can be bought in a wide variety of denominations, including small amounts. There is no limit on the size of your purchase.

TIPS

WITH GREAT FANFARE and even more debate, the U.S. Treasury introduced a brand new security concept on January 29, 1997. It appears that the name of this security, Treasury Inflation-Indexed Securities, escaped scrutiny by acronym coiners. The marketplace quickly corrected what could have been an awkward name of TIIS by dubbing the newcomers as TIPS, which stands for Treasury Inflation-Protected Securities.

As stated previously, Treasury notes and bonds pay out a fixed amount of cash, based on the coupon rate, every six months. In contrast, TIPS pay out a *variable* amount of cash every six months that is initially lower than that paid by Treasury notes and bonds. As described below, this generally more modest coupon is designed to allow for the substantial principal accrual that is supposed to exactly offset the variability of the future cost of living. In this way, TIPS are designed to provide a guaranteed return over and above the inflation rate. Although the value of the principal varies over time, all TIPS are initially sold at auction in minimum amounts of $1,000.

The return on TIPS, then, consists of two parts:

1 The dollar amount of the semiannual cash interest payment changes every six months and is computed as follows: The coupon interest rate that is fixed at the time of auction is multiplied by the sum of (A) the original principal of the bond plus (B) any inflation adjustment to the bond's value.

2 The value of the TIPS principal increases daily at a rate of inflation based on the Consumer Price Index (CPI) as described below. The TIPS' accrual during any month is based on the difference between the two most recent monthly nonseasonally adjusted U.S.

City Average All Items Consumer Price Index for All Urban Consumers figures. There is a three-month lag in the application of the CPI to the Treasury calculation of the TIPS principal amount.

If you hold the TIPS until it comes due, the Treasury will pay you the sum of (A) the face amount of the security plus (B) an amount equal to the inflation (as measured by the CPI) that has occurred over the life of the security. Think of the semiannual inflation adjustment as a bonus that is added to the face amount of the bond. These inflation adjustments are not paid out until the security comes due. If you sell your TIPS before its due date, you will get a price that is set by the bond market. This price may be higher or lower than the bond's face value.

The inflation adjustment works in reverse if there is deflation rather than inflation. (*Deflation* is when the CPI basket literally drops in price each month, as it did for much of the 1930s. In contrast, the more common term *disinflation* refers to the situation where inflation, the increase in the price of the basket, becomes smaller over time. For example, in 1990 the basket increased in price by about 5 percent; by 1998 that increase dropped to 2 percent, which meant that there was disinflation, not deflation.) If there is deflation rather than inflation or disinflation, the value of the TIPS is adjusted downward, and the coupon interest payments that are paid in cash semiannually are calculated using the reduced principal value. However, in the case of deflation, all is not lost because the Treasury guarantees that upon maturity when the bond comes due, the minimum price that you will receive is the face value of the TIPS. This eliminates the risk that a severe deflation will substantially reduce the value of your TIPS.

This sounds more complicated than it actually is. Let's see how it works by using a simplified example. Assume that you bought a $1,000 TIPS on January 1 that has a fixed coupon rate of 4 percent. Further assume that the CPI increased by 1 percent for the period January 1 to June 30 (that is about a 2 percent per annum inflation rate). As we said, the 4 percent coupon rate will stay the same for the life of the bond, while the amount of the semiannual interest payments to you will vary with inflation.

With the above assumptions, the calculation of the interest payment for the first six months that you own the bond would be as follows: The value of the principal of your TIPS would increase $10 from $1,000 to $1,010 because of the 1 percent inflation increase ($1,000 x .01). The actual amount of cash interest that you would be paid would be calculated as follows: The adjusted principal amount of your bond ($1,010) would be multiplied by 2 percent (or, one-half the annual rate), because the calculation is for six months (or, one-half of the year). Thus, the amount of the first cash interest payment to you would be $20.20 ($1,010 x .02).

If for the second six months of the year inflation remains the same, the inflation-adjusted principal amount of the TIPS would rise to $1,020 and the interest payment for that period would be $20.40 ($1,020 x .02). Therefore, if there were inflation every six months as measured by the CPI, the principal amount of your bond would increase, and the amount of interest paid to you in cash would also increase. If the bond were a 10-year TIPS and you held it until it came due, the Treasury would pay you the principal amount of the security as adjusted upward for inflation. In this case, the bond you paid $1,000 for would be worth about $1,344 if the rate of inflation increased and averaged 3 percent and about $1,790 if the rate of inflation increased further and averaged 6 percent. In addition, the interest payment paid to you semiannually would rise every six months in proportion to the CPI.

The *Wall Street Journal* and the *New York Times* provide two values each day for each TIPS. First, the amount of the principal of the security as increased by inflation is stated. Second, the market value of the bond is also provided. The market value of the TIPS fluctuates with the rise and fall of other interest rates and the supply and demand for the security.

>>ADVANTAGES

TIPS provide a way to diversify your portfolio as well as three levels of protection. First, interest payments rise with inflation. Second, the principal amount increases with inflation. Third, the Treasury guarantees that when the bond comes due, the minimum price that you will receive is the face value of the bond. Thus, the risk of a severe deflation reducing the face value of the bond is eliminated. As a result, TIPS should be less volatile than other same-maturity bonds.

TIPS are traded by all primary dealers, though not as much as other Treasuries.

>>RISKS

What you gain in inflation protection on one hand, you lose in current cash flow on the other. A TIPS coupon rate is typically lower than what you would receive from other interest-paying Treasury notes and bonds because the TIPS provide inflation protection. Furthermore, if inflation is low over the life of your TIPS, you would receive a lower overall return on this bond investment than if you purchased other Treasury securities. And, as discussed above, should deflation occur, the amount of your semiannual interest payment would decrease along with the security's principal value, but not below the face value.

While TIPS are designed to protect you against inflation, they do not guard against market risk. General increases in interest rates that are not accompanied by inflation may result in a decline in the value of your TIPS if you need to sell it before it comes due. In fact, in 1997, the first year the bonds were issued, they declined in value.

There is also the tax risk of phantom income which is discussed immediately below.

>>TAX IMPLICATIONS

TIPS have tax consequences similar to those applicable to STRIPS. The upward adjustments to the principal of your TIPS will result in no current cash distributions to you until you either sell the bond or it comes due. However, unless the TIPS are held in a tax-sheltered retirement account such as an IRA, you are required to report this upward adjustment in your federal income tax return as taxable income over the period from the date of the adjustment to the earlier of the maturity date or the date you sell the TIPS, even though you do not currently receive the value of the upward adjustment in cash. Correspondingly, a downward adjustment in the principal amount (in a period of deflation) will give rise to a deduction against the interest income paid to you. If you are in a low tax bracket, you might own these bonds in any account. However, if you are in a high tax bracket, you should consider owning TIPS in a tax-sheltered retirement account.

There are different consequences if you own your TIPS through mutual funds. Please see Chapter 11 for a discussion of TIPS owned in a mutual fund.

TIPS are not subject to state or local income tax.

>>SPECIAL FEATURES AND TIPS
TIPS can be used as collateral for a loan.

TIPS allow investors the opportunity to speculate on changes in inflation and interest rates. TIPS have a low correlation to other financial assets and thus may help investors reduce risk as part of their asset allocation.

Since 1926 inflation in the United States has averaged about 3 percent. For this same period, U.S. government bonds have yielded about 5 percent. Thus, the so-called real yield on U.S. government bonds has been about 2 percent. If you can get a real return on TIPS that exceeds 2 percent, you might consider TIPS favorably compared to other Treasuries of the same maturity.[1]

Some advisers believe that TIPS are good for retirees because they will be hurt if their purchasing power starts to erode with inflation. Thirty-year-olds, by contrast, do not need as much inflation protection, because their salaries are expected to go up over time, and the bulk of their earnings are ahead of them.[2]

Jeff Metz, a financial adviser located in Marlton, New Jersey, said that his strategy in buying TIPS is to compare them to comparable maturity Treasuries and to buy TIPS only at Treasury auction. That way it is easier to compare the rate of return on the Treasury to the rate of return on TIPS. You will also save transaction fees, because there is no cost to buy TIPS at Treasury auction. Metz compares the coupon on the TIPS to the yield-to-maturity on the Treasuries and then makes an estimate for inflation. For example, if the yield-to-maturity on a 10-year Treasury bond is 4.5 percent and the coupon on the TIPS is 3 percent, it makes sense to buy the TIPS if you estimate that inflation over the 10-year term of the TIPS will exceed 1.5 percent (4.5 percent minus 3 percent).

CHAPTER 4

U.S. SAVINGS BONDS

U.S. SAVINGS BONDS are the most widely held security in the world, with over 800 million, valued at $186 billion, being held by 55 million Americans.[1] The U.S. government markets them as a patriotic and profitable investment for the so-called little guy. In fact, in December 2001, the series EE Savings Bond was renamed the Patriot Bond. Although U.S. savings bonds have the reputation of being simple and straightforward, nothing could be further from the truth. Therefore, we start this chapter with the following warning.

The structure of savings bonds is complex. Their tax consequences are even more complex. You can't predict what your return on EE and I Savings Bonds will be because they have floating rates. The yield calculation on EE Bonds has changed three times since 1990. Not only that, the way you register ownership of any of the bonds has important tax consequences.

The good news is that we have described the best way to capitalize on the various savings bonds under each individual description. For despite their complexity, savings bonds may be great investments, and we believe you should take the time to understand them. There are no fees, loads, or commissions to buy them. They are fully guaranteed by the U.S. government and are not callable. They are free of state and local income tax and may be free of federal income tax if used for certain educational expenses by qualified taxpayers.

All savings bonds are nonmarketable, which means that they cannot be sold to anyone else or used as collateral for a loan. However, after you own them for a minimum of six months, you can sell (redeem, in bond language) your savings bonds back to the Treasury Department at any time. Just take them to your financial institution with proper identification and you will be helped with the redemption process.

All savings bonds are registered with the Treasury Department, which provides a certificate of ownership stating the name of the owner. Should a bond be lost, destroyed, or stolen, you can receive a replacement free of charge. To facilitate replacement, you should keep a record of the serial numbers, issue dates, registration information, and the Social Security number(s) that appear on them.

You must choose one of three ways to register savings bonds:

1 Single ownership. With single ownership registration, only the registered owner, such as John Doe, can cash or make a gift of the bond. On John Doe's death, the bond will become part of his estate and will go through probate.

2 Co-ownership. With co-ownership registration, either co-owner, such as John Doe or Robert Smith, may cash the bond without the knowledge or approval of the other. When the first co-owner dies, the second becomes the sole owner of the bond. This is similar to a joint account at a bank and avoids probate. You should determine whether there may be gift tax consequence of registering a bond in the name of someone who has not provided the cash to purchase the bond.

3 Beneficiary. With beneficiary registration, such as "John Doe, payable on death to Mary Doe," only the owner, John Doe in this case, may cash the bond. The beneficiary, Mary Doe, if she survives John, automatically becomes the sole owner of the bond when John dies. This type of ownership avoids probate, unless Mary were to predecease John.

Savings bonds can be bought through a bank, an employee payroll savings plan, or directly from the government through its TreasuryDirect program. For a superb information source on this program, as well as many other up-to-date aspects of savings bonds, check these websites: www.savingsbonds.gov and the Bureau of Public Debt at www.publicdebt.treas.gov.

Series EE Savings Bonds

THIS DESCRIPTION IS FOR EE Bonds with issue dates of May 1997 and later. For the yields and other rules related to EE or E Bonds with earlier issue dates, visit the U.S. government's public debt website at www.publicdebt.treas.gov and look for the heading "For Series EE/E Savings Bond Investors."

EE Savings Bonds are one of the most popular Treasury issues. They are called accrual securities because interest is accumulated monthly but not paid out in cash until the bonds are redeemed. They sell at a 50 percent discount to their face value, which means you pay $25 for a $50 EE Bond.

The interest rate on EE Bonds compounds on a semiannual basis. It changes every May 1 and November 1 and is set at 90 percent of the average yield on 5-year Treasury securities for the preceding six months. Thus, you never know what long-term return you will be getting when you buy these bonds. The bonds do, however, currently feature two very important guarantees: (1) they reach their face value in a maximum of seventeen years, and (2) they will not yield below 4.2 percent for this seventeen-year period. Thus, no matter how low the 90 percent average falls, purchasers of EE Bonds are guaranteed a minimum 4.2 percent compounded interest rate of return at the end of seventeen years, when they can also receive the face value of the bond. Should the 90 percent average turn out to be greater than 4.2 percent, EE Bond purchasers benefit by receiving a correspondingly greater return than 4.2 percent. Between May 1997 and May 2002, for example, the six-month returns varied from a low of 3.96 percent to a high of 5.68 percent. Each time the interest is added, the redemption value of the bond increases.

While there is no requirement that you must redeem your EE Bonds after a set period, the bonds stop earning interest thirty years from their issue date.

>>ADVANTAGES

EE Bonds have numerous attractions. Chief among them are that they provide protection against inflation and deflation, plus a guaranteed lump sum distribution. Further, their initial investment is as low as $25, rather than $1,000 for a Treasury security. As discussed below, they can provide several tax advantages, particularly with regard to higher education expenses.

>>RISKS

There is a small reduction in liquidity in that you cannot redeem your EE Bonds for the first six months that you hold them and if you redeem them in the first five years from your purchase date, you will lose the last three months of interest.

>>TAX IMPLICATIONS

You can defer reporting all of the taxable income from EE Bonds by exchanging them for HH Bonds. This can be done any time before your EE Bonds reach their thirty-year maturity. This is reviewed under HH Bonds below.

If you elect not to exchange your EE Bonds for HH Bonds, the difference between their purchase price and the amount you receive when you cash them in is regarded as taxable interest income. The interest income earned on EE Bonds may be reported on your federal income tax return in one of two ways. The first and usual way is to report it in the year in which the bond is cashed. The alternative is to report the increase in redemption value as interest income each year even if you do not receive any cash. The second way can have advantages. For example, when an EE Bond is owned by a child or other taxpayer who has no other taxable income, it might be advantageous to report the interest income yearly. This would enable such a holder to avoid paying tax when the bond is redeemed.

If the taxpayer is your child and is over fourteen and elects to cash in the bonds, he or she will pay tax on the postponed interest income at a presumably lower tax bracket than yours. But keep in mind the possible exclusion of taxes on all EE Bond interest if you qualify to use the bonds for college tuition, described under "Special Features" below.

If you want to change your method of reporting savings bond interest from the usual way to the alternative way, you can do so without notifying or getting permission from the IRS. However, when filing your federal income tax return for the year you change, you must include on that return all savings bond interest accumulated to date that hasn't previously been reported.

If you want to do the opposite, change your method of reporting savings bond interest from the alternative way to the usual way, you can do so by filing IRS Form 3115 with the IRS and following the procedures in the savings bonds section in IRS Publication 550, *Investment Income and Expenses.*

If you are a surviving co-owner and the decedent had postponed reporting the interest income while he or she was alive, there are two choices for reporting the deferred interest income:

1 All the postponed interest income can be reported on the decedent's final income tax return. In this case, you will not have to include any of this income in your tax return. You would include only interest earned after the date of death.

2 All of the interest income earned before and after the decedent's death can be reported in your tax return.

>>PRICING INFORMATION

You can invest as little as $25 in an EE Bond. The yearly maximum that you can invest is $15,000, which would purchase $30,000 in face value of EE Bonds. EE Bonds come in eight denominations, $50, $75, $100, $200, $500, $1,000, $5,000, and $10,000.

>>SPECIAL FEATURES

The Education Savings Bonds Program, which applies to both EE Bonds and I Bonds, offers significant tax advantages to qualifying individuals. The program was introduced by the Treasury Department in 1990 as a response to the soaring costs of higher education.

If you qualify, this program allows you to exclude from your income all or part of the taxable interest income you receive on the redemption of EE or I Savings Bonds. The transfer of redemption proceeds to a qualified tuition program, 529 plan, or Coverdell Educational Savings Account for you, your spouse, or dependent also qualifies.[2] This exclusion applies to qualified higher educational expenses that you pay for yourself, your spouse, or any dependent for whom you are allowed a dependency exemption on your federal income tax return at an eligible institution or state tuition plan in the same calendar year that the bonds are redeemed.

You must meet all of the following requirements for the exclusion of taxable interest income to apply:

1 Year of purchase. EE Bonds must have been purchased by you in January 1990 or later. All I Bonds are eligible for this program. You are not required to indicate that you intend to use the bonds for educational purposes when you buy them.

2 Age. You must be at least twenty-four years old on the first day of the month in which you bought the bonds.

3 Registration. When using the bonds for your child's education, the bonds must be registered in your name and/or your spouse's name using one of your Social Security numbers. Your child can be listed as a beneficiary on the bond, but not as a co-owner. If your child is listed as a co-owner, the bond does not

qualify for the exclusion. When using bonds for your own education, the bonds must be registered in your name. If you are
married, you must file a joint return to qualify for the exclusion.

4 Year of redemption. The bonds must be redeemed in the year
the tuition is paid. You must use both the principal and interest
from the bonds to pay qualified expenses in order to exclude
the interest from your gross income.

5 Qualified institutions. Post-secondary institutions, including
colleges, universities, and vocational schools that meet the
standards for federal assistance (such as guaranteed student
loan programs) qualify for the program.

6 Qualified expenses. Qualified educational expenses include
tuition and fees (such as lab fees and other required course
expenses) at an eligible educational institution. The expenses
may be for the benefit of you, your spouse, or a dependent for
whom you are eligible to claim an exemption on your federal
income tax return. Expenses paid for any course or other education involving sports, games, or hobbies qualify only if
required as part of a degree or certificate-granting program. The
costs of books and room and board aren't qualified expenses.

7 Income limits. The full interest exclusion is available only if
your income is under a certain limit in the year you use EE or
I Bonds for educational purposes, not the year in which you
buy the bonds. In tax year 2002, for example, the exclusion
was eliminated for single taxpayers with modified adjusted
gross incomes of $72,600 and above and for married taxpay-
ers filing jointly with modified adjusted gross incomes of
$116,400 and above. Married couples must file jointly to be
eligible for the exclusion.

If you meet all of the above requirements when your child is
ready for college and you cash in your EE or I Bonds and use
them for tuition, all of the interest earned on the bonds will
be tax free. Thus, EE or I Savings Bonds become as tax-efficient as investing in tax-free municipal bonds. Moreover, you
might receive a higher return on savings bonds than on municipal bonds.

>>RECOMMENDATIONS AND TIPS

If EE Bonds pay only 90 percent of the average of 5-year Treasury securities, why not buy 5-year Treasury securities and make the extra return? If you can afford the minimum purchase price of $1,000 for a 5-year Treasury security, it might provide a higher return. On the other hand, if you qualify to use the proceeds of the EE Bonds for college tuition, you might be better off buying EE Bonds. The EE Bonds will provide a tax deferral and, if you qualify, a tax exclusion feature. In addition, while 5-year Treasures are subject to annual federal income taxes and market risk, EE Bonds have no market risk.

EE Bonds increase in value on the first day of each month. Thus, if it is near the end of the month when you plan to redeem your bonds, you may want to wait until the first day of the next month to earn a full month's interest. For example, if you planned to cash your bonds on March 28, you would lose interest for the entire month of March. If you could wait until April 1 to redeem your bonds, you would earn interest for the entire month of March.

When held for a long time, EE Bonds may result in a large tax liability in the year they are redeemed. Consider two tax reduction options:

1 Give the EE Bonds to individuals in tax brackets lower than yours before the bonds are cashed. If you are making a gift of EE Bonds, you should supply the Social Security number of the recipient. If you do not know that person's Social Security number, you must supply yours. The person who cashes in the EE Bonds must report the interest income on their federal income tax return.

2 Exchange the EE Bonds for HH Bonds (discussed below). HH Bonds provide current income while continuing to defer any taxes due on the EE Bonds.

Series HH Savings Bonds

HH SAVING BONDS are markedly different from EE Bonds in that HH Bonds provide current income and are issued at full face value. (Recall that Series EE Bonds pay income only at redemption and are sold at a discount to face value.) Thus, the redemption value of an HH Bond is always the same as its issue price. You cannot buy HH Bonds for cash; rather you can only get them in exchange for eligible E Savings Bonds, EE Savings Bonds, or upon reinvestment of the proceeds of matured HH Bonds. For example, if your EE Bonds currently have a value of $1,000 (and you bought them for $500), you could exchange those EE Bonds for $1,000 face value amount of HH Bonds. In order to exchange an EE Bond for an HH Bond, the following broad requirement must be met: the EE Bond must be at least six months old and no older than a year after the month in which it stopped earning interest. Remember that EE Bonds stop earning interest thirty years from their issue date.

HH Bonds do not increase in value. Instead, every six months you receive a payment in cash by a direct deposit to your checking or savings account equal to six months of interest on your HH Bond. The interest rate on HH Bonds is set at a fixed rate. On the day you obtain the bond, you "lock in" this rate for the first ten years you hold the bond. Interest rates are reset on the tenth anniversary of the HH Bond's issue date. The first interest payment is due six months from the issue date shown on the bonds, and subsequent payments are made every six months.

HH Bonds reach final maturity and stop earning interest twenty years from their issue date. You then have two options: You may redeem them or exchange them for new HH Bonds. However, you can only take advantage of the latter option once.

>>ADVANTAGES
HH Bonds are risk free because they are guaranteed by the U.S. government. They have no liquidity risk because they can be redeemed at face value at any time. If you exchange EE Bonds for HH Bonds, you can continue to defer paying federal income taxes on the interest accrued on your EE Bonds. (See the discussion below under "Tax Implications.")

>>RISKS
HH Bonds generally feature an interest rate that is less than what you can earn on corporate or longer-term Treasury bonds.

Consider the risks, rewards, and tax consequences of each before investing.

Cashing in HH Bonds may result in a large tax liability in the year they are redeemed if you held the EE Bonds that you exchanged for them for a long time. Thus, exchanging EE Bonds for HH Bonds might result in a bunching of income in one year and a higher federal income tax than if the income had not been deferred.

>>TAX IMPLICATIONS

You must report the payment you receive as interest income on your federal income tax return for the year it is earned. This income is not subject to state or local income taxes. An interest income statement (Form 1099-INT) will be issued to you each year showing how much you must report on your federal income tax return.

There is a significant tax advantage available if you elect to exchange your EE Bonds for HH Bonds. If you make this exchange, you can continue to postpone paying tax on the interest that has accrued on the EE Bonds. However, you must begin to pay tax on the interest that you earn from your HH Bonds. Even if your EE Bonds were accruing interest at a higher rate, the rate you will receive on the HH Bonds is the current HH Bond rate. You would make this exchange by using exchange application Form PDF 3253.

Any deferred interest from savings bonds that you exchange to buy HH Bonds must be reported as taxable income on your federal income tax return at the earlier of (1) the year in which your HH Bonds reach final maturity unless you exchange them for new HH Bonds or (2) if you cash your HH Bonds prior to final maturity.

An example might be helpful. Assume that you bought an EE Bond twelve years ago for $500 and it is now worth $1,000. If you trade your EE Bond for an HH Bond worth $1,000, you would continue to postpone reporting the $500 of interest income that you earned on your EE Bond until you cash in your HH Bond or the HH Bond reached final maturity. Remember that you can exchange your HH Bonds for new HH Bonds after the former come due in twenty years. However, the interest income that you now earn on your $1,000 HH Bond every six months will be subject to tax each year.

>>PRICING INFORMATION

Series HH Bonds are issued in four denominations: $500, $1,000, $5,000, and $10,000. A minimum of $500 redemption value in eligible savings bonds is required in order to make an exchange of EE Bonds for HH Bonds. If the cash received from the EE Bonds is not in even $500 units, then the owner of the EE Bonds must either take the difference and pay taxes on the money received or add more money to purchase another $500 unit. As an example, assume that your EE Bonds are redeemed for $2,328. There are two options:

Option 1. Purchase four $500 HH Bonds for $2,000 and pay taxes on the remainder of $328.

Option 2. Purchase five $500 HH Bonds for $2,500 and pay the difference of $172 in cash.

There is no limit on the number of HH Bonds you can acquire in a calendar year.

Series I Savings Bonds

THE I BOND, first issued in September 1998, is the newest and most complex of the three types of savings bonds issued by the Treasury Department. It is an inflation-indexed accrual security that is bought at face value. Interest is accrued and added to the I Bond monthly. However, the interest is not paid until the bond is redeemed.

The I Bond earnings rate is composed of two separate rates: a fixed rate of return and a variable semiannual inflation rate. When these two rates are combined, they produce the composite earnings rate on the I Bond.

The fixed rate of return is set by the Treasury Department twice a year, each May 1 and November 1. The announced fixed rate applies only to bonds purchased during the six months following its announcement. The fixed rate that is in effect for the six-month period during which you buy your I Bond remains your fixed rate for the thirty-year life of your I Bond. Thus, the fixed rate of return announced in May, for example, of a given year is the same over the entire life of the I Bonds you purchased between May 1 and October 31 of that year. Between September 1998 (when I Bonds were first introduced) and May 2002, for example, the fixed rate has ranged from a low of 2 percent to a high of 3.6 percent per year.

The semiannual inflation rate changes every six months and is also announced each May 1 and November 1 by the Treasury Department. The inflation rate is computed using the Consumer Price Index for All Urban Consumers, published by the Bureau of Labor Statistics. The semiannual inflation rate announced in May is a measure of inflation over the preceding October through March; the inflation rate announced in November is a measure of inflation over the preceding April through September. From September 1998 to May 2002, the inflation rate has ranged from a low of 0.57 percent to a high of 1.91 percent.

As noted previously, the composite earnings rate on your I Bond is computed by combining the fixed rate and the inflation rate according to a set formula. An I Bond's composite earnings rate changes every six months after its issue date. For example, the earnings rate for an I Bond issued in August 2002 changes every August and February. However, the formula used to calculate the composite rate is more complicated than simply adding together the fixed rate and the semiannual inflation rate.

For those of you who are mathematically inclined, the formula for I Bonds issued from November 1, 2001 to April 30, 2002 are as follows:

Fixed rate for I Bonds issued from November 1, 2001 to April 30, 2002 = 2 percent

Inflation rate for I Bonds issued from November 1, 2001 to April 30, 2002 = 1.19 percent

Composite rate = [fixed rate + 2 x inflation rate + (inflation rate x fixed rate)] x 100

Composite rate = [.02 + 2 x .0119 + (.0119 x .02)] x 100

Composite rate = [.02 + .0238 + .000238] x 100
Composite rate = [.044038] x 100
Composite rate = .044 x 100
Composite rate = 4.4 percent

The composite rate of 4.4 percent applies for the first six months after the issue. This composite rate combines the 2 percent fixed rate of return with the 1.19 percent semiannual inflation rate as measured by the Consumer Price Index. In effect, if you purchased I Bonds issued between May 1, 2001, and October 30, 2001, you would earn a 2 percent fixed rate of return over and above inflation for the thirty-year life of the bond.

The above example and explanation assume that each year there will be at least some inflation. However, it is possible that in the one or more years that you hold your I Bond there may be deflation. In the case of deflation, your I Bond's composite rate will be lower than its fixed rate. This is because instead of an inflation rate being added to your fixed rate, the deflation rate will be subtracted from your fixed rate. Deflation will cause an I Bond to increase in value slowly, or not increase in value at all, during the period of deflation.

If the deflation rate exceeds your fixed rate there is a safety guarantee built into the I Bond. The terms of the I Bond provide that no matter how bad deflation gets, the composite rate will never be reduced below zero. In the case in which the deflation rate exceeds the fixed rate, the redemption value of your I Bonds will remain the same until the composite rate becomes greater than zero. For example, if your fixed rate is 2 percent and the deflation rate is 1 percent for the year, your composite rate for the year will be 1 percent (2 percent minus 1 percent). If your fixed rate for the year is 2 percent and the deflation rate is 3 percent, your composite rate for the year would be 0, because the composite rate cannot be reduced below zero.

All of the rates and detailed calculators are provided by the Treasury Department on its website, www.savingsbonds.gov. Go to Savings Bond Calculator to find the value of your bonds and what they are earning currently.

>>ADVANTAGES

I Bonds are guaranteed to protect against the risks of inflation and are also guaranteed to keep their value even if there is deflation. I Bonds have no market risk because you can redeem them at their computed value from the Treasury Department at any time after six months. In addition, I Bonds generally have all of the same advantages as noted above for EE Bonds.

>>RISKS

Unlike EE Bonds, which guarantee a minimum rate of return, I Bonds do not guarantee a minimum level of earnings. In addition, although I Bonds generally increase in value monthly, they can stop accumulating interest in periods of deflation.

There is a small reduction in liquidity in that you cannot redeem I Bonds for the first six months that you hold them, and if you redeem them in the first five years from your purchase date, you will lose the last three months of interest.

I Bonds stop earning interest thirty years from the issue date. When your I Bonds reach final maturity in thirty years, you must redeem them and report all of the interest in the year of redemption. You may not exchange I Bonds for HH Bonds to defer your payment of tax on the interest income.

>>TAX IMPLICATIONS

The taxation of I Bonds is generally the same as noted above for EE Bonds except that you cannot exchange your I Bonds for HH Bonds when the I Bonds come due in thirty years. The Education Savings Bond Program is the same for I Bonds as for EE Bonds.

>>PRICING INFORMATION

I Bonds are sold at face value in denominations of $50, $75, $100, $200, $500, $1,000, $5,000, and $10,000 and earn interest for as long as thirty years.

>>RECOMMENDATIONS AND TIPS

I Bonds are tax efficient. Consider using I Bonds as a tax-deferral vehicle if you have contributed fully to all of your tax-sheltered retirement accounts—such as your 401(k), 403(b), IRA, etc.—and you still want an investment that will provide a tax deferral.

You can buy as much as $30,000 per year of I Bonds in addition to any other series of savings bonds. If you are married and want to buy more, you and your spouse can buy as much as $60,000 per year of I Bonds; you may each register $30,000 of these bonds in your names as single owners. Another way to register the bonds as a couple is as follows: Put your name as the first co-owner together with your Social Security number and your spouse's name (without Social Security number) as the second co-owner on the first bond. On the other bond, do the opposite: Put your spouse's name and Social Security number as the first co-owner and your name (without Social Security number) as the other co-owner.

U.S. AGENCY DEBT SECURITIES

CHAPTER 5

ONE OF THE LASTING LEGACIES of the Great Depression

of the 1930s is the increased use of U.S. federal agen-

cies to aid a wide variety of consumers. Enacted under

the auspices of Congress, agencies reduce borrowing

costs for homeowners, farmers, agricultural interests,

and students, among others. The number of agencies

and their subsequent outstanding bonds has ballooned

over the years, creating a huge amount of agency debt.

There are two basic kinds of agency financial instruments. One is a debt security, which is similar to a Treasury note or bond, and the other is a mortgage pass-through security. The latter is issued by both government and nongovernment organizations and is discussed in the next chapter.

Agencies issuing debt securities are generally classified in one of three categories: government owned, government sponsored, or the ubiquitous "other." Government-sponsored enterprises are popularly known as GSEs. They are shareholder-owned, privately managed corporations that are regulated by the U.S. government.

Of the many agencies, four are major issuers in the liquid, easily traded bond markets:

◆ **Fannie Mae** (formerly titled the Federal National Mortgage Association)

◆ **Freddie Mac** (formerly titled the Federal Home Loan Mortgage Corporation)

◆ **Farm Credit System** (sometimes referred to by its acronym of FCS)

◆ **Federal Home Loan Bank System** (an agency that has yet to acquire an acronym, let alone a popular name).

Other agencies are Financing Corporation (FICO), Resolution Funding Corporation (REFCORP), Student Loan Marketing Association (Sallie Mae), Tennessee Valley Authority (TVA), and Federal Agricultural Mortgage Corporation (Farmer Mac).

While most agency debt instruments are not backed by the full faith and credit of the U.S. government, all have an implied AAA rating and are considered exceptionally safe investments. Most agency bonds, however, are callable and often have very short calls. (In contrast, Treasuries issued after November 1984 are not callable.) Agencies generally have slightly higher yields than Treasuries because they are viewed as being slightly more risky than Treasuries.

Major Debt-Issuing Agencies

FANNIE MAE AND FREDDIE MAC

THESE AGENCIES ARE GSEs that are regulated by the Secretary of Housing and Urban Development. Fannie Mae was chartered in

1938 and Freddie Mac in 1970. Both assist low- and moderate-income families to buy homes. In order to obtain funds to underwrite such mortgages, they issue discount notes and medium-term notes. The proceeds are then used to buy mortgages, mortgage securities, and other home loans from banks and other lenders. The mortgage activities of these two GSEs are described in detail in the next chapter.

In 1998 both Fannie Mae and Freddie Mac began benchmark securities programs, known respectively as Benchmark Notes and Reference Notes. These programs offer large and regularly scheduled issues of debt securities ranging between $2 billion and $5 billion. The issues provide greater liquidity to the agencies and offer a higher yielding alternative to Treasury bonds. Fannie Mae and Freddie Mac are two of the largest issuers of debt in the United States. Fannie Mae issues debt in a minimum purchase amount of $10,000 and in increments of $1,000. Freddie Mac issues debt in a minimum purchase amount of $25,000 and in increments of $1,000.

FARM CREDIT SYSTEM (FCS)

ESTABLISHED IN 1916, the Farm Credit Administration regulates this GSE. It is a nationwide system of borrower-owned banks that lend directly and indirectly to ranchers, farmers, and certain farm-related businesses. Banks in the system issue three kinds of securities: (1) short-term discount notes with maturities that range from five to 270 days with a minimum denomination of $50,000; (2) short-term bonds with maturities that range from three to nine months with a minimum denomination of $50,000; and (3) medium notes with maturities that range from one to ten years with a minimum denomination of $1,000.

FEDERAL HOME LOAN BANK SYSTEM

ESTABLISHED IN 1932, this GSE is under the jurisdiction of the Federal Housing Finance Board and is responsible for regulating savings and loan banks. The system's membership consists of private savings and loan banks, and these in turn own the twelve regional Federal Home Loan Banks. The banks borrow in the open market and lend this money to savings and loan banks, which then lend it to home buyers. The banks issue short-term, non-callable, discount securities in minimum amounts of $50,000 and longer-term bonds, which may be callable, in denominations of $10,000, $25,000, and higher amounts. Any bond issued in the system is a joint obligation of all twelve Federal Home Loan Banks; thus, if there is default by one, the others are legally liable to cover it.

FINANCING CORPORATION (FICO)

FICO BELONGS IN the "other" agency category in that it is a mixed ownership government corporation chartered by the Federal Home Loan Bank Board. It was begun in 1987 to finance the recapitalization of and to help create liquidity for the Federal Savings and Loan Insurance Corporation (FSLIC) after the stability of the savings and loan banks was threatened. Although FICO's borrowing authority was terminated in 1991, many of its obligations—backed by two insurance funds and carrying attractive coupon rates—still exist, though they are hard to locate. We have found it worthwhile to have our broker track down FICO bonds for our own portfolios and have purchased them in small and large pieces. In 1997, for example, our broker was able to locate and sell to us FICO strips, which are zero-coupon bonds, that had face values between $2,000 and $23,000 and a yield-to-maturity between 7 and 7.5 percent. We bought these bonds for our tax-sheltered retirement accounts so that we would not be adversely affected by the phantom income that they throw off.

RESOLUTION FUNDING CORPORATION (REFCORP)

THIS IS ANOTHER mixed-ownership GSE. It was established in 1989 to fund the Resolution Trust Corporation. It provided financing to bail out the large number of thrifts that failed in the 1980s. Although the bonds issued by REFCORP are not direct obligations of the U.S. government, the U.S. Treasury guarantees the interest and Treasury bonds secure the principal. Thus, there is little if any default risk on these bonds. There are only a few of these bonds available for purchase today. If you can find them, they are in

$1,000 minimum amounts, although most sellers would not want to sell such small pieces to you.

STUDENT LOAN MARKETING ASSOCIATION (SALLIE MAE)

THIS GSE, ESTABLISHED IN 1972, is regulated by the Farm Credit Administration. It is scheduled to lose its status as an agency on September 20, 2008, at which time it will be solely a shareholder-owned, privately managed corporation. Sallie Mae's mission is to guarantee and purchase student loans, thus providing liquidity for banks, educational institutions, and others who lend to students. Sallie Mae issues various securities, including discount notes, medium-term notes, and floating-rate and zero-coupon bonds. Sallie Mae issues its securities in minimum amounts of $100,000 and in increments of $5,000.

TENNESSEE VALLEY AUTHORITY (TVA)

CREATED IN 1933 to develop the resources of the Tennessee Valley and its adjacent areas, the TVA is wholly owned by the U.S. government. Despite this ownership, TVA bonds are not backed by the full faith and credit of the U.S. government. The principal and interest of the bonds are payable only by the TVA from the proceeds of its power program. The TVA issues discount notes and long-term bonds. The TVA issues its securities in minimum amounts of $100,000 and in increments of $1,000.

FEDERAL AGRICULTURAL MORTGAGE CORPORATION (FARMER MAC)

FARMER MAC IS A GSE established in 1988 that promotes liquidity for agricultural real estate and rural housing loans. It does this by buying loans from lenders and creating pools of these loans, against which it issues securities that are purchased by investors. Farmer Mac issues various securities, including discount notes and medium-term notes, in minimum amounts of $1,000 and in increments of $1,000.

>>ADVANTAGES

Although most agency bonds are not well known, they are very attractive investments because of their high credit rating and yields that are higher than Treasuries. Agency securities have negligible credit risk and are considered extremely safe because the federal government is unlikely to let one of its sponsored enterprises default.

Agency bonds can be used as collateral for loans.

>>RISKS

While there is no significant liquidity or tax risk associated with agency bonds, they are subject to a small amount of event and political risk.

With regard to the latter, Congress has periodically become concerned about the mushrooming amount of agency debt and has sought to curtail the amount of lending. Such a situation occurred in the summer of 2001, when Fannie Mae's obligations of $675 billion came to the attention of several congressmen. Their futile efforts to curtail the agency were headlined in the *Wall Street Journal* of July 5, 2001, under the title of "How Fannie Mae Gave the Slip to Adversaries Seeking to Rein It In."

Most agency securities have call provisions, and these constitute the major risk of this type of investment. Many of these calls are extremely short; e.g., one, two, or three years. Thus, even if your agency bond has a good return, it can be called away before you really have a chance to fully benefit from it. The short calls subject you to reinvestment risk because they are generally exercised at times when interest rates are declining. When you buy a 20-year or 30-year agency bond with a one-year call, you are also—perhaps unknowingly—buying a significant downside market risk should interest rates go up, and a call risk if interest rates go down. You can easily deal with this concern by not buying long-term agency securities with very short calls.

>>TAX IMPLICATIONS

All agency bonds are subject to federal income taxation. However, the following agency bonds may not be subject to state and local income taxation:

◆ Farm Credit System
◆ Federal Home Loan Banks
◆ Financing Corporation (FICO)
◆ Resolution Funding Corporation (Refcorp)
◆ Student Loan Marketing Association (Sallie Mae)
◆ Tennessee Valley Authority (TVA)

The following agency securities are subject to state and local income taxation:
◆ Fannie Mae
◆ Freddie Mac

>>SPECIFIC INFORMATION SOURCES

Excellent bond-specific websites are www.fcs.com, www.fhlb.com, www.freddiemac.com, www.fanniemae.com, www.salliemae.com, and www.tva.com.

>>SPECIAL FEATURES AND TIPS

Bonds issued by Fannie Mae, Freddie Mac, Federal Home Loan Banks, and Farm Credit System are quite liquid and, as such, are easy to buy and sell, which results in lower trading transaction costs.

Consider zero-coupon agencies for your tax-sheltered retirement accounts. For example, in 1997 the yield on 15-year agency zeros was 7.5 percent while the overall stock market was racking up 20 percent per year gains. Bond aficionados that we are, we ignored the techs and tucked into our IRAs an assortment of call-protected zeros with the 7.5 percent yield. These securities will double in less than ten years without any further action or monitoring on our part as well as without any need to reinvest the coupons. In essence, we bought a risk-free investment that is guaranteed to double in less than ten years. It doesn't sound as sexy as a new high-tech concept, but it sure has proved rewarding for us.

While early call features are a risk, they can also present an opportunity, especially in an atmosphere of rising interest rates. Based on the fact that agency securities with early calls generally have higher yields, a major brokerage firm presented the following plan, which shows how one can achieve reasonable returns while maintaining a high level of credit quality, even in a low interest rate environment. In September 2001 interest rates were as follows:

	Yield-to-Maturity
Money Markets	3.1%
1-year CD	3.2%
2-year U.S. non-callable Treasury	3.5%
5-year U.S. non-callable Treasury	4.2%
10-year U.S. non-callable Treasury	4.8%
5-year non-callable Fannie Mae	4.8%
5-year Fannie Mae with first call	5.5% if not called in 2 years; 5.1% if called in 2 years

The firm wrote: "Even if the bond is called away in two years, it will have yielded 5.1 percent, which is 160 basis points (1.6 percent) higher than a comparable U.S. Treasury, which yields 3.5 percent. If the bond is not called, and is held to maturity, it will yield 5.5 percent, versus 4.2 percent for a comparable U.S. Treasury."

These data present a good example of the attractiveness of agency securities even though some, as in this case, Fannie Mae, are subject to state and local income taxes while Treasuries are not. Of course, the yield on the agencies was not as high as that on totally taxable corporate bonds at the time. However, as noted throughout this book, corporate bonds are much riskier than agencies and because of this risk must offer more attractive yields to entice buyers.

We feel that if the yield difference between an agency and a Treasury is only 20 basis points (0.2 percent), you should consider buying the Treasury because of its greater liquidity and safety, particularly if you can advantageously use the state tax exemption. If you can earn more than 50 basis points (0.5 percent) on an agency bond compared to a similar maturity Treasury, we believe the agency is more attractive in that situation.

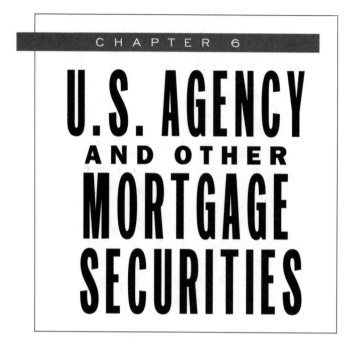

CHAPTER 6

U.S. AGENCY
AND OTHER
MORTGAGE
SECURITIES

IN ITS BASIC FORM, a mortgage pass-through security

(generally known as a mortgage security) represents a

share, technically referred to as an *undivided interest,* in

an investment pool consisting of many mortgage loans.

The cash flow—consisting of both principal and inter-

est payments—from the mortgage loans, reduced by

fees, is passed through to holders of the mortgage securities. While there's a lot of money to be made from these financial instruments, understanding them is not particularly easy due to their complex structure.

It helps first to understand how a mortgage security's underlying asset, a simple mortgage, is created. Mortgages came into being because most people only have enough money for a down payment when purchasing a home. They require help, in the form of a mortgage loan, to pay the balance. Banks provide this sort of help. For example, let's say you borrow $100,000 for thirty years to finance the purchase of your house. Your loan agreement is documented by a mortgage, and it stipulates how much and how frequently you will make payments. The bank might charge a series of fees for making the loan.

After receiving your $100,000 mortgage document, your bank—without your knowledge or consent—will probably turn around and sell it to another entity. If the bank agrees to collect your mortgage payments and provide you with payment records even though it no longer owns your mortgage, it receives a fee from the buying entity for doing so. The bank now has its $100,000 back and can lend the $100,000 to another borrower.

In its turn, the purchasing entity creates a mortgage pool and either guarantees the creditworthiness of that pool or obtains such a guarantee from another institution. The resulting financial package, highly desirable because of the credit guarantees, is divided into shares that are sold to investors. The majority of these securities are either issued or guaranteed by one of three government agencies, as noted previously: Fannie Mae (originally named Federal National Mortgage Association), Freddie Mac (originally named Federal Home Loan Mortgage Corporation), and the Government National Mortgage Association (which has yet to officially shorten its name but which is widely known as Ginnie Mae).

There are benefits for everyone in the transaction. The homeowner is able to borrow money at the lowest rate available because an agency guarantees the repayment of the mortgage loan. The bank earns its fees and takes no risks. The investors in the mortgage securities are happy because they have an easily traded security that is guaranteed by an agency and that will generally yield

more than an equivalent Treasury bond. And the agencies are ful-
filling their function, which is to increase home mortgage liquidity and to encourage banks and other lenders to finance mortgages
for low-income and middle-income families.

It is important to note that the agencies are barred by their charters from originating mortgages. The mortgages in the pools are
originated by a network of lenders, which includes mortgage
bankers, savings and loan associations, and commercial banks.
After ensuring that the mortgage loans meet established credit
quality guidelines, the agencies either directly or indirectly convert—*securitize* is the term used in financial language—the loans
into mortgage securities. The resulting mortgage securities carry a
guarantee of timely payment of principal and interest to the
investor, whether or not there is sufficient cash flow from the mortgage pool. Agency mortgage securities provide investors with an
investment that offers liquidity, safety of principal, and attractive
yield. They are one of the most widely held and safest mortgage
securities in the world.

A little history will be useful in understanding why the agencies were created and how they differ. Until the late 1930s, afford-
ing a home was difficult for most people because a prospective
homeowner had to make a down payment of 40 percent and then
pay the mortgage off in three to five years. During the three- to
five-year period only interest on the mortgage was paid. At the
end of that time, the principal was paid in one lump sum, called
a *balloon payment.* As the boom of the 1920s turned into first a
stock market crash and then a depression, more and more people
defaulted on their mortgages because they could not meet the
final balloon payment. Thus, while prospective homeowners preferred long-term, fixed-rate mortgages, banks and other mortgage lenders were reluctant to offer them because of the risk of
default on the mortgages.

The government stepped in and created the Federal National
Mortgage Association as part of the Federal Housing Administration (FHA) on February 10, 1938, and charged it with bolstering
the housing industry. Throughout the association's first years of
operation, it primarily bought mortgages issued to lower-income

people; banks held on to the lucrative returns from mortgages issued to more prosperous customers. This situation changed during a credit squeeze in which banks and savings and loan institutions were receiving 6 or 7 percent annual interest on 30-year fixed-rate mortgages and paying out 9–12 percent interest on bank deposits. By the late 1960s, banks found the idea of selling a greater number of mortgages more attractive because of their realization that holding them could be risky.

Once again the government stepped in. In 1968 it split the Federal National Mortgage Association into two separate legal entities. One became a shareholder-owned, privately managed corporation supporting the secondary market for conventional loans. This entity became popularly known as Fannie Mae, a nickname legally sanctioned in 1997. Though a private corporation, its ties with the government were not completely severed because it operates under a congressional charter and is subject to oversight from the U.S. Department of Housing and Urban Development (HUD) and the U.S. Department of the Treasury. The association with HUD and the Treasury gives Fannie Mae a powerful backing in the event of any financial problems; the aura of the association is extended to its securities, which, as noted previously, carry an implicit AAA rating.

Fannie Mae has two primary business activities: (1) portfolio investment, in which it buys mortgages and mortgage securities (this activity is funded by the debt securities it issues and which were described in the last chapter); and (2) credit guarantee, in which it charges fees to guarantee the credit performance of single-family and multifamily loans.

The second entity resulting from the government's 1968 split of the original Fannie Mae is known as Ginnie Mae. Ginnie Mae, the Government National Mortgage Association, differs from Fannie Mae in four important respects:

1 It is a government corporation located within HUD;

2 Its obligations are fully rather than implicitly backed by the full faith and credit of the United States;

3 Its purpose is to serve low-income to moderate-income home buyers as opposed to all home buyers; and

4 It does not form mortgage pools but rather guarantees the timely payment of principal and interest on qualified pools, which are known as Ginnie Mae pools. There are about 400 issuers of qualified pools, and they administer over 400,000 Ginnie Mae mortgage pools. All mortgages in a Ginnie Mae pool are insured by the Federal Housing Administration (FHA), the Veterans Administration (VA), or other governmental entities.

In 1970 Congress further increased mortgage activity by chartering the Federal Home Loan Mortgage Corporation as an active participant in the secondary mortgage market. In 1989 it followed Fannie Mae's footsteps and became a shareholder-owned, privately managed corporation subject to oversight from HUD and the Treasury. In 1997 it once again copied Fannie Mae's example and legally changed its name to the popularly known Freddie Mac. While there is little discernable difference between Fannie Mae and Freddie Mac, competition between the two ensures that the benefits of the secondary market are passed on to home buyers and renters in the form of lower housing costs.

Each agency has a website that provides helpful information: www.fanniemae.com, www.freddiemac.com, and www.ginniemae .gov.

Mortgage-Backed Securities

NOW LET'S TAKE a closer look at mortgage pools and how securities are created from them. In our example at the beginning of this chapter, your mortgage was combined with many other similar mortgages to form a mortgage pool. Assume that your mortgage is in the amount of $100,000 and there are nine other similar mortgages also in the amount of $100,000 each. In this case the value of the mortgages in the pool is $1 million. This mortgage pool will receive cash flow from three sources:

◆ First, the homeowners pay interest on their mortgages.

◆ Second, the homeowners pay scheduled principal payments on their mortgages.

◆ Third, and most important to understand, the homeowners may make nonscheduled prepayments on their mortgages, creating additional cash flow. These nonscheduled prepayments are the result of home owners refinancing or prepaying their mortgages, selling their homes, or defaulting on their mortgages. Refinancing is particularly prevalent when interest rates go down and home-owners pay off existing mortgages to obtain new, cheaper ones. As a result, a 30-year mortgage pool might be paid off in twelve to fourteen years. Thus, while debt securities such as bonds are traded in terms of their due dates, mortgage securities are traded in terms of their assumed "average life."

If and when any nonscheduled prepayments take place, additional cash comes into the mortgage pool. All of the cash flow is collected by the originator/servicer of the mortgage pool. The originator/servicer charges a fee of about 0.5 percent for this work. The originator/servicer then distributes each month all of the cash collected minus its fee pro rata to the owners of the mortgage securities.

Put another way and restated to make sure the point is clear, when you hold a mortgage security, you receive a monthly, rather than a semi-annual, cash flow from three sources: interest on the mortgages; principal payments on the mortgages; and nonscheduled payments resulting from homeowner refinancings, prepayments, sales, and defaults.

Keep in mind that not all this cash flow is income. The principal payments and prepayments are an early return of your principal. As an investor in a mortgage security, you are in the position of a bank that lends money on a mortgage to a homeowner. When you are repaid, you receive back mostly interest in the early years and mostly principal in the later years.

>>ADVANTAGES

Agency mortgage securities are very attractive because of their high credit rating and yields that are often higher than Treasuries. Typically, if a 10-year Treasury is yielding 5 percent, the mortgage security will yield around 6 percent.

Although there is a difference in the underlying credit of each agency, all agency mortgage securities are very safe and have AAA ratings. The U.S. government *directly guarantees* the Ginnie Mae mortgage securities as to timely payment of interest and principal, giving them a strong AAA rating.

Although the U.S. government does not directly guarantee the Fannie Mae and Freddie Mac mortgage securities, they have an implied AAA rating because it is assumed the federal government will stand behind the debt. Fannie Mae and Freddie Mac can borrow directly from the U.S. Treasury if conditions so warrant. In addition, it is considered unlikely that the U.S. government would let one of its government-sponsored enterprises, such as Fannie Mae or Freddie Mac, default. Fannie Mae and Freddie Mac themselves are the only guarantors of their own mortgage securities. It is interesting to note that in 2001 Standard & Poor's Corporation issued a credit rating report for the two saying that if they were viewed on their own without the support of the U.S. government, their credit rating would be double A minus (AA-), rather than AAA.

Finally, keep in mind that in practice there has been no difference in the safety record of the three agencies' securities. None has ever defaulted or missed a payment of interest or principal to an investor.

>>RISKS

Mortgage securities have a number of significant disadvantages when compared to Treasuries, the major one being their uneven and unpredictable cash flow that results from prepayments. These prepayments are a wild card in analyzing mortgage securities because they make it impossible to predict the overall cash flow. If you can't predict cash flow, you can't predict current return, and you certainly can't compute a yield-to-maturity. Thus, it is difficult to compare the yield on a mortgage security to the yield on a Treasury or corporate bond. In fact, it is the unpredictability of cash flow that causes the mortgage securities to yield more than Treasuries.

The prepayment assumptions used for mortgage securities are based on complicated statistical models. Usually, the payment history of the mortgage securities is compared to prepayment patterns prepared by the FHA. If interest rates change markedly, the FHA may issue new prepayment guidelines.

Unless you purchase mortgage securities through a fund, the relatively small blocks that an individual can purchase might actually be statistical aberrations from the norm. Another concern that individual investors have is that they might get an unfavorable price on the mortgage security that they buy because of the difficulty in evaluating the price.

Unpredictable prepayments may cause other problems. If the estimated yield on the mortgage security is based upon the mortgage pool remaining in existence for, say, twelve years, prepayments may result in a pool coming to an end in only nine years. This might result in a lower yield on the mortgage security. In this scenario, if you purchased a mortgage security at a premium, you could lose money.

Capital depletion is a potential problem for the inexperienced investor in mortgage securities. The large cash flows look like manna from heaven. But, if you spend all of the cash flow that you receive from the mortgage security as it comes in, you will deplete your capital and you will have nothing to reinvest when the cash flow stops. Thus, a mortgage security is similar to an investment in an oil well—large cash payments in the early years, but declining payments in the future as the oil is depleted. By comparison, a debt security pays you the principal at its maturity date as well as interest payments twice a year.

Mortgage securities also have interest rate risk. If interest rates rise, homeowners will generally not refinance their mortgages, thus keeping the mortgage pool alive for a longer period of time. This might result in a yield lower than originally estimated because it will take longer for you to get your capital back to reinvest at a higher rate. Mortgage securities perform the best when interest rates remain within a narrow range.

Finally, there is not much daily information available to investors about mortgage securities. The *Wall Street Journal* only provides a small number of Ginnie Mae quotes and none for Fannie Mae and Freddie Mac. The *New York Times* has no quotes.

>>TAX IMPLICATIONS

All of the agency mortgage securities are subject to federal income tax and state income tax on all interest income and original issue discount. Your broker will report the amount of interest income and original issue discount to you on Forms 1099-INT and 1099-OID. The portion of any payment from a mortgage security that represents a return of the principal that you originally invested is received tax free.

>>SPECIAL FEATURES AND TIPS

It is difficult for individual investors to evaluate information about specific mortgage securities being offered by brokers and to commit enough cash to properly diversify a portfolio of mortgage securities. For these reasons, mortgage securities may not be suitable for individuals to purchase on their own. Some investors, however, may find buying individual Ginnie Mae certificates to be attractive if they want a large cash flow and do not care if their principal is returned unpredictably.

For most investors, the best way to invest in mortgage securities is through buying a Ginnie Mae open-end mutual fund. This approach utilizes the expertise of the fund's investment adviser and provides diversification among different Ginnie Mae securities. Buying both high and low interest rate Ginnie Mae securities for the long term and the short term smoothes out the returns and reduces the market risk. We personally invest in mortgage securities through open-end mutual funds and recommend them to our clients. You might wish to consider the following Ginnie Mae funds: Vanguard GNMA Fund (800-835-1510), Fidelity Ginnie Mae (800-544-8888), and USAA Invest-GNMA Trust (800-382-8722).

Collateralized Mortgage Obligations (CMOs)

CMOS ARE SIMILAR to mortgage securities in that they are based on underlying mortgages. CMOs were created by financial engineers within the investment-banking world in 1983 to alleviate the problem of how to deal with the prepayment uncertainties associated with mortgage pools. The CMO solved the prepayment problem, at least in part, by allowing a greater certainty of return for those willing to accept a lower yield, while rewarding those who assume an unpredictable return and maturity with a higher yield. CMOs created a whole new range of profitable financial products for Wall Street.

If mortgage-backed securities seem complicated, CMOs are even more complex. They consist of endless variations of combined cash flows originating from mortgage pools. Michael Vranos, the former head of mortgage securities at Kidder Peabody, boasted to the *Wall Street Journal* that his job is to sell securities to the dumb guys. Some of his clients understandably resented the assessment. Grudgingly, however, many investors concede that Vranos's tactless remark contained a kernel of truth.

For those wishing to explore the attributes of CMOs, the following is a simplified explanation. While holders of mortgage securities receive cash through pro rata monthly distributions, owners of CMO securities receive cash from a mortgage pool on a prioritized basis. That prioritized basis is called a class or a *tranche,* with the latter word being derived from the French word for *slice.*

Let's consider a simple example of a CMO with three classes of securities and see how it works. In practice there may be up to fifty different classes, the thought of which can induce nightmares for people trying to understand this product. We will call our three classes the *A-Class,* the *B-Class,* and the *Z-Class.* The term *Z-Class* originally referred to the last class to be paid; today, it is often used to describe an accrual bond that may or may not be the last in the CMO to be paid. This class is also known as an *accrual tranche* or a *Z bond.*

In our example assume that $1 million has been invested in the three classes as follows:

◆ **A-Class.** The face value of the securities in the A-Class is $600,000. Interest at the annual rate of 6 percent is paid monthly on the face value of the securities until they are paid off. All scheduled principal payments and all prepayments are paid monthly to the A-Class until $600,000, representing the full face value of the A-Class, is paid off. No principal payments or prepayments are paid to the B-Class or Z-Class until all the A-Class securities are paid off.

◆ **B-Class.** The face value of the securities in the B-Class is $300,000. Interest at the annual rate of 8 percent is paid monthly on the face value of the securities even when the A-Class is still outstanding. All scheduled principal payments and all prepayments are made monthly to the B-Class, but only after all the A-Class is paid off. No principal payments or prepayments are made to the Z-Class until $900,000, representing the full face value of the A-Class and B-Class securities are paid off.

◆ **Z-Class.** The face value of the securities in the Z-Class is $100,000. Interest at the annual rate of 10 percent is accrued but not paid on the face value of the securities until $900,000, representing the full face value of the A-Class and B-Class, is completely paid off. Such interest as well as scheduled principal payments and all prepayments are made monthly to the Z-Class only after all the A-Class and B-Class are both paid off. Thus, the Z-Class gets the remainder of the payments from the mortgage pool. The Z-Class bears some similarity to a zero-coupon bond in that interest is accrued but not paid. The Z-Class may have a very long life and no definite maturity. It may also be difficult to determine the tax consequences of the Z-Class.

Note the higher interest rates for the B-Class and Z-Class to make up for the longer life and higher risks in these classes as compared to the A-Class.

The A-Class security is similar to a short-term bond. Since the A-Class receives a share of the interest and all the prepayments initially, it will turn out to be a shorter-term security and will have a more predictable return than the B-Class or the Z-Class securities. It might be possible to predict with a high degree of reliability that the A-Class will be retired in, say, three years. The life of and thus the return on the B-Class will be more difficult to predict than the A-Class, and thus the B-Class should earn a higher return.

As noted above, the last class, the Z-Class, will receive no interest or principal payments until all of the other classes are repaid in full. While the A-Class may have an expected life of three years, the Z-Class may not be retired for twenty or thirty years. The return on the Z-Class obviously is the most difficult to predict and value. It should have the highest yield because of its uncertainties. It will lose value quickly when interest rates rise because prepayments decline and lengthen the life of the Z-Class. Many CMO investors have lost money when their estimates were not met with respect to Z-Class securities.

There are two major types of CMO structures. One, as in the above example, provides that only principal payments are redirected, and interest goes pro rata. In the other type, principal as well as interest payments are redirected. The pattern for the latter, while byzantine, is similar to that described above and makes later tranches even more volatile.

CMOs can be, and often are, categorized by type of issuer. The term *agency CMOs* refers to those issued by the agencies. The mortgages in the agency CMOs are already pooled mortgages and in securitized pass-through form. They are of similar size, age, and quality. Investors in agency CMOs have only prepayment risk, but not credit risk.

The terms *private-label CMO, nonagency CMO,* and *whole-loan CMO* refer to investments comprising mortgages that do not have an agency guarantee. Some private institutions, such as subsidiaries of investment banks and other financial institutions, issue nonagency CMOs, usually consisting of jumbo loans. Jumbo loans are not used in agency CMOs. Nonagency CMOs are often rated AA or AAA due to credit enhancements. Within the same issue individual tranches may be rated differently.

>>ADVANTAGES

If you buy agency CMOs there is minimal credit risk, and you may receive a higher return than on Treasuries because of the market risk relating to the uncertainty of the CMO's maturity. In the absence of a government or other guarantee, nonagency CMOs may provide a significantly higher return than agency CMOs or agency debt bonds of comparable maturity, reflecting the greater credit risk on the nonagency CMOs.

If you buy the A- or B-Classes in a CMO (i.e., the top classes), the cash flow should be more predictable than for other agency mortgage securities. This is why CMOs were developed. If you buy the A-Class, it should, as noted, resemble a short-term bond, although with less predictable maturities. The A- or B-Class CMOs will provide high monthly cash flows.

You can buy CMOs in $1,000 pieces, rather than the $25,000 minimum required for a Ginnie Mae security.

>>RISKS

The attractiveness of CMO securities varies considerably because of repayment unpredictability. The safest are the A-Class and B-Class agency CMOs. Predictions relating to the life of the CMO and thus the yield predictions may be very far from the actual outcome. What may appear to be a short-term investment could lengthen by many years if interest rates later rise sharply (resulting in smaller prepayments). Even the shortest classes are not immune to maturity extensions.

The Z-Class nonagency CMO is generally the riskiest and should not be approached unless you or your financial adviser can do a careful analysis of the risks. Indeed, any Z-Class security may be hard to analyze. Called "toxic waste" in the trade, the Z-Class will also be more volatile than other mortgage securities, particularly when interest rates are moving rapidly. The Z-Class has poor liquidity. Finally, the Z-Class may have difficult accounting and tax aspects.

Even if private insurance backs the credit on a CMO, these insurers are not as creditworthy as the agencies. If your CMO has a credit rating of AAA because of the backing of an insurance company, the credit rating of your CMO will decline if the credit rating of the insurer declines. This is not an uncommon occurrence.

It is very difficult to find information about CMOs. Neither the *New York Times* nor the *Wall Street Journal* provides price quotes on these securities.

>>TAX IMPLICATIONS

The tax treatment for CMOs is complex, and you must consult your tax adviser for specific advice. The portion of the payment treated as interest will be subject to federal, state, and local income tax, whereas that treated as return of principal or original cost is not subject to tax. However, if the CMO securities are purchased at a discount from their original issue price, part of the discount may be taxed as interest income, and some may be taxed as capital gain.

For CMOs held in a brokerage account, your broker will report the tax consequence to you. However, there is a risk that the outside source that is reporting to your brokerage firm may not report the tax consequence of the CMO before March 15, and you might be delayed in preparing your income taxes.

>>PRICING INFORMATION

You can buy CMO securities in minimum amounts of $1,000. Many CMOs are created for institutions, however, and their minimum purchase price is much higher. You might also buy CMO securities by buying a mutual fund or unit trust that invests in CMO securities. Many of these entities have minimum prices of $1,000.

>>SPECIAL FEATURES AND TIPS

Because of the inherent disadvantages in CMOs, particularly nonagency CMOs, you should proceed with caution and seek answers to the following questions:

◆ Is the CMO an agency CMO? If not, what is its credit rating? Can I lose some of my principal?

◆ Can you get a full prospectus for the CMO? If not, where can you get detailed information on the CMO?

◆ Are you buying the CMO at original issuance or on the secondary market? If on the secondary market, how can you assure yourself that the price is appropriate?

◆ If the CMO has a trading history in the secondary market, has it met its original assumptions? If not, why not?

◆ What is the exact class of CMO that you are buying, and what are the exact terms of the payout?

◆ Does the return on the CMO yield a sufficient amount more than comparable Treasury or agency debt security to merit the additional risk of the investment?

◆ What are the tax consequences of the CMO?

◆ Is there an active market in this CMO if you want to sell it? Keep in mind that what looks like a high yield might be a high return of your principal. Don't make the mistake of spending that principal because you think it is income.

◆ Are these CMOs proprietary products, i.e., products that are created by a particular brokerage house? If so, you might receive a relatively low price if you need to sell your securities, because the broker that originally sold you the CMO might be the only interested buyer.

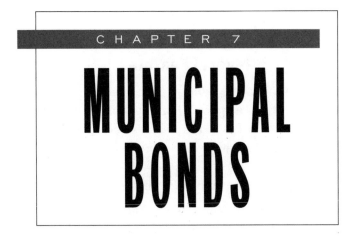

CHAPTER 7

MUNICIPAL BONDS

WHEN IT COMES TO tax-advantaged investments, it's hard

to beat municipal bonds, or munis as they are popularly

called. The American public, particularly those in

income brackets over 25 percent, has been quick to cap-

italize on this fact—so much so that the municipal bond

sector is the only bond category in which individuals, as

opposed to institutions, are the most frequent buyers. At

the beginning of 2002, some $1.6 trillion worth of these bonds was outstanding in the marketplace.

General Features

DESPITE THEIR POPULARITY and significant tax advantages, munis remain a mystery to most people. In large part this is due to the fact that munis encompass a universe of bonds of varying quality and return. In other words, if you've seen one muni, you *haven't* seen them all.

The first variable about munis in this regard is that they are issued by states, local governments, or special public entities such as school districts and sewer authorities. In large part, the credit-worthiness and revenue sources of these various issuers determine the financial attractiveness of their bonds.

Second, the term *tax free* is relative when it comes to munis. While most munis are exempt from federal income taxes, some are taxable and some are subject to the alternative minimum tax. Further, many munis find it impossible to escape the clutches of state or city tax departments. Fortunately, the Bond Market Association has taken a giant step in clarifying this situation by creating a website, www.investinginbonds.com, that provides the information you need to compare a tax-free yield to the taxable yield. For example, this site can help you determine if a 4.5 percent muni or a 6.5 percent corporate yield is more attractive in tax terms. Also see Chapter 13 for a simple formula you can use to calculate the comparison yourself.

Third, munis are generally issued in serial form. This practice protects the issuer from paying out a huge lump sum. For example, when issuing $10 million worth of construction bonds, a school district will sell them all at once but have blocks with different redemption dates. In this case, you could buy two blocks of bonds from the same issue, yet each would be redeemed at a different time. This allows you to target the bonds to mature at a time that suits your needs.

Fourth, bonds pay interest either semiannually or only when the bond matures. The issuer, in conjunction with the underwriters, decides whether the bonds are issued as paying current interest or as deferred-payment zero-coupon bonds. If the bonds are paying current interest, they could be issued at a discount, at a premium, or at face value.

Fifth, municipal bond pricing is a bit like that in an "oriental bazaar." Although muni bonds all start with a minimum $5,000 face value and are quoted in decimals, market forces quickly take over and raise or lower the purchase price. These prices are difficult to track because munis are traded in an over-the-counter market that is not widely publicized.

And here's a big catch: Municipal bonds tend to have fixed call options, with a first call usually between five and ten years from their date of issue, and then are callable every year thereafter. Others are noncallable for their entire lives. Some have a sinking fund. Some revenue bonds have extraordinary calls that are very active or only exercised in specific catastrophic situations. Any call exposes you to reinvestment risk.

Finally, while most issues are in book-entry form and must be held at a brokerage house, some appear as bond certificates you can hold in your hands.

It is our goal in this chapter to render any seemingly mysterious features both intelligible and manageable for investors. We have been buying and selling many millions of dollars worth of munis for our own personal needs and for our clients for the past twenty-five years and in the process have made a lot of money for both our bank accounts and theirs. We hope the information in this chapter will help you do the same.

Risk Features

WE FIND MUNIS TO BE not only profitable but also comparatively low risk viewed as a whole. Fitch Ratings, the international rating agency, agrees with us. The firm examined data from 1979–1999 and found that the overall default rate was less than 1.5 percent. Even if there is a default, there is a workout period. Defaulted bonds returned somewhere between thirty cents and eighty cents on the dollar. As with other aspects of life, quality counts. Thus, in another study, Standard & Poor's found that not one of the highest-rated bonds—those with double-A or triple-A designations—defaulted in the 1986–2000 period.

There is a wide spectrum of risk in municipal bonds. Some categories are extremely safe: general obligation bonds, because they require voter approval, and revenue bonds with substantial and multiple sources of funds. You can be comfortable buying these categories if they have an A rating or better or they are insured by one of the major muni bond insurance companies.

Some munis are extremely risky, on the other hand, with narrow streams of revenue that may not be secure. They will have a low rating or none at all. A nonrated bank may guarantee them. Through the media, you will learn about problems in an industry, although they may not mention bonds specifically. For example, note the regular drumbeat of articles on the problems of hospital reimbursements and tobacco settlements. That general information tells you that those market sectors represent a weaker sector in the muni market. Tread cautiously. In good times, lower-grade bonds may yield only slightly more than better quality paper—maybe 15 or 20 basis points—but the spreads open up in bad times. This means that buyers lower the price they are willing to pay when there is negative economic news, while sellers maintain the price at which they are willing to sell.

Municipal bonds are subject both to risks that they all have in common, as well as specific risks particular to a particular class of bonds. Risks common to all munis include the following:

◆ **Fluctuations in state and federal aid.** Such fluctuations have destabilizing effects on municipal budgets and can impair their ability to repay fixed debt. Federal programs often provide only start-up costs or a portion of capital costs. Relying on the traditional last-minute state appropriation to fund its ailing schools and city, Buffalo, for example, was devastated to find the state's cupboard empty at the close of 2001 because money had been diverted to disaster activities as a result of the September 11, 2001, attack. Having already spent the $54 million they were seeking, the city and school district had to drastically cut services to cover the shortfall.[1]

◆ **Lack of diversified tax base.** Dependence on a restricted revenue source increases the vulnerability of both general obligation (G/O) and revenue bonds. Airline terminals, for example, saw their revenue decline after the September 11 attack, and, as a result, many of the bonds backed by this revenue were downgraded.[2]

◆ **Fiscal imprudence.** Putting political decisions before fiscal responsibility has frequently resulted in rating downgrades or worse. The California fiasco of recent years—in which the state's debt ballooned after poorly conceived legislation resulted in the purchase of electricity at prohibitively high prices—severely affected local municipalities, not to mention the effect on the private utilities. After the state's debt was downgraded in 2001, Moody's put fifty-eight county governments on credit watch because it felt that the state aid received by these governments would be significantly curtailed.[3]

◆ **Excessive debt.** Creation of debt mountains soaring over the tax base or revenue source is not a good sign. Indications of possible problems include increases in the amount of debt, the requirement of paying sizable issues in one year, and increases in the amount of annual interest due. New York City is a case in point. Following the September 11 attack, the city was put on credit watch after its revenues from taxes throughout the city plunged while its need for money for rebuilding and essential services skyrocketed.

Ratings and Other Security Enhancements

THE INVESTMENT ATTRACTIVENESS of munis is frequently gussied up with the addition of insurance and/or ratings. An insured bond—which means the face value and interest payments are guaranteed—is given a higher rating than one that is not insured. It is this aspect, extra coverage that guarantees payment, that makes munis especially attractive. Sometimes only specific maturities of a bond issue are insured. Insurance, however, costs money, and issuers often seek to do without it if they can obtain a double-A rating or better on their own. For example, in December 1994 the Wissahickon School District in Pennsylvania issued $5 million of bonds. The district received a double-A rating that made it possible to save the $60,000 that would have been required to purchase bond insurance had it received a lower rating.

The insurance firms themselves are rated, and their ratings are automatically transferred to the bonds they insure. Thus a firm receiving a triple-A designation from a major rating agency bestows a triple-A designation on the bonds it insures. Let it be noted that the firms do not willy-nilly insure bonds. They carefully scrutinize the creditworthiness of each and only insure those that they deem likely not to default. These are private and public companies with no government backing—no relation to FDIC that insures your bank deposits. Naturally, the insurance does not cover any premium over par that you pay for a bond.

Sophisticated buyers always ask what the rating on an insured bond would be without any insurance, although this information is not always available. All things being equal, it is better to have insured bonds that are of better credit quality than insured weaker credits. If the underlying rating is strong, you can rely on the underlying strength of the bond as well as on the insurance for protection. This is called belt-and-suspenders protection.

Here is as good a place as any to note that while insurance guarantees return of principal, it does not necessarily protect against a falling price for trading purposes—market risk. When "the Street" heard that a nonprofit bond issuer for student apartment complexes was withdrawing money from operating expenses to build up its reserve fund, the rumor mill cranked into high gear on the fear that there might be a technical default. The price of the actively traded bonds plummeted 8 percent in a day.[4] Since these were insured bonds, if there had been a default, the bond insurers would have continued to pay interest and principal when

Triple-A Ratings

CURRENTLY, FIVE BOND insurance companies carry the triple-A rating: American Municipal Bond Assurance Corporation (AMBAC), Financial Guaranty Insurance Company (FGIC), MBIA Inc., Financial Security Assurance Inc. (FSA), and XL Capital Assurance Inc. (XLCA).

due. Despite this assurance, if you sold the bonds into the bad news market, you would have suffered a loss. As they say in the marketplace, the moral of this story is that "Insurance does not make a bad bond good."

Some bonds are offered with attractive security enhancements known as escrow or prefunded features. Municipalities generally add these features as an approved accounting method for reducing debt exposure. In this scenario, U.S. government bonds, U.S. agency bonds, or other obligations are placed in a bank escrow account created solely to meet the interest and principal requirements of the outstanding municipal bonds. Prefunded bonds—popularly dubbed *pre-rees*—are priced to the first call date and will be redeemed on that date. Although many traders assume escrowed bonds are protected from early calls, several loopholes have allowed the occasional early recall of these bonds.

Mechanics of Purchasing Munis

MUNIS ARE PURCHASED through large, all-purpose brokers or through bond boutique houses. The buyer must pay for them three days after the date of purchase.

Since most municipals trade infrequently, municipal traders in the secondary market use price matrixes to determine what a bond is worth. Traders see where other similar bonds are trading and price the bonds accordingly. Brokerage houses use the price matrix to evaluate a bond portfolio. This approach is like pricing an existing house for sale by looking at what comparable houses have sold for recently. In an unstable market, those prices can be very misleading.

Taxable Status of Munis

IN THIS BOOK, we have broadly grouped municipal bonds by their taxable status: taxable munis, which are completely taxable even though they are issued by municipalities; private activity bonds, which are subject to the alternative minimum tax, which came into being as a result of the 1986 Tax Reform Act; and tax-exempt bonds, which are not subject to federal income tax, and sometimes not to state income tax as well. Included in the tax-exempt grouping are the major categories comprising general obligation bonds and revenue bonds.

TAXABLE MUNICIPAL BONDS

MUNICIPALITIES HAVE ISSUED a staggering amount—about $60 billion worth—of bonds that are subject to federal income tax. These bonds have been on the scene since the 1986 Tax Reform Act and are the result of the federal government's attempt to limit the use of the municipal tax exemption. The bonds are issued for private purposes that are not eligible for tax-exemption, such as stadiums funded by gate receipts and investor-led housing. Lease revenue bonds can also be taxable if the private sector is occupying public space.

>>ADVANTAGES
Municipal debt subject to federal income tax may be free of taxes in the state of issuance. Pennsylvania residents, for example, don't have to pay state taxes on the interest derived from taxable munis issued in their state. This feature gives taxable municipal debt a leg up when comparing it to corporate debt or certificates of deposit. In addition, taxable munis are eligible for bond insurance, unlike most corporate bonds.

>>RISKS
Though not really a risk, you'll find that taxable munis are not widely available because insurance companies and banks usually buy up the issues. Many brokers do not sell them at all—which leads to the next problem, namely liquidity. Because they are not plentiful, they do not trade well. Do not plan on buying them to resell.

>>TAX IMPLICATIONS
The bonds are subject to federal and, for nonresidents, state and local income tax. If you purchase bonds issued in your state of residence, they may be exempt from state income tax.

>>SPECIAL FEATURES AND TIPS

Insured! That is what most taxable municipal debt is, which is always a great comfort. Most other taxable bonds are not insured.

Like other municipal debt, taxable munis can be prerefunded to their earliest call date. Taxable municipal debt may have fixed calls.

When we compare taxable munis to corporate bonds, the risk/reward ratio says buy insured taxable munis whenever possible.

PRIVATE ACTIVITY BONDS

PRIVATE ACTIVITY is a relatively new designation, describing bonds that are subject to the alternative minimum tax (AMT). One of two aspects of a bond will trigger this designation: (1) more than 10 percent of the proceeds will be directly used for private trade or business, or (2) more than 5 percent of the proceeds will be loaned to private entities.

Since January 2002, school districts became free to issue private activity bonds for school construction purposes. Unlike G/O or revenue school bonds, discussed later, these bonds are subject to the AMT. This development reflects the takeover of public schools by private companies such as Edison Schools and the addition of charter schools operating within public school districts.

When a school district issues bonds for a charter school, the bonds may be subject to the AMT because it is partly for the benefit of a private entity. Public entities, such as state and local governments, may also issue bonds for charter schools, and they would not be subject to the AMT.

>>ADVANTAGES

Private activity bonds provide a real benefit to you if you are not subject to the AMT. They must provide a higher return because so many muni buyers do not find it advantageous, in tax terms, to purchase them.

>>RISKS

One very risky type of private activity bond goes by the name of Industrial Development Bonds (IDBs). These are issued for economic development and pollution control, including solid waste and resource recovery issues in which private entities are responsible for debt service. Of all the types of bonds issued, these have had the highest default rate in recent history, representing 29 percent of the defaulted debt during the 1990s according to a Standard & Poor's 2001 study. Most of those bonds were unrated. Muni bonds subject to the AMT are less liquid than other tax-exempt munis.

>>TAX IMPLICATIONS

As noted previously, private activity bonds may be subject to the alternative minimum tax (AMT).

TAX-EXEMPT BONDS

THE MOST COMPELLING FEATURE of tax-exempt bonds is their immunity from federal income taxes. However, although tax-exempt bonds are exempt from federal income taxes, they are not uniformly exempt from state and local taxes. Only bonds issued by U.S. territories, namely Guam, the Virgin Islands, and Puerto Rico are tax exempt in all states. That's the good news. Unfortunately, only Puerto Rico has a high-rated triple-B. Using the services of a knowledgeable bond broker or a financial adviser may provide the best way to take advantage of the tax breaks inherent in munis.

It is important to know the kind of tax-exempt bond you may be purchasing. Following are capsule descriptions highlighting the advantages and risks of the many choices offered among general obligation and revenue bonds. As with all other bonds, it is essential to check the rating before you commit to buy these types of munis.

General Obligation Bonds

THERE ARE TWO CATEGORIES of bonds that finance traditional government responsibilities: general obligation bonds (G/Os), which are supported by the taxing power of the issuing entity, and revenue bonds, which are supported by specified revenue streams, generally consisting of fees paid by users of the project being financed. Sometimes they are jointly financed.

Until the late twentieth century, G/Os constituted the majority of munis that were issued. Then they slowly began to fall out of favor as governments found it politically more acceptable to issue debt backed by dedicated streams of revenues rather than tax receipts. Furthermore, G/Os have to be approved by public referendum whereas revenue bonds do not.

Unless specifically limited by law, the full faith and credit and all the financial resources of the issuer back these bonds.

Municipalities of any kind and size may issue G/O bonds, from the largest state to the smallest township. Bonds backed by the broadest taxing power are called *unlimited tax G/Os (UTG/Os)*. Munis sometimes are supported by a specific taxing power. These are called *limited tax G/Os (LTGOs)*. Voters might support a limited tax designated for the construction of a prison, for example.

An issuer's strength is based on the breadth of its tax base—a diversified economy drawing from many revenue sources—and a low level of debt. States, as opposed to counties and municipalities such as towns and cities, generally feature the broadest tax base and the most flexibility, and this is reflected in the ratings assigned to their bonds. In 2001 the average Standard & Poor's G/O rating for states was about double-A, with ten states having the gilt-edged rating of triple-A.[5]

School district bonds, issued for school construction and other educational requirements, employ a variety of revenue sources and may be classified as G/O, revenue, or private activity bonds.

School district bonds that are G/O bonds are backed by the ad valorem taxes levied on school district residents and are frequently augmented by state support. Pennsylvania and Arkansas, for example, have state intercept programs that direct state aid to bond payments in the event the school district cannot meet its obligations. Texas has a Permanent School Fund based on oil revenues to back the debt of its schools.

General obligation school district (SD) bonds are similar but distinct from Public School Building Authority bonds. The latter are revenue bonds. The authority represents many schools at one time; however, the bonds are usually the responsibility of the specific school for which the debt is issued. They pay the authority, and the authority pays the trustee who directs the paying agent to pay you. The quality of the schools and the price determine whether these bonds are a good buy.

>>ADVANTAGES
Fitch ranked general obligation bonds among the safest in a 1999 study. Since these bonds require voter approval, they come with a broad commitment for debt repayment.

State debt sells well because of its sterling track record, no matter what the rating. This means that should you need cash, you should be able to quickly sell a state G/O at a reasonable price.

State legislatures limit the amount of school district G/Os that can be issued by raising the bar regulating the percentage of voters who must approve a bond issue. As such, these bonds are generally viewed as very safe debt because they are voter approved and supported by ad valorem taxes. School district bonds are frequently registered in the name of the owner, so that the purchaser can receive a certificate and interest payments directly.

>>RISKS
The advent of a recession and the consequent drop in tax revenues from all sources poses one of the greatest risks to G/Os. In addition, serious restrictions can be put on the ability of legislatures to raise taxes.

>>SPECIAL FEATURES AND TIPS
General obligation bonds tend to be very "clean." That is, they do not have many special provisions, and there are no long stories used to describe them. G/Os generally do not have extraordinary calls. Buy state G/Os whenever possible unless state politics take the bloom off the rose.

State G/Os are generally more liquid because they are known

quantities and very safe. Given this reputation, there is generally a smaller spread between the asking and selling price. The next best are G/O school district bonds and those issued by counties, cities, and local governments.

Revenue Bonds

AS PREVIOUSLY MENTIONED, revenue bonds are supported by specified revenue streams. Their rise in popularity over the past few decades has led to the creation of several variations and twists on how entities can package and sell bonds. These bond packaging approaches include:

◆ **Authorities.** These are political entities, originally thought to be above politics, which are conduits for the issuance of bonds. Huge conglomerates known as authorities issue transportation bonds, water and sewer bonds, housing bonds, and so forth. The term is said to have originated in England, when the creators of the Port of London sought a way to differentiate it from other entities. In the enabling legislation where the powers of the port were granted, the document repeatedly referred to the word *authority,* as in "Authority is hereby given …"[6] In the United States, the use of authorities to issue debt began in 1921 with the formation of the Port of New York Authority (later renamed the Port Authority of New York and New Jersey). After 1960 when revenue bonds began to replace general obligation bonds, authorities became more prevalent.

◆ **Bond banks.** These are entities structured by states to lower the cost and to improve the marketability of debt issued by small municipalities. The banks purchase bonds from the municipalities with funds raised through the sale of their own bonds. The local municipalities then repay the bond bank.

◆ **Leases.** Using this financial structure, a municipality or its agency issues bonds to build a facility, which is then leased to the issuer. The rent paid is sufficient to pay off the bonds, at which time the lessee is usually granted the right to purchase the facility for a nominal sum. A possible hitch in this scheme is that the rent payments are usually dependent on the vagaries of annual appropriations in the state's budget, although facility usage fees may also support the debt. If the money is not appropriated, the bonds will be called.

On a cautionary note, in 2002 Kmart filed for bankruptcy, and $215.2 million worth of lease-backed and mortgage revenue bonds originally issued in 1981 went into default. Although the bonds backed by mortgages were expected to fare better, those backed by leases of closed stores had no value. Since 1986, municipal issuers are no longer permitted to sell bonds backed by retail stores.

When issued by the state, lease debt is usually rated one notch below that given to the sponsoring state's general obligation debt. In some states, leaseholders may not have priority status as creditors in bankruptcy situations without taking action in court.[7]

◆ **Certificates of participation (COPs)** are debt instruments that are typically backed by lease payments, although they are legally different than bonds. Like leases, COPs require annual appropriations by the state legislature. In the recent past there have been rare cases of attempts by issuers to renege on these obligations. The most infamous was in double-A rated Orange County, California, where citizens voted down a sales tax increase to pay for losses in an investment portfolio. There were losses, and the county was downgraded. Brevard County, Florida, citizens tried to walk away from COPs backing a municipal building because they did not like its location. Eventually, the pressure of the bond market rating and insurance companies led to the refinancing of these bonds.

◆ **Special tax districts.** These provide infrastructure improvements for residential and/or commercial real estate development. In Colorado they are called *special improvement districts.* Florida calls them *community development districts.* In Texas, special sewer districts are called *municipal utility districts* (MUDs). These districts are based on the idea, "If I build it, they will come." Alas, they don't always come. Problems arise more frequently with these kinds of loans than with more traditional munis.

The issuing entity, then, is the key distinguishing factor among municipal revenue bonds. As such, knowledge about this entity should help you distinguish, for example, among three triple-A rated insured bonds with one supporting a housing development, another a stadium, and the third an electric utility. In good times, it probably won't matter what you buy. It is when unemployment is rising, sales are dropping, and mortgages are defaulting that how you allocated your assets makes a difference. Remember, traders consider the underlying ratings of insured bonds and value them accordingly.

The following presents brief descriptions, including advantages and risks, of the major types of revenue bonds issued by various entities, arranged alphabetically for easy reference.

AIRPORT BONDS: See "TRANSPORTATION BONDS"

CHARTER SCHOOL BONDS: See "EDUCATION BONDS"

CONVENTION AND CASINO BONDS: See "ENTERTAINMENT INDUSTRY BONDS"

EDUCATION BONDS

CHARTER SCHOOLS ARE PRIVATE SCHOOLS that receive funding from the existing school districts and federal funds through the Department of Education. Each state must separately authorize the establishment of charter schools, and the terms of the charters vary. As of 2001, thirty-seven states and the District of Columbia had authorized them.[8]

School construction may be financed through the establishment of a lease issued by an authority or a building corporation. Funding is provided by grants from the federal government, as well as by the school district in which the charter was granted and through student fees. Charter school bonds may be more likely to attract an investment-grade rating if their main purpose is to relieve overcrowding. Some charter schools have been able to secure insurance for their bond issues as well.

Bonds for colleges and universities are usually issued under the auspices of state authorities. The authorities are pass-through entities enabling the debt to be issued. The security for college and university bonds is based on a variety of income sources. They include government grants and private endowments, revenue from student housing rents, private and federal research contracts, and entertainment such as sporting events and theatrical productions. The bonds that receive the highest ratings are those issued by larger, well-known institutions that are better endowed and more financially secure than smaller, less influential schools. State supported schools get funding from state appropriations, student enrollment fees, and other sources.

>>ADVANTAGES
Buying college and university debt adds diversity to your portfolio. Public higher education debt was deemed to be the least risky class of debt in this category by Fitch Ratings in its 1999 study and in a 2001 study by Standard & Poor's.

>>RISKS
The downside of charter school bonds is that, for the most part, they have no track record. Their survival could be threatened if existing school districts are able to restructure and reform. The Fitch Ratings points out that waiting lists at charter schools could evaporate if students were attracted to a public school with a strong athletic program or some other special features. Poor community relations, publicity, governance, leadership, and a negative demographic change could affect the charter schools' viability.[9] For these reasons, existing charter school debt is mostly classified as high risk.

For higher education bonds, in addition to the usual risks such as poor fiscal management and bad publicity leading to a decline in enrollment (usage fees), the primary risk is that the cost of education will outweigh the perceived benefits. In an economic downturn, private colleges with small endowments may have difficulties staying afloat.

>>SPECIAL FEATURES AND TIPS
Do not confuse junior college debt with community college debt. The former is private and the latter public. A junior college may or may not be well endowed. Privately funded junior college debt therefore may not be as strong a credit as publicly funded community college debt.

ENTERTAINMENT INDUSTRY BONDS

MUNICIPALITIES, PARTICULARLY THOSE in urban areas, find it beneficial to attract tourists and suburban residents to downtown hotels, restaurants, and stores and do so by sponsoring the construction of convention centers, cultural centers, and sports arenas to draw these outside spenders. Entertainment debt supports such construction activities and is funded by dedicated tax revenues and usage fees.

>>ADVANTAGES

Municipal officials view stadiums, hotels, and convention centers as ways to jump-start a depressed area. As such, municipalities are committed to their establishment.

>>RISKS

Both dedicated taxes (such as hotel occupancy taxes) and usage fee revenues can be adversely affected by declines in economic activity. When travel and leisure revenues dry up, so too do the taxes that are dedicated to pay for entertainment projects.

Tribal casino debt has its own unique issue. Since Native American tribes are sovereign countries that exist within the United States, it is not clear if a debt can be collected if there is a dispute. Many tribal governments are in disarray, and the reservations are economically impoverished. Not all tribal debt is of the same caliber.

>>SPECIAL FEATURES AND TIPS

Personally, we don't like to purchase bonds that are nonessential in nature. While you may consider attending a sporting event or playing golf essential when times are good, in hard times that may not be the case. Insurance is highly advisable when considering investing in these entertainment deals because you can't judge the likelihood of their ongoing success.

HEALTH CARE AND HOSPITAL BONDS

HOSPITALS HAVE A CONTINUAL NEED to upgrade facilities and buy new equipment. Bonds to finance much of this improvement are issued through state health authorities, which act as financing conduits for hospitals as well as for nursing homes and the relatively new continuing care retirement communities (CCRCs). Bonds for the latter, which are residences for elderly citizens who require some assistance, are frequently not rated. Nursing home bonds also are frequently nonrated. Whether or not the bonds are rated, the authorities assume no responsibility for the repayment of their issues.

>>ADVANTAGES

Hospital bonds tend to yield more than similarly rated bonds of other types. CCRCs and nursing home bonds likewise typically yield more than hospital bonds. When they are unrated, it is not uncommon for the yields to be positively through the ceiling.

>>RISKS

The financial health of hospitals is reeling under the onslaught of rising costs and restricted managed care payments. In 2001 there were more downgrades than upgrades of hospitals by rating agencies. Smaller regional providers in particular are having great difficulty in addressing financial and operational challenges.

In Standard & Poor's study of defaults in the 1990s, many of the nonrated bonds in this sector defaulted, with nursing home bonds defaulting more frequently than any other sector.[10] Insurance companies paid if the bonds were insured. If you are considering buying nonrated bonds, it is essential to know a good deal about the issuer.

>>SPECIAL FEATURES AND TIPS

Hospital bonds are subject to extraordinary calls in addition to regular calls. They also may have sinking funds. The higher yields resulting from downgrades can make hospital bonds attractive for junk bond buyers. Insurance may reduce some of their characteristic risk, but remember the adage: Insurance does not make a bad bond good.

The long-term financial viability of CCRCs remains to be proven, and bonds for their purposes are relegated to the high-yield market. CCRCs supported by financially solvent religious and nonprofit institutions are more attractive than those without such backing.

HIGHWAY BONDS: See "TRANSPORTATION BONDS"

HOUSING BONDS

MUNICIPAL HOUSING BONDS support the creation of multifamily or individual housing units for the poor and elderly. There are three kinds, with each having a different purpose and special security provisions. All are managed through state and local housing finance agencies.

◆ **State housing agencies** float bonds for builders of multiunit apartment buildings for the elderly. Some of these have federal insurance and are very creditworthy. The others are difficult to evaluate.

◆ **State housing finance agencies** sell bonds to secure funds for the purchase of mostly single-family mortgages from banking institutions. The mortgage revenue and a variety of insurance policies back these bonds.

◆ **Local housing authority bonds** support the development of multiunit apartment buildings and are secured by comprehensive rent subsidy packages.

Housing bonds are funded by underlying mortgages and may be insured or subsidized by the federal government. Federally insured housing bonds are rated double-A or triple-A depending upon the extent of the coverage provided by the Federal Housing Administration or the Veterans Administration. The Department of Housing and Urban Development (HUD) subsidizes rent payments for qualified individuals. Some housing bonds also carry a moral obligation pledge from the state in which they are issued. In addition, there may be insurance on the properties in case they are damaged or destroyed and insurance on the contractors for proper performance in construction.

While single-family mortgage bonds are quite safe from default, they have a very high probability of being called away early. *Super-*

sinkers are single-family mortgage revenue bonds with maturities between twenty and thirty years that will probably be redeemed within ten years. A sharp drop in interest rates could result in bond calls after a year. In extreme cases this could result in a cash short-fall because the revenue fund did not appreciate sufficiently to pay the costs of bond issuance.

>>ADVANTAGES
Housing bonds for single-family homes tend to have higher yields than other munis. Default risk is minimized on housing bonds that carry federal support and other kinds of insurance. Still, according to a Standard & Poor's review of default rates in the 1990s, single-family housing had a relatively high default rate for muni bonds. The highest concentrations of those defaults were in Florida, Minnesota, and Texas.[11] Many multi-family housing deals are backed by federal insurance, carry a single-A to double-A rating, and have additional private insurance as well.

>>RISKS
Although federal rent subsidies provide a reliable stream of income supporting the bonds, HUD reserves the right to stop paying if the rental unit is vacant for more than a year or if the housing administration does not follow HUD rules. Public Housing Authority bonds issued in anticipation of federal payments from HUD run the risk that the funds to pay the debt service will not be appropriated in sufficient amounts. However, expecting that this might be a problem, the issuer can build in safeguards. The rating should reflect them.

Housing bonds are subject to unpredictable, so-called extra-ordinary calls that can occur any time after the bonds are issued. Some bonds might be called from unexpended proceeds. In this case, the issuer would be unable to utilize all the money that was raised from the bond issue. Bonds can also be called because the mortgages backing the bonds have been retired. When interest rates are declining, calls tend to increase with home refinancing activity.

>>SPECIAL FEATURES AND TIPS

Single-family housing bonds should be purchased at or near par due to the likelihood that they will be called away early through an extraordinary call. For this reason, they have limited upside price potential. They may also have fixed calls.

Supersinkers are attractive to investors who prefer the high yield of long-term bonds and are willing to deal with unpredictable early calls.

NURSING HOME BONDS: See "HEALTH CARE AND HOSPITAL BONDS"

PUBLIC POWER BONDS

PUBLIC POWER BONDS were initially floated to subsidize electrification of underdeveloped rural areas of the country. The use of municipal bonds for this purpose began in the 1930s in California, Nebraska, and the Northwest. The first authority that grew out of federal legislation aimed to harness the Columbia River to produce hydroelectric power.[12] One of the major bond defaults of the twentieth century occurred when the Washington Public Power Supply System undertook the construction of five nuclear power plants to supplement that power.

>>ADVANTAGES

Formerly included in every widow and orphan portfolio, electric utility bonds fund a basic need to supply heat, cooling, and light for homes and businesses. Some very well managed utilities are available; however, one needs to pick and choose carefully today to find a power bond with both an attractive yield and protection against default.

>>RISKS

A power provider must comply with federal and state regulations, restricting its flexibility. Deregulation of the power industry in California, for example, led to runaway costs for the utilities while limiting the prices charged to consumers. California Edison teetered on the brink, and Pacific Gas and Electric declared bankruptcy. Although all muni bonds are subject to changes in political climates, the years 2000 and 2001 highlighted the particular vulnerability of public power bonds to this risk factor.

>>SPECIAL FEATURES AND TIPS

Like other revenue bonds, utility bonds are subject to extraordinary calls that could result in their being called away early.

TOBACCO BONDS

INDUSTRY PAYMENTS to state and local governments to settle legal claims against the industry secure tobacco bonds. An arrangement between R. J. Reynolds Tobacco Co., Philip Morris Inc., and Brown and Williamson Tobacco Corp. and forty-six states established by a master settlement agreement has given those states the right to payments from tobacco profits for twenty-five years. The process of issuing bonds to access the use of the anticipated revenue now is called *securitization*. Tobacco bonds typically have a single-A rating. Few individuals own these bonds because they have been scooped up by fixed-income mutual funds to boost overall yield.

Not all tobacco bonds are the same. The debt service may be secured by only tobacco proceeds or tobacco mixed with other revenue sources. Arkansas, for example, has issued revenue bonds where only 5 percent of the proceeds come from tobacco.[13]

>>ADVANTAGES

There are two advantages in purchasing tobacco bonds: They tend to offer higher yields than other munis, and they also provide an element of diversification to a bond portfolio.

>>RISKS

While the current stream of income from tobacco is quite good, revenue will decline if people stop smoking. The revenue could also be undermined by huge punitive damages awarded to plaintiffs in malpractice suits. Given the special nature of these bonds, they are not as liquid as other types of munis. If you are a buy-and-hold investor, that is not a problem.

>>SPECIAL FEATURES AND TIPS

Authorities were created specifically to issue the large deals backed only by the tobacco revenue, passing on the risk and the reward to you. You have to decide if you are being compensated for that transfer of risk with the extra 30 to 40 basis points that you are paid for buying them.

Tobacco bonds may be structured more like mortgage bonds, rather than straight debt. The bonds have "turbocharged" redemption provisions, so they are best purchased at par or at a discount.

TRANSPORTATION BONDS

TRANSPORTATION AUTHORITIES engage in just about every aspect of bringing goods and services into and out of a region. Some even include real estate activities among their portfolios.

Transportation bonds include bonds issued for ports, roads, trains and buses, and airports. A key factor in considering transportation bonds is not the name of the authority issuing them but rather what entity is paying for them. Highway revenue bonds, for example, are of two types: toll road bonds and public highway improvement bonds. The latter are financed by earmarked funds from gasoline taxes, automobile registration payments, and driver license fees. A recent source of funds available to states for accelerating road and bridge construction is in the form of grant revenue anticipation notes, an expectation of payments from federal grants. These so-called *garvees* are used in conjunction with other sources of bond payments.

Trains and buses rely on usage fees to fund their bonds, although federal grants are occasionally available for such purposes. One current federal program, dubbed Bus Rapid Transit, supports the construction of bus-only lanes, traffic lights that stay green as a bus approaches, and bus-boarding platforms, among other ideas.

Airport bonds are financed from three different sources of revenue: (1) ticket fees paid by passengers, (2) a wide number of airport usage fees (including flight fees paid by airlines for air travel; concession fees paid by shops, stands, and restaurants; parking fees; and fueling fees), and (3) lease income from the use of hangars or terminals.

>>ADVANTAGES

Transportation bonds represent the full range of credit quality, from established, broad-based issuers and solid debt coverage on one end to some of the more vulnerable issuers with lower collateralization and coverage on the other. Investors can pick up some high yields here, but you always have to balance the yields with their risk.

>>RISKS

Downgrade and default is possible for transportation bonds funded by revenues. Although reliable streams of income support most revenue bonds, the issuers may be overtaken by adverse political actions and events beyond their control. Florida, for example, has two bridges that are not producing enough revenue to support their upkeep and payment on the bonds. The Santa Rosa Bridge in the Florida Panhandle and the Garcon Point Bridge spanning Pensacola Bay have had trouble meeting their debt payments, and the Florida legislature has been unwilling to grant state loans to bail them out.

Airports are acutely sensitive to the fiscal fortunes of airlines using them as major hubs.

>>SPECIAL FEATURES AND TIPS

Transportation bonds usually have extraordinary calls that can be exercised in the event of a catastrophe. Sometimes they have stated calls and sinking funds.

When considering transportation issues, ask yourself if you would use the services being provided by the issuer and backed by the bonds. Ask if there are any alternative providers of the same service in the same area.

WATER AND SEWER BONDS

WATER AND SEWERS ARE ESSENTIAL to civilized living, and the entities that provide these services have little trouble collecting bills. In addition to usage fees, water and sewer districts charge assessment fees to determine the placement of the sewers and connecting fees that are collected before the sewers are built. The water and sewer bonds issued to support these activities are generally regarded as being among the safest municipal investments, a finding confirmed by Fitch Ratings in its 1999 study.

The bonds are generally issued by a municipality, or by municipalities within a given area in the case of the wastewater bonds. An authority, a water conservancy district, or a state bond bank may also issue bonds. Bonds issued through a state bond bank may carry a moral obligation pledge protecting cash flow against loan defaults. When the funding source is the federal government, the money is channeled into a state infrastructure bank, and the municipal project is subject to state and federal guidelines.

>>ADVANTAGES

Considered, as was noted, among the safest of municipal investments, water and sewer bonds are often double-barreled. The payment sources for the bonds are twofold: the revenue from water usage and a pledge of the municipality's tax revenue. Such double-barreled bonds may be sold as general obligation bonds or, with a more restricted revenue source, as limited-tax general obligation bonds.

>>RISKS

These bonds come with a wide range of ratings, with each determined by how established an area is and the solvency of customers who will pay for the bonds. As with other types of bonds, start-up situations tend to be riskier than bonds floated for repairs of established systems. Default potential is also higher in areas where utilities are not allowed to discontinue service even in the event of nonpayment of bills. Problems might also arise if bonds financed an existing antiquated system, in that more money than initially projected might be required to repair it.

Note that the introduction of conservation programs can cause a decline in revenue. Changes in legislation can also negatively affect water revenue if payments for purchased water are somehow restricted. For example, a Utah state senator proposed legislation in 2001 that would prevent the use of property tax revenue for the repayment of water and sewer bonds, reasoning that the tax lowered the cost of water, thus encouraging careless consumption. If that legislation had passed, it would have undermined the credit quality of future water and sewer bond issues in the state.

>>SPECIAL TIPS AND FEATURES

Traders value water bonds more than sewer bonds, and sewer bonds more than wastewater bonds, although they may be offered to you at the same yield.

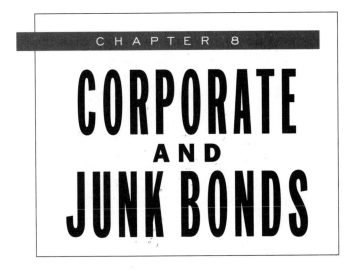

CHAPTER 8

CORPORATE
AND
JUNK BONDS

AT $2.2 TRILLION in outstanding debt, the corporate

bond market is huge. Bought by institutions and indi-

viduals alike because of their high yield, corporate

bonds span the spectrum of maturities and finance just

about every aspect of the economy. As such, their cred-

it ratings range from good-as-gold triple-A to down-

and-out junk.

General Considerations

GOOD-AS-GOLD CORPORATE BONDS are hard to find. According to Kamalesh Rao of Moody's Investor Service, the number of triple-A rated companies has shrunk over the past thirty years.[1] In the late 1970s fifty-eight companies had triple-A ratings and accounted for 25 percent of corporate debt. In 2001 only nine had the triple-A rating, and these companies accounted for only 6.2 percent of corporate debt. The stellar nine consisted of four corporate descendants of 1970s triple-A rated companies—Merck, Bristol-Myers Squibb, General Electric, and Exxon Mobil—and five newcomers—Berkshire Hathaway, American International Group, Johnson & Johnson, Pfizer, and United Parcel.

Of course, the higher a bond's rating, the less you are supposed to worry about a corporate bankruptcy and vice versa. With the collapse of Enron in 2001, the ratings assigned by agencies came under increased scrutiny. Moody's responded to the critical nature of the scrutiny by sending out a request for information about off-balance-sheet financial arrangements to about 4,200 companies in January 2002. The last time Moody's took this action was in 1994 when Orange County, California, filed for bankruptcy.

With a dearth of triple-A rated companies, credit protections have become increasingly important. Secured bonds offer such protections because they have a first claim on specific assets if the corporation is unable to pay. Examples of secured bonds are mortgage bonds, collateral trust bonds, and equipment trust certificates. If you see one of these names in the title of a bond, you will know that you have a secured bond. For example, a description might read: "Duke Power, First Mortgage Bonds." This means that the issuer, Duke Power, a utility company, issued a bond that is secured by a first mortgage on certain of its property. Collateral trust bonds are secured by securities of other companies (usually subsidiaries) owned by the company issuing the bonds. Equipment trust certificates are liens against the rolling stock of railroads or the airplanes owned by an airline company.

Guarantees are also a form of credit protection. Though usually featured on munis, they are sometimes on corporate bonds as well. The guarantees often appear as letters of credit (LOC), which are credit guarantees issued by banks. LOCs provide funds to pay off the corporate bond issue should the corporation default. Another form of a guarantee is when a parent company guarantees the bonds of one of its subsidiaries. Some corporate bonds are insured by the companies that also insure municipal bonds.

Unsecured bonds are known as debentures and are protected only by the full faith and credit of the company. Debentures can receive high bond ratings if the issuing company is financially strong. Bonds with a lesser claim on assets are called subordinated debentures.

In order to protect their creditability and to inform investors at the same time, rating agencies have developed "watch lists" that indicate when a company's rating might be either raised or lowered. Moody's provides its list on its website, www.Moodys.com. You can enter the name of the bond, or identify it by CUSIP. The Securities and Exchange Commission has the most current information from company filings at www.SEC.gov/edgar/quickedgar.htm.

While the overwhelming majority of corporate bonds feature a fixed interest rate, there are some offered with variable rates. Long featured in European bonds, variable rates have been attached to U.S. securities only since the 1970s. The rates are tied to some other measure, usually a Treasury bond rate or the European LIBOR (London Interbank Offer Rate) and are adjusted at specified intervals. As with other debt instruments, corporate bonds may be sold as zero-coupon bonds, which means they pay no interest until maturity.

The taxation of corporate bonds is very complicated, and you should consult your tax adviser on the specifics. However, we can offer the following generalizations:

◆ The interest that you receive on corporate bonds is generally subject to federal and state income tax at ordinary income tax rates. If you own zero-coupon bonds and they are not in a tax-sheltered retirement account, you may have to report phantom income each year even if you receive no current interest.

◆ If you sell your bonds before they come due, you must report either a short-term or long-term capital gain or loss on your federal and state income tax returns.

◆ If you bought a corporate bond at a premium (i.e., more than face value), you can generally amortize the premium over the life of the bond. This means that you can deduct a piece of the premium each year as an interest deduction on your income tax returns.

Corporate bonds are traded in one of two ways: either on the New York Stock Exchange (NYSE) or in the over-the-counter (OTC) market. While OTC trades are generally not reported, NYSE quotes frequently appear in the financial sections of newspapers. A hypothetical entry, in this case for an AT&T bond, might read as follows:

ATT 7¾ 07 Cur Yld 7.3 Vol 56 close 105½ Net Chg.- ½

Decoding the description, here is what we find out:
◆ AT&T has issued a bond with a coupon rate of 7¾ percent that comes due in 2007. Notice that there are pieces of information not presented, such as whether the bond has any calls or a sinking fund, the credit rating, and bond collateralization. This information is available from the bond guides published by Moody's or Standard & Poor's, or from your broker.
◆ The current yield (Cur Yld) is 7.3 percent. The more significant yield-to-maturity or yield-to-call is not presented. Thus, be aware that the current yield can be misleading. The novice bond investor mistakenly tends to view this yield as "the yield" that is quoted among brokers. However, bond calls can complicate the picture. As explained in Chapter 2, it is the yield-to-call and the yield-to-maturity that is the professional's basis for trading bonds.
◆ The volume (Vol) shows that fifty-six bonds ($56,000) of this issue were traded.
◆ The paper lists the closing price for the day at 105½, or $1,055 per bond.
◆ The change from the closing price on the previous day is off ½. This means that the closing price the prior day had been 106.

With the above as a general background, the following section will discuss different kinds of corporate bonds.

Key Categories of Corporate Bonds

THERE ARE TWO MAJOR INDICES, one compiled by Dow Jones and the other by Lehman Brothers, that track corporate bonds, and each has its own variation on how to categorize the bonds. The categories help to clarify the type of risk that you take when you buy corporate bonds. Bond sectors are of more than theoretical interest to bond buyers, as bad news affecting one issuer in a sector can affect all other bonds within the sector.

We have followed the Lehman example and have cut the corporate universe into Financials, Industrials (under which transportation falls), Utilities, and Yankee bonds. These are described below.

◆ **Financial institutions.** Included here are banks, finance companies, brokerage houses, insurance companies, REITs (real estate investment trusts), and other related types of firms. In some classifications, banks are separated from other financial companies because they do not always move in tandem.

◆ **Industrials.** This is a catchall category including manufacturing, mining, retail, and service-related companies. Transportation companies are also included. Their creditworthiness has been negatively affected by deregulation and new technologies. Railroad bonds were at one time some of the safest but have progressively seen their attractiveness erode. Airlines are one of the latest industries to suffer the effects of government deregulation, and the new freedom provides management the opportunity to make horrendous mistakes.

◆ **Utilities.** This category, which includes telephone and communications companies, gas distribution and transmission companies, water companies, and electric power companies, is reeling under the effects of deregulation. Historically considered stable investments, utilities have been forced from cozy, monopolistic surroundings into free-market environments that are not always friendly to their well being. Under the Telecom Act of 1996, for example, AT&T was left with the long-distance business and the Baby Bells were given aegis over local telephone calling. A combination of increased competition in the long-distance business and imprudent investments in cable, wireless, and Internet businesses resulted in AT&T assuming a staggering $36.5 billion of debt.[2] By the fall of 2001, the former incredibly staid and conservative Ma Bell found that its access to commercial paper was closing. It was only able to sell $10.9 billion of bonds by offering hefty interest rates and special credit enhancements.

◆ **Yankee bonds.** These are foreign bonds that are dollar denominated, thereby eliminating the currency risk. Yankee bonds are registered with the SEC and issued and traded in the United States. Included in this category are bonds issued by Canadian provinces and utilities; supranational agencies, like the World Bank; sovereign bonds, such as bonds issued by Australia and Sweden; and, to a lesser extent, corporate bonds.

Yankee bonds may yield more than similarly rated U.S. corporate bonds due to investors' lack of familiarity with the credit. They may also be issued with shorter maturities and better call protection, making them particularly attractive to U.S. and foreign buyers of dollar-denominated bonds.

Brady bonds are a kind of Yankee bond and are issued by emerging market countries. Named after Treasury Secretary Nicholas Brady, they were introduced in 1980 as a way for commercial banks to repackage their nonperforming emerging market loans.[3] Some of the debt backed by the Brady name is collateralized. U.S. zero-coupon bonds back the principal, and eighteen months of interest is guaranteed on a rolling basis.

In 1999 Ecuador became the first country to default on its Brady payments; Russia and Argentina have since followed. The last has been the most spectacular of all. Before the Argentinian default, an expected loss of principal—otherwise known as the haircut—was between 30 and 50 percent on the dollar. Argentina's loss is estimated to be 70 percent or more and sets a disturbing example for other third-world countries because it demonstrates that declaring bankruptcy can be one way to escape crushing debt loads.

>>ADVANTAGES

Corporate bonds provide a predictable stream of income. Interest is usually paid semiannually, although some bonds pay interest monthly. They yield more than Treasury and agency bonds and usually more than other taxable fixed-income investments. They are a suitable investment for tax-sheltered retirement accounts and for those in low tax brackets.

>>RISKS

Event risk is no stranger to corporate bonds. They may be subjected to leveraged buyouts (LBOs) or takeovers. In an LBO the employer or a purchaser takes the company private, often creating a windfall for the stockholders. However, an LBO may result in great uncertainty for the bondholders because their bonds are no longer liquid. LBOs have turned investment-grade bonds to junk overnight, in the process smearing the bonds of similar companies that are identified as potential acquisition candidates. In 1988, for example, when RJR Nabisco was taken over, prices of many large corporate bonds plummeted across the board as traders reacted to the realization that even large companies were not safe from such hostile actions.[4]

Bonds often lose out when corporations try to boost their stock prices. In 2000, for example, scores of companies raised the reported per share earnings by the simple expedient of buying back their shares, even though their earnings did not increase. After all, when you have four shares outstanding and you earn one dollar, your per share earnings are twenty-five cents. This earning report is doubled to fifty cents when you buy back two shares and thus have only two shares outstanding. While the companies were beefing up their per share earnings, however, they were acquiring boatloads of debt to buy back their shares. This heavy debt led Moody's to downgrade three times as many bonds as it upgraded in that year, a ratio not seen since the recession of the early 1990s.[5]

Floating-rate bonds have their own specialized risks. Although the coupon payments adjust to the changes in the marketplace interest rates, they do not adjust to changes in the credit quality of the issuer. Thus the interest rate being paid is based on the credit quality of the issuer when the floating rate was established.

>>PRICING INFORMATION

Although generally issued with a minimum face value of $1,000, corporate bonds are frequently sold in lots of $5,000.

Prices for frequently traded issues are currently reported after a four-day lag at the website www.investinginbonds.com; however, the market is moving toward greater price transparency.

While companies generally have only one class of common stock, they usually have many distinct bond issues. Bonds that trade often are easy to evaluate, whereas bonds that seldom trade are more difficult to price.

>>SPECIAL FEATURES AND TIPS

Corporate bonds come with one of three alternatives:
1 callable, which can vary from every thirty days to several years or be of a type known as *extraordinary,* which is triggered by the sale of assets or other special provisions;
2 noncallable, which covers the life of the bond; and
3 convertible, which means the bond can be turned in for shares, the number of which is stipulated by the indenture. You can pick what is best for you.

Sinking funds are a frequent provision of some types of corporate bonds and not of others. They are frequently found in the indentures of industrial bonds and public utilities, but not in telecommunications and finance companies.[7] Although sinking funds might redeem your bonds at an unwanted time, they do provide for the orderly repayment of debt. With zero-coupon bonds, on the other hand, no debt is repaid at all until the bonds come due. In that case you place your faith in the issuer's ability to pay all the debt at once.

Puts are a relatively new feature in corporate issues. They are the opposite of calls in that they allow buyers to redeem their bonds before maturity at face value and without penalty. One variant is the death put. If the bondholder dies, his estate can redeem the bond at face value. By its very nature, the death put increases the attractiveness of long-term bonds.

Unadorned puts are often used as an added inducement when an issuer is on credit watch. Another provision is the "step-up," which increases the size of the coupon by a fraction of a percentage point for a stated reason, like a rating agency downgrade. AT&T used both these inducements, plus a juicy yield, to attract buyers for its November 2001 issue.[8]

On a cautionary note, it is important never to equate a company's rising stock price with its financial health or willingness to support its outstanding debt.

Corporate Medium-Term Notes (MTNs)

HAVING READ ABOUT the complexities of bonds, it should not be too surprising to learn that medium-term notes are not always medium term. Once upon a time, when they first appeared in the 1980s, they did have maturities that fell between short-term commercial paper and long-term bonds and deserved their medium-term designation. They were noncallable, unsecured, senior debt securities with fixed coupon rates and investment-grade ratings with maturities of five years or less.

Now, however, their maturities range from nine months to thirty years. The Walt Disney Company even issued a medium-term note with a 100-year maturity in 1993. Starting as small niche offerings of the automobile industry, MTNs are now issued by hundreds of corporations both within the United States and in Europe. Not only are they not necessarily medium term, they may be callable, variable-rate, asset-backed, or debentures.

An aspect of MTNs that has remained true since their inception is their distribution process. Under the traditional system, underwriters buy the bonds themselves and take on ownership risk. With MTNs, brokers needn't do so. They act simply as middlemen in selling the bonds directly from the company to an investor, in the process pocketing a fee from the company for its services.

A second constant feature of MTNs is that they are offered on a continuous basis, rather than as one lump sum. This was made possible through SEC Rule 415, which went into effect in March 1982. The ruling allows a corporation to register at one time all bonds that it plans to sell over a two-year period. This is called a *shelf registration*. It gives corporations great flexibility in issuing bonds and is especially useful in allowing them to take immediate advantage of drops in interest rates. The value of each shelf registration generally ranges from $100 million to $1 billion. Once all bonds in a registration have been sold, the company can "reload" by filing for more debt in another registration.

>>ADVANTAGES

Unlike corporate bond offerings that are issued all at once, MTNs are available on a continuous basis, so you can purchase them at a time that is convenient for you. In addition, coupon rates can be quite attractive for maturities that are beneficial to the issuer.

>>RISKS

Because of their flexibility, MTNs are issued both privately and publicly, and this allows corporations to conceal some of their debt. MTN offerings are often issued simultaneously with derivatives to hedge company risks.

>>PRICING INFORMATION

Investors in MTN offerings must have deep pockets, because these offerings are usually in the range of $1 million to $25 million. Many brokers step in and buy them for trading purposes. They sometimes slice the MTNs into bonds with much smaller face values, generally in the $1,000 to $5,000 range. These bonds are then sold in packages, whose total size is determined by an investor's needs.

>>SPECIAL FEATURES AND TIPS

Medium-term notes are issued intermittently when the time is most propitious. Institutional buyers of corporate notes purchase them in blocks of $1 million or more. The small investor will usually not have access to this market except as noted above.

Structured notes are used in conjunction with swap transactions. You will probably not be aware of how the proceeds of the loan will be used when you are purchasing a note. However, if there are call options on structured notes, you can be sure that the bonds will be called if interest rates drop.

Corporate Retail Notes

CORPORATE RETAIL NOTES are shelf-registered notes that are the equivalent of MTNs for little guys. These notes are posted on the Internet and purportedly sold directly to you as original issue securities through a broker.

The issuer adjusts the coupon so you will always buy them at or near par in the initial offering. Whether you purchase them through a "discount" broker or a full-service broker, the price will be the same when they are newly issued, unless the broker tacks on a fee.

Corporate retail notes are also distinguished from MTNs in that you always know when they are going to be issued. In an MTN shelf registration, the issuer can release the bonds at its discretion. Retail note issuers commit to releasing a set number of bonds each week during the life of the registration. The issuer does have discretion to adjust the coupon rate, call features, and maturities in response to market fluctuations. The company might offer the same kind of bonds week to week, or change the type or maturity of the offerings. It might offer monthly pay or semiannual pay bonds, interest-bearing bonds or zero coupons, and callable or noncallable bonds.

General Motors Acceptance Corporation (GMAC), the financial arm of General Motors, was a pioneer in issuing corporate retail notes and used the moniker of SmartNotes to make them particularly attractive. The GMAC prospectus dated June 1, 2001, for example, is a shelf registration for the issuance of $8 billion. They are unsecured and unsubordinated debt. The prospectus does not detail the total amount of outstanding debt issued by the company.

Americans love brand names, and retail note issuers have capitalized on this, with many creating their own logos. Caterpillar Financial Services Corporation has PowerNotes; Tennessee Valley Authority, Electronotes; United Parcel Services, UPS Notes; and Freddie Mac, FreddieNotes. The bond rating agencies give each of these issuers high rating, though that is not a criterion for issuing these notes.

Corporate retail notes are usually offered on a Friday and the prices are good until the next Thursday, although the days of the open order period may vary from one issuer to another.

>>ADVANTAGES

Simplicity is the hallmark of corporate retail notes. You do not have to understand bond basics to purchase one. Since they are always issued at par, you do not have to understand the differences between premium, discount, and par bonds. You do not have to understand accrued interest.

Large, highly rated corporations usually issue them. They are convenient, come in a variety of maturities and payment options, and are sold in small lots.

You do not have to decide quickly if you want to purchase them, because the offering will remain stable for five business days despite market fluctuations. And, there's always next week, as corporate retail notes are continuously available.

>>RISKS

You can lose money on the sale of corporate retail notes. Their price and yield will bounce around just like that of any fixed-income investment. They also may have lower yields than institutional corporate notes due to features geared to attract the retail market.

They may have a senior lien or a subordinated lien on assets. In the event of a failure to pay in a timely fashion, holders of senior lien bonds can demand accelerated repayment, while holders of subordinated lien bonds must wait until an actual bankruptcy filing for assets to be allocated to creditors.

Corporate retail notes provide liquidity for the company when the commercial markets may be closed to them. For company survival, liquidity is always good. From the investors' perspective, it is the amount of debt the company assumes that could raise questions as to risk considerations.

>>PRICING INFORMATION

Corporate retail notes are priced at or near par, which is usually $1,000. That is also the minimum purchase amount. They have no accrued interest when first issued.

>>SPECIFIC INFORMATION SOURCES

For information on corporate retail notes look at Direct Access Notes (DANs) through ABN AMRO Financial Services at www.directnotes.com and Internotes from Incapital LLC at www.internotes.com. You can get a prospectus from any participating broker/dealer listed on either website, or you can visit the website of the individual issuers. You can also visit the SEC site at www.sec.gov/edgar/quickedgar.htm. Alternatively, you can call 800-SEC-0330 to receive documents or visit public reference rooms at SEC offices in Washington, D.C.; Chicago; and New York.

>>SPECIAL FEATURES AND TIPS

With the introduction of online information, it is very easy to check out corporate retail notes offerings each week. The offering sites are happy to e-mail you information on new offerings as they are formulated.

If you purchase monthly pay bonds, they have a slightly higher yield than equivalent semiannual bonds because you receive cash sooner. Not all issuers of these notes will necessarily be identified by a brand name when they are sold, so inquire whether you are purchasing a bond, an MTN, a Direct Access Note, or an Internote.

Most corporate retail notes contain a survivor's option, or death put, permitting the estate of the beneficial owner the right to put (that is, sell) the note back to the issuer at face value. There are some restrictions as to the dollar amount of notes accepted for this purpose.

This is a buy-and-hold investment because the spreads may be quite wide on the sale, although they are negotiable, as with any other bond.

Corporate High-Yield Bonds:
AKA Junk Bonds

THE TERM JUNK BOND is often equated with the term *high-yield bond*. While there are bond merchants who prefer that no distinction be made between the terms, they are in fact not synonymous. A bond may be high yielding without being junk, and a junk bond may not be high yielding.

A high-yield bond is simply one that currently yields more than other available bonds. It does so for any number of reasons, including (1) It is perceived riskier than other bonds and so must offer a higher return to attract investors; (2) It has an early call date and must offer a higher return to compensate investors for the short amount of time the bond will be held.

Junk bonds are the debris of failing or distressed companies. Often paying no interest income because their coupon payments have been abandoned, they are frequently the playthings of speculators. Buyers of these bonds are betting that they will eventually be sold for more than their current market price. Thus, unlike all other bonds, junk bonds are bought more for their capital appreciation potential and not for their interest payouts. As the saying goes: "Thar's gold in that thar junk!"

Junk bonds have had a long, if not always honorable, history in American financial markets. The term first appeared sometime in the 1920s and was used to describe bonds that few would touch because they were below investment grade. As has been noted, such bonds were also known as *fallen angels,* a term reflecting the fact that the bonds had once been respectable, investment-grade instruments and then had lost that designation when the issuing companies encountered extreme financial difficulties. Both analysts and investors avoided junk bonds not only because of their likelihood of default but also because the investment policies of many financial institutions excluded the bonds from their approved lists.

Since the 1980s, however, the application of the term *junk bond* has broadened. It now applies to bonds issued by established companies undergoing restructurings or leveraged buyouts (LBOs). An LBO is the purchase of a controlling interest in a company through the use of borrowed money. Sometimes, a company will buy itself, changing from a publicly owned to a privately owned entity. When that happens, the once publicly traded bonds are no longer traded and become illiquid; holders then have to wait until the bonds mature to obtain the principal. When Seagate Technology Inc., the world's biggest manufacturer of computer disk drives, announced it would go private in 2001, for example, the trading price of its bonds fell by half.

The term *junk* also covers the bonds of rising stars, new start-up companies turning to the bond markets for additional capital. While the majority of these start-ups have no, or the most speculative, risk rating, some are promising enough to be in the double-B category and have what the investment community considers interesting possibilities. These bonds can be called *junk* or, as some prefer, *businessman's risk bonds*.

Finally, some corporate managements deliberately create junk bonds as a protection against hostile takeovers. They make themselves unattractive by saddling themselves with debt from bond offerings and using the resulting funds to pay out high dividends to stockholders, thus depleting company assets. Suddenly, highly rated bonds become junk bonds, much to the dismay of the bondholders. Who wants to buy a debt-ridden company? The answer is no one if the acquiring company cannot ascertain the depths of the problem. The American International Group, the world's largest insurer, was ready to sign on the dotted line in a $833 million foreign investment in Hyundai Group, but Korean regulators refused to provide protection in the event hidden debt bombs exploded.[9] The deal fell apart.

Two other developments came to the fore in the 1980s. In the first, the concept of modern portfolio theory became widely embedded in financial planning. In very broad terms, this approach holds that diversification smoothes out risks. In practical terms, it made holding junk bonds more attractive because it meant that the portfolio could capture the high yield of the bonds while reducing the risk of holding them through diversification.

And then, of course, there was Michael Milken. He was, as the well-known quote explains, in the right place at the right time: junk bonds were acceptable portfolio components, and many companies were ripe for hostile takeovers and dismemberment. From his bastion at Drexel Burnham and Lambert, Milken saw to it that high-yielding bond issues became the hottest items in town. They financed merger and acquisitions activities that were used to take over companies and milk them dry, as some put it—or, according to others, to unlock their unrecognized values.

Without question, Milken was an innovative financier and created new debt instruments. Alas, he skirted a few too many regulations in doing so, with the result that he went to jail, Drexel Burnham and Lambert went bankrupt, and the junk bond market became seriously tarnished.

At the time Milken was at his high-flying prime, junk bonds were considered good investments not only for their money-making potential but also because their default rate was quite low. In fact, they were so good that there was a narrowing in the difference between their yields and that of Treasuries. With the scandal surrounding the collapse of Drexel Burnham and Lambert and the onset of the recession in 1990–1991, investors fled from junk bonds, selling them for whatever price they could get. Where once the spread between junk bonds and Treasuries had been about 200 basis points, it ballooned to 1,200 basis points in November 1990.

Modern portfolio theory, however, remained unaffected. Throughout the 1990s increasing amounts of high-yield bonds were bought for mutual funds. The attractiveness of their yields was such that even staid investment institutions such as Vanguard and TIAA-CREF introduced funds consisting solely of these bonds.

Junk bonds attract a unique clientele and require analysis that differs from that used with investment-grade bonds. As well-known investment-grade bonds began to slide (including Dole Food company, Hasbro, and AMR, the corporate parent of American Airlines) and with the default rate calculated by Fitch Ratings at 12.9 percent in 2001, up from 5.1 percent in 2000,[10] analysts who formerly only focused on either high-grade or high-yield bonds began to cover both types. In 2001 Moody's Investors Services downgraded the ratings of forty-nine such companies as the country slid into a recession.[11] With telecom companies investors were lucky to get the quoted price of 14–20 percent of face value.[12]

>>ADVANTAGES

For knowledgeable players, junk bonds can be very lucrative. In addition to their high yields, they also offer the potential for substantial capital appreciation.

>>RISKS

Junk bonds share with other bonds all the same risks and then some. Interest rates may rise, depressing the prices at which the bonds are sold. Downturns in the economy affect all business, but the weakest companies suffer the most. Liquidity dries up just when you really need it.

The special risk for junk bonds is the heightened possibility of default and further rating downgrades. Credit watch or actual downgrades mean that the value of your bonds decline and their salability diminishes. Default may lead to your losing every dime of your investment.

More frequently you will have some recovery of assets that are paid in cash and securities. Moody's found that the recovery rate on junk bonds was 38 percent across the board in their 1970–1991 study. The analysts calculated the recovery rate by using the trading price at the time of default divided by the par value of the bonds.[13] However, if you hold only a few junk bonds—something few professionals would recommend—this might not be your experience.

>>PRICING INFORMATION

Credit issues mainly affect the yield on junk bonds. The price of junk bonds generally does not respond to the movement of interest rates in the same way as better credits. Treasury yields might change, but yields on junk bonds may not move or will move only fractionally. Traders value junk bonds principally on price discovery: that as the prospects of the company improve and the risk of default is reduced, the value of its bonds will increase.

The thin market for these bonds makes them expensive to trade. Junk bonds are difficult to price unless they are actively traded. Their price is set based on a total return approach, taking into account likely interest payments and return on capital invested.

>>SPECIAL FEATURES AND TIPS

Some investors make a lot of money trading junk bonds. They are frequently individuals who are retired and have time to closely follow bankruptcy proceedings. They make a bet on the reorganization of the company. A lot of bonds trade at the bottom of a bankruptcy when many holders want to get out and are willing to sell at ten to fifteen cents on the dollar. If the bet pays off, the return could be forty to fifty cents on the dollar. This type of trading, however, is not for the faint of heart.

Defaulted bonds generally trade flat, that is, without accrued interest. If the bond is only heading for default, you might be able to negotiate a sale with a due bill. A due bill is attached if a seller sold securities with interest due that the trustee identifies as belonging to the seller rather than the buyer. If a due bill is attached, the buyer's broker can claim the interest. You get a proportionate share of the next interest payment, if there is one, if you have a due bill designation. If the buyer's purpose is to become a player in the restructuring by amassing a large block of bonds, they won't care about the interest.

If you want to purchase junk bonds, consider purchasing them through a mutual fund. Don't forget, however, that junk bonds are especially risky when the economy is heading into a recession. In the six months ending July 1, 2001, for example, the Vanguard High-Yield Corporate Fund was the only one of the firm's ten bond funds to register a decline.

Corporate Convertible Bonds

CONVERTIBLES! BACK IN OUR dating days, we loved riding along with the top down and the wind blowing through our hair while we debated if that big black cloud up ahead really meant rain. If you like that kind of racy feeling, then convertibles are for you. They start off as simple, interest-paying bonds that yield less than the market rate, and they may wind up as dividend-paying stocks.

The raciness comes in when you get to convert bonds into equity for a fixed number of common stock shares. For example, your $1,000 face value convertible bond might say that it will become ten shares of common stock. Alternatively, your convertible bond might specify a conversion price rather than a number of shares. If the price is $100, then the security can be exchanged for ten shares. The term *parity price* is used to describe the price at which the shares are convertible. In this example, the parity price is $100. There may be a step-up feature that increases the price of conversion after a specified amount of time.

The majority of convertible issuers are below investment grade. Convertibles represent one of the few remaining funding sources available to companies saddled with large debt loads or with very volatile earnings. The management is reluctant to raise new funds through issuing stock because this would dilute and thus lower per share value. By issuing convertibles, a company can have its cake and eat it, too. Often a convertible bond will carry a stipulation that it can be called if the stock appreciates significantly, a process called *forced conversion*. This gives the company leeway to issue either new convertible bonds or new equity shares based on the higher stock price.[14]

>>ADVANTAGES

Convertibles offer the safety of a bond with the upside of a stock. They feature interest payments, which provide a stream of income, and a maturity date when the principal will be returned. In the event of bankruptcy, convertible bonds have senior status over preferred and common stock. If the stock drops, the bonds will theoretically cushion the fall for the convertible holder, while allowing an upside participation if the stock soars.

>>RISKS

If a company is increasingly looking like a candidate for bankruptcy, you will find its bonds will not hold their value. And, in the event of bankruptcy or a sinking share price, you will have given up a substantial yield for the benefit of an unattractive conversion feature.

If a company is doing well and the indenture provides that the bonds are callable, you can be sure that a call will happen if the stock dividends are less than the interest payments on the bonds. Depending upon the price you paid for the bonds, you may suffer a loss as well as miss an opportunity for a big upside.

If you purchase an individual convertible bond and decide: "Now is the time to get out," you might have difficulty finding a buyer. This is primarily an institutional market populated by fund managers and insurance companies. You probably do not have a block of bonds that is attractively sized for them. Who is going to buy ten apples when they are looking for a truckload?

>>PRICING INFORMATION

Although the face value for corporate convertibles is generally $1,000, the price you pay for such a bond is based on valuation factors that are complex even for sophisticated investors. The purchase price is affected not only by call and put options, but also by stock splits and dividend payouts that reduce the value of the stock. There may or may not be antidilution provisions in the indenture.

>>SPECIAL FEATURES AND TIPS

Convertibles will behave more like a bond if the bond price is above par, which happens if the bond has a high coupon rate or is a zero-coupon bond selling at a premium to its current value. The bonds may be puttable (that is, sellable back to the issuer), which is good for you, or callable, which is not, because it takes away your options.

If you want to purchase convertible securities, you might want to consider buying them through a mutual fund, whose management has done all the work in assessing what is and what is not a good valuation.

Some convertibles have features that permit the issuer to decide when to raise the roof by allowing the company to dictate the timing of the bond conversion to stock. While rating agencies like a debt conversion based on what is best for the company, it is better for the bondholder to be able to decide when and if to convert.

A conversion price is frequently 20–35 percent above the share price at the time of issue. In order for that to be appealing, you must believe that the stock has good upside potential. Investors eagerly purchased technology convertibles in the 1990s in anticipation of rapid stock appreciation. The "tech wreck" in 2000 derailed windfalls from bond conversions and left many with neither income nor a full return of principal.

CHAPTER 9

BOND LOOK-ALIKES

THEY LOOK LIKE BONDS, and they often act like bonds,

but they are not bonds. These are the financial instru-

ments that compete with bonds and complement bonds.

Investors often become interested in these alternatives

when they seek more cash flow or a different kind of

cash flow to satisfy their financial needs.

And when investors are interested, financial firms and

brokerage houses are quick to rush in with fancy-sounding products geared to such interests. Two of the many recent offerings go by the names of Principal-Protected Securities (a great name in a sliding stock market) and Equity-Linked CDs (not so great in a sliding stock market). No matter what the name, we feel these so-called new financial products are often no better or worse than the old ones. Many, in fact, are blatant appeals to investors who are called yield hogs. These people see yield and yield alone in examining investments and ignore other considerations such as safety, liquidity, and tax implications.

We have limited this bond look-alike chapter to five classic bond alternatives and present the uses, advantages, and disadvantages of each.

Bank Certificates of Deposit

BANK CERTIFICATES OF DEPOSIT (CDs) are time deposits, one of the simplest and most common investments. With them you deposit cash with a bank for a stated time period and earn a stated rate of interest. When you buy a $100, 12-month bank CD with a 5 percent interest rate, for example, you will receive all your principal plus $5 in interest for a total of $105 at the end of twelve months when the CD comes due.

Bank CDs offer a variety of interest payment options, including monthly, quarterly, semiannually, yearly, and when the CD comes due, as in the above example. Bank CDs are generally nonnegotiable, which means that you can't sell them to a third party. You must either wait until the CD comes due or must sell the CD back to the issuing bank before maturity and pay a penalty.

Bank CDs may have fixed or variable interest rates, may have call features, and may also be sold as zero coupons.

In order to make the CDs more attractive than Treasury securities, banks may offer them at a higher interest rate than that paid on comparable Treasuries.

>>ADVANTAGES
Bank CDs are one of the safest investments to be found because your principal is protected. The Federal Deposit Insur-

ance Corporation (FDIC) insures up to $100,000 of principal and interest per ownership category deposited in an account at an insured savings institution. Banks that display the FDIC or eagle sign at each teller window are FDIC insured.

In addition, bank CDs are free of market risk because the principal is always returned if you redeem them before their due date.

>>RISKS

Many financial institutions that sell CDs are not insured by the FDIC. These institutions often offer higher rates, but their CDs come with the risk that the institution could fail. In addition, if the face amount of the CD plus accrued interest exceeds $100,000, the excess is not insured. Thus, if you are concerned about safety, make sure that the FDIC insures the issuing bank and that your principal and interest do not exceed $100,000.

Although you can generally withdraw cash from a bank CD before it matures, there is a penalty. Typical bank penalties for early withdrawals are as follows:

◆ Maturity of 7 to 90 days: generally all interest earned.

◆ Maturity of 91 to 364 days: generally equal to 90 days' interest.

◆ Maturity of 365 days or greater: generally equal to 180 days' interest.

These penalties can eat into your principal. For example, suppose you bought a 24-month CD at the bank and needed to cash it in after three months. In this case you would pay a six-month interest penalty even though you only earned three months of interest.

>>TAX IMPLICATIONS

Interest from CDs is subject to federal, state, and local income tax. In addition, there is a tax disadvantage to long-term (more than 12-month) bank CDs that pay interest at maturity rather than annually. The interest earned each year must be reported in your federal income tax return, even if you don't receive it until a later year, unless the CD is held in a tax-sheltered retirement account.

Withdrawal penalty payments are deductible whether you itemize your deductions or not.

>>PRICING INFORMATION

CDs can be purchased in amounts from $50 to $100,000 and possibly more at certain banks.

>>SPECIFIC INFORMATION SOURCES

Good sources of information on current CD rates throughout the country and a CD calculator can be found at www.bankrate.com and www.bauerfinancial.com. The latter is sponsored by Bauer Financial (2655 LeJeune Road; Coral Gables, FL 33134; 800-388-6686), which also publishes *Jumbo Rate News* that covers 1,300 CD Rates. The *Jumbo Rate News* Internet home page site is www.bankrater.com/topjumbocdrates.asp.

>>SPECIAL FEATURES AND TIPS

Jumbo bank CDs in amounts of $100,000 or more often earn more interest than nonjumbo bank CDs.

Unless given instructions to redeem a CD when it comes due, bank CDs roll over automatically. There is often a ten-day window between the maturity of the last CD and the start of a new one, and this gives you time to shop around to see if there are better returns elsewhere. Sometimes the bank itself might be offering specials on its CDs. If you simply roll over your CD without asking about specials, you may miss a more attractive rate.

Keep in mind that each financial institution is free to have its own penalty provisions, and you should ask about the penalty for early withdrawals.

While no one can predict the future of interest rates, if you feel interest rates will fall, a bank CD allows you to lock in favorable rates.

If you are investing $1,000 or more, compare CD rates with Treasury offerings before making your decision to invest.

Be aware that some bank CDs are callable. This is important

if you think you are locking in a high rate. Indeed, callable CDs are only attractive if their rates are significantly higher than those at prevailing levels.

Broker Certificates of Deposit

IN THE 1980s major brokerage firms began to sell bank CDs to their customers. It has proven to be a happy arrangement for all parties. Small banks are able to tap into a larger market by having a national firm sell their CDs, and the brokerage firms receive a fee from the banks for doing so.

Let's see what a typical broker CD looks like and compare it to a typical bank CD.

◆ **Insurance.** Brokers will generally only sell CDs of banks that are FDIC insured. However, you must make sure that the bank issuing the CD has FDIC insurance.

◆ **Maturity.** Broker CDs have maturities that generally range between one month and twelve years since brokers deal with many banks. In comparison, many banks offer CDs that have lives of only five years or less.

◆ **Maximum amount.** The face amount of many broker CDs will not exceed $90,000 in order to make sure that the principal and interest do not exceed the $100,000 insurance limit. Many banks will sell you a $100,000 CD.

◆ **Interest payout.** Brokered CDs generally pay semiannual interest, like a bond. Some banks will pay you interest monthly, semi-annually, yearly, or when the CD comes due. You must ask the bank what its payout possibilities are.

◆ **Resale.** The key difference between a bank and a broker CD is that the broker CD is negotiable. This means that you can generally sell the broker CD back to the broker without a penalty prior to its due date at its market price rather than its face value. The market price that you receive may be higher or lower than the CD's face value. Thus, if interest rates decline after you buy the broker CD, you may be able to sell your CD back to your broker at a gain. If interest rates have gone up over your holding period, you can hold the broker CD until it comes due and receive its face value or sell the CD to the broker at a loss.

◆ **Fees and commissions.** There is generally no stated commission charged to the broker's customers on the sale of a CD. The broker earns its fee from the bank.

>>ADVANTAGES

When buying a broker CD from a large firm, you are offered a veritable shopping mall of offerings. The firm can locate advantageous prices and a variety of CD offerings that you would be hard put to find on your own. This can lead to excellent buying opportunities. For example, the interest rate on a typical 5-year broker CD in November 2001 was 4.65 percent, and the yield on a 5-year Treasury bond was 3.85 percent.

>>RISKS

As discussed above, broker CDs are subject to market risk when sold before their due date.

>>TAX IMPLICATIONS

Interest income from broker CDs is fully taxable. When they are sold early, however, the difference between the sale price and the purchase price is treated as either a long-term or short-term capital gain or loss.

>>PRICING INFORMATION

Broker CDs can generally be purchased in amounts from $1,000 to $90,000 from brokers.

>>SPECIAL FEATURES AND TIPS

There are many varieties of broker CDs, including zero-coupon CDs that are similar to zero-coupon bonds.

There are also "step-rate" CDs. A "step-down" CD will generally pay an above-market interest rate for a stated period and then will pay a lower, stated rate until it comes due. A "step-up" CD will generally pay a below-market interest rate for a stated period and then will pay a higher, stated rate until it comes due. Step-rate CDs might wind up with more or less interest than a CD without these features. As with all broker CDs, if you sell them back to the broker before their due date, you may have a gain or a loss. Get the buy-back terms from the broker before you buy unless you are sure you can hold the CD until maturity.

The U.S. Securities and Exchange Commission has warned investors in a release dated April 13, 2001, entitled *Certificates of Deposit: Tips for Investors,* that some brokers are selling broker CDs that say they are "one-year noncallable." Some investors believe that this means that the CD comes due in one year. In fact it means that the CD can be called after one year. If the CD is of longer duration and the investor wants his money back sooner, he must redeem the CD and may lose some principal. The SEC also warned CD investors that they should make sure that they understand when and how the CD rate can change. (See www.sec.gov/investor/pubs/certific.htm.)

Single Premium Immediate Fixed Annuities

AN ANNUITY IS A CONTRACT between you and an insurance company in which you give the company cash in exchange for an agreed-upon stream of payments. Immediate annuities are financial instruments with a simple premise: You make one lump sum payment for which you immediately (within thirty days) start to receive a fixed monthly amount for a fixed number of years, for life, or until a fixed total amount of money is paid.

Think of the immediate annuity as an insurance policy in addition to being an investment. When you purchase an immediate annuity there will be no money to return to you when the policy terminates because the money will have been spent on the purchase of an insurance benefit: the scheduled stream of fixed payments to you.

Each insurance company has its own variations on the following four distribution options. The most common options are the first two.

1 Life only. Payments are made for as long as you live. Your annuity contract can also provide for a joint and survivor annuity. If this distribution option is elected, payments will be made for your life and the life of your spouse or another named person. If you (and the other) both die prematurely, you lose the remaining value that you paid for in your annuity contract. You receive the highest payout for a single life annuity since it will terminate in the shortest amount of time and the lowest payout for a joint and survivor annuity since it will generally pay out for a longer period of time.

2 Life with period certain. You or your beneficiary will receive payments for the longer of (a) your life (or lives) or (b) a stated minimum number of years even if you die prematurely. Under such a policy, the beneficiary would inherent the remaining amount of the policy if you die before the stated number of years.

3 Period certain but not life. This guarantees payments for only a specified number of years, but not for life.

4 Accumulated amount only. This option provides for payment of a specified amount per month until the annuity account is exhausted.

>>ADVANTAGES

An immediate annuity provides you with a guaranteed stream of income for life (assuming you select one of the first two options), no matter how long you live. No other investment is so well constructed for this purpose. An annuity is a kind of longevity insurance. The purpose of a fixed annuity is to shift to the insurance company the risk of outliving your money.

The payments from an immediate annuity are fixed and unaffected by financial market gyrations or interest rate fluctuations. If your immediate annuity provides for a payout of $1,000 per month for life, that is what you will get no matter what is happening in the financial markets.

Unlike many other investments, the stated returns on immediate annuities are net of any fees. What you see is what you get.

>>RISKS

Immediate annuities are irrevocable and, thus, worse than illiquid. Once you buy an immediate annuity for, say, $100,000, you have completely lost control of that $100,000. You have exchanged your $100,000 for a stream of payments, and your deal is done. Before you buy the annuity you should read the annuity contract to determine if you can get a prepayment for medical emergencies or for some other purpose. If there are no such provisions, assume your money is locked up for good. This is a reason to commit only a portion of your capital to an immediate annuity.

There is a risk that the insurance company could go broke and thus default on your annuity contract. This risk can be greatly reduced if you buy only annuities of highly rated insurance companies.

Finally, there is inflation risk. This is associated with all long-term fixed income investments, and it can be a serious one when your income is steady but its purchasing power is declining drastically.

>>TAX IMPLICATIONS

Although most annuities offer tax-deferred growth, this is not true of immediate annuities, because you receive a stream of cash from their inception, and there is no accumulation phase. Part of the cash you receive is considered taxable income, and the remainder is a nontaxable return of your principal. The IRS provides tables that tell you how much of an immediate annuity is subject to federal income tax. See IRS Publication 939, *General Rules for Pensions and Annuities.*

Many charities tout the tax implications of buying annuities known as *charitable gift annuities.* In this case you buy the annuity contract from the charity and the charity promises to pay you an income for life, starting either immediately or when you reach a certain age. In this case you might receive a tax deduction as well as lifetime income. Keep in mind that you are counting on the charity remaining solvent.

>>PRICING INFORMATION

The cost of an immediate annuity ranges from $1,000 to generally as much as you want.

>>SPECIFIC INFORMATION SOURCES

There are a number of websites to research annuities that include an annuity calculator to determine yields. See www.annuityadvantage.com and www.annuity.com.

>>SPECIAL FEATURES AND TIPS

Fixed annuities are the wallflowers of the insurance world. Although widely recognized as bond alternatives because they offer a fixed rate of return on a cash investment, their charms are rarely touted. Why? Because salespeople receive much higher commissions for selling variable annuities, and you'll find that, not unreasonably, where there are large fees to be made there are many salespeople praising the product. We recommend fixed annuities.

Consider using an immediate annuity to supplement your income when your earned income is falling because you are working part time or are nearing retirement.

Look at insurers who have earned the highest ratings for at least ten years and then compare their quoted monthly distributions per $1,000 purchase. You can check the ratings of insurance companies by contacting A.M. Best at 908-439-2200 and Weiss Research at 800-289-9222. A.M. Best is paid by insurance companies for doing ratings. Weiss Research is paid by consumers and is a more stringent evaluator. To get a final check on ratings, you might call Moody's at 212-553-0377 and Standard & Poor's at 877-481-8724. You might also check the Insurance News Network website, www.insure.com. We find TIAA-CREF to be a good company with good rates.

If you have a significant health problem, ask about impaired risk annuities. Impaired risk underwriting is a process by which physicians or underwriters evaluate your life expectancy based on your health. If it is projected that you will not live as long as your life expectancy, you may get a higher payout.

Check out immediate annuities that provide an increasing payout over the years. These annuities start with a below-market payout for the first number of years and then increase by a set percentage over the later years.

Instead of buying one large, lump sum immediate annuity, buy several with smaller amounts at different time periods. This allows you to capture any rising rates.

Finally, buy the immediate annuity when you are older. The

older you are when you buy an immediate annuity, the shorter your life expectancy and thus the higher the payout and rate of return. Since part of this income is deemed a return of principal, it will not be taxed. We recommend serious consideration of immediate fixed annuities after age seventy.

Deferred Fixed Annuities

WHEREAS THE IMMEDIATE ANNUITY premise is simple, that of the deferred fixed annuity is not. The "deferred" in the name is what makes it attractive to many investors, because the tax on its income can be deferred as long as you stay invested in an annuity. The "fixed" refers to a fixed rate of return on your cash investment during the accumulation phase. Finally, this instrument may never become an "annuity" if you so choose. On the other hand, it can be structured to provide significant tax advantages as well as a lifetime stream of income. It is, in our opinion, a financial instrument worth considering. Others are starting to agree with us, particularly since deferred fixed annuities were one of the most profitable investment instruments during the stock market declines in 2000 and 2001.[1]

We suggest you think of deferred fixed annuities in terms of four phases: investment, accumulation, nonfixed distribution, and fixed distribution.

◆ **Investment phase.** In this phase, you sign an annuity contract with an insurance company. The contract specifies that you make either a lump sum payment or a number of payments over a period of time.

◆ **Accumulation phase.** The terms of this phase are stipulated in your annuity and state the fixed rate of return on the cash that you invest for a fixed number of years. The contractual term may vary from one to ten years. This is similar to the contractual return you would get on a CD from a bank for a fixed number of years. At the end of a contractual term, the insurance company will make another offer in which the fixed return will remain or be adjusted upward or downward. At this point, and at the end of any further contractual terms, you have three choices:

1 Cash out your deferred fixed annuity. If you cash out, you may be subject to insurance company penalties and federal income tax penalties.

2 Transfer your deferred fixed annuity to another annuity company. If you do so, you may trigger an early withdrawal penalty clause in your annuity contract. (Some annuity companies do not levy withdrawal penalties.) However, there would be no federal taxable income generated or tax penalties if you follow the tax rules for a tax-free exchange.

3 Extend the term of your current deferred fixed annuity. You may get a higher or lower interest rate on the extension.

◆ **Nonfixed distribution phase.** Many annuity contracts allow you to make systematic or possibly irregular withdrawals from your contract. You can receive regular payments based on a variety of factors, including a fixed dollar amount, a percent of your account value, or your life expectancy. You can also change how the payments are to be made or stop the payments altogether.

If you make systematic withdrawals before your fixed distribution date, keep two points in mind. First, if you take too much cash out of your contract, you may not have enough to meet your distribution goals in the future. Second, withdrawals from your deferred fixed annuity might trigger penalties from the annuity company as well as federal income tax and tax penalties.

◆ **Fixed distribution phase.** In insurance circles, this is known as annuitization, the time when you and the company agree on a permanent payment option. As with immediate annuities, the options are life only, life with period certain, period certain but not life, and accumulated amount only.

Deferred fixed annuities are most suitable for individuals who wish to increase tax deferral above that offered through qualified plans such as 401(k)s and IRAs and who are not concerned that their heirs may not inherit any of the proceeds.

>>ADVANTAGES

In addition to ultimately providing you with a guaranteed stream of fixed income, the deferred fixed annuity has a number of other advantages. While the income is accumulating, it is tax deferred. Thus, if you hold the annuity for twenty years, you will not pay tax on the accumulated income for twenty years. Tax will only be payable on the amount of a portion of the distributions from the policy.

The deferred fixed annuity has more flexibility than the immediate annuity in that you can set the size and timing of the distributions and you can transfer the annuity from one company to another.

You have no market risk with a deferred fixed annuity. Your principal is guaranteed in the same way as with a CD.

>>RISKS

The rate, particularly the renewal rate, may not be competitive with other suitable investments. This is a particular problem if you invested at one rate (sometimes called a teaser rate, because it is high) which is followed by a renewal rate clearly below market. At this point you are faced with either taking a below-market rate of return or possibly having to pay annuity company penalties and possible tax penalties if you want to take a distribution or switch to another company.

If the annuity company becomes financially troubled, you may lose some principal and/or your money may be tied up for a period of years. Because of this possibility, you should consider investing a portion of your cash with two or more companies to spread the risk of default.

Penalty payments for early withdrawals can be substantial in the early years of an annuity contract. A typical penalty schedule starts at 7 percent the first year, going down 1 percent each year until there is no penalty in the eighth year.

>>TAX IMPLICATIONS

If the value of the annuity is paid out as a lump sum distribution, all of the earnings are subject to tax as ordinary income for federal income tax purposes. Thus, if you invest $50,000 in the annuity and there is a lump sum distribution of $70,000, $20,000 will be subject to ordinary income tax.

If there are partial withdrawals before the annuity date, taxable earnings are deemed to be paid first, so that payment of taxes will be accelerated.

If the deferred fixed annuity is annuitized and is paid out as a series of payments, the tax result is the same as for the immediate annuity.

If you are younger than 59½ at the withdrawal date, you will be subject to a 10 percent IRS penalty. There is no tax penalty if you are age 59½ or older at the date of distribution.

>>PRICING INFORMATION
Minimum purchase is usually $1,000. There is usually no upper limit to the amount purchased.

>>SPECIFIC INFORMATION SOURCES
For the tax implications of annuity income, see IRS Publication 939, *General Rules for Pensions and Annuities.* You can find this publication and all other IRS publications on the IRS website, www.irs.gov.

>>SPECIAL FEATURES AND TIPS
Deferred Fixed Annuities are most suitable for individuals in the following situation: They have contributed the maximum to their qualified plans such as 401(k)s and IRAs. They want a tax deferral on their investment return. They will keep the deferred fixed annuity for at least fifteen years, and at that time they will be at least 59½. They are not concerned that their heirs may not inherit any of the proceeds from the deferred fixed annuity. They expect to be in a lower tax bracket at the time they draw on the deferred fixed annuity.

Some annuity contracts provide for a free withdrawal privilege. Check to determine how much of your cash might be taken out without paying a penalty to the annuity company each year; some allow you to take out 10 percent each year without a penalty. However, taxable income will still be generated and possibly a tax penalty.

Even if there were capital gains recognized in your annuity, when there is a distribution, it is all taxed as ordinary income. Thus, an annuity converts capital gains into ordinary income.

Nonconvertible Fixed-Rate Preferred Stock

PREFERRED STOCKS COME in many shapes and forms: convertible; nonconvertible; variable rate; and numerous kinds of fixed-rate, including fixed-dividend, auction market, and remarketed preferreds. There are also fancy, preferred stock packages created by large brokerage firms. With billions of dollars in these instruments outstanding, these are not small players in the overall markets.

Of the many preferred stock variations, the one known as a nonconvertible fixed-rate preferred stock is most like a bond and is often sold as a bond alternative. For brevity's sake, we refer to this simply as the Preferred, which beats the acronym NFRPS any day.

Although the Preferred has a number of bond-like aspects, it is legally a form of equity. Unlike a bond, there is generally no redemption due date at which time the Preferred must be paid off. Where redemption due dates do exist, they are usually so far in the future as to be irrelevant. There is no contractual legal obligation to pay dividends on the Preferred; if the issuer misses a payment, it is not considered a legal default, but such an action would constitute a default on a bond.

In one way, the Preferred is like a perpetual bond in that it pays dividends at a fixed rate per share each year. For example, if the par value of your Preferred is $50 per share, and the dividend rate is 8 percent per share, you would receive a dividend of $4 per year ($50 x 8 percent). Since Preferred dividends are generally paid quarterly, you would receive $1 per quarter. This dividend will never be increased, even if the earnings of the company grow, because it is fixed. By comparison, the dividends on common stock may grow as the company becomes more profitable.

While a Preferred generally pays its dividends in cash, there are certain kinds of Preferred called PIKs. This kind of Preferred pays dividends in kind, i.e., additional shares of preferred stock, rather than cash dividends. PIK Preferreds are risky securities.

Most issues of Preferred are what are known as *cumulative Preferred*. This means that if the issuer does not pay the preferred dividend when it is due, the amount of the dividend accumulates and will be paid when the issuer is financially able to do so. Thus, in the above example, if dividends are not paid for a year on the Preferred, the $4 is accrued and will be paid in the next year, if financially possible, together with an additional $4 for that next year.

If there is a failure to pay interest or principal on a bond, this is considered a default and a bankruptcy or reorganization will result. By contrast, if a dividend is not paid on the Preferred, no such serious consequences ensue. The following, however, may be triggered if a Preferred dividend is not paid:

1 The Preferred is immediately given priority over common stock dividends and none of the latter will be paid until all unpaid dividends on the Preferreds are paid in full.

2 There may be a restriction such that the corporation can't use corporate funds to buy back common stock. The point is to conserve cash for the payment of dividends on the Preferreds.

3 Sinking fund payments may be halted. The point here again is to conserve cash for the payment of dividends on the Preferreds.

4 The Preferred shareholders receive voting rights that they did not have before.

Some Preferred stocks are designated as noncumulative preferred. This is an unusual kind of preferred since it allows management to skip a dividend and never make it up. Noncumulative Preferred have generally come about as a result of a corporate reorganization or bankruptcy, where debt holders were given this kind of stock in exchange for their debt securities.

If there is a bankruptcy, liquidation, or other financial failure of the corporation, the Preferred shareholders will be paid before there is any payment to the common shareholders. However, in this case the debt holders will be paid before there is any payment to the Preferred shareholders.

Almost all Preferred issues are callable at some time at a set price. The price might be the issue price or could be a higher price that declines over the years to provide some protection from an early call. Many Preferred issues grant call protection by providing that the issuer cannot buy them back for a period of years, often five years. Before you buy a Preferred, you should examine closely when the Preferred is callable and what specific protection you might have against an early call.

Generally, calls occur when interest rates have dropped, and there is an advantage to the issuer in calling in the Preferred. Of course, if interest rates are falling, you don't want to have a call. If the issue has no call provision, then the Preferred will generally provide for a sinking fund. If the Preferred has a sinking fund, then the issuer will be required to redeem a certain number of Preferred shares annually until all shares are retired.

Three nationally recognized rating organizations rate Preferreds: Moody's Investors Service, Inc.; Standard & Poor's Rating Group; and Fitch Ratings. These ratings are useful in comparing one Preferred to another, but not in comparing Preferreds to bonds.

>>ADVANTAGES

Many Preferreds offer a high rate of current return. In many cases the current return from the Preferreds is higher than the return from highly rated corporate bonds and considerably higher than dividends from common stocks. This income is generally predictable and stable. In addition, there is a low minimum investment since many Preferreds are issued in face amounts of $25 per share or lower. Most bonds are issued in minimum amounts of $1,000 per bond. Many Preferred stocks are listed on the New York or American Stock Exchanges, making them easier to trade and track than most bonds.

>>RISKS

With the higher return on the Preferred comes a greater risk. If there is a default in the payment of interest or if the issuer becomes insolvent, there may be little or nothing left for Preferred shareholders after all of the issuer's other debt is paid. There is a similar but smaller risk if the issuer is downgraded by one of the rating services. In this case the value of the Preferred may decline in the stock market. Keep in mind that there is generally no due date for the Preferred, so that the decline in the value of the shares may be permanent.

Since the Preferred generally never comes due, there is a significant amount of market risk if interest rates are rising. The fixed yield becomes less attractive in such an environment, and, thus, the Preferred's trading price drops.

Since almost all Preferreds are subject to call provisions, these instruments are vulnerable to reinvestment risk, which is serious when interest rates are falling and you must reinvest at a significantly lower rate. Remember it is because of the higher current return that you made the decision to invest in the Preferred in the first place.

>>TAX IMPLICATIONS

If you are an individual, dividends from Preferred stock are reported as ordinary income on your federal income tax return. The sale of Preferred stock results in short-term or long-term capital gains treatment. If a corporation holds the Preferred, it may exclude 70 percent of qualified preferred stock dividends from its federal income tax return.

>>PRICING INFORMATION

Preferreds trade flat, which means that their price incorporates the accrued dividend and goes down after the quarterly ex-dividend date, just as it does with any stock. (The ex-dividend date is the date on which the buyer of a stock is no longer able to receive a specific dividend payment.) In comparison, bonds trade on an accrual basis; i.e., the quoted trading price does not reflect accrued interest.

Some Preferred shares are listed on the New York or the American Stock Exchanges. The rest trade in the over-the-counter market in a way similar to that of many corporate bonds. The price for Preferreds can be as low as $10 per share.

>>SPECIFIC INFORMATION SOURCES

The best information source on Preferreds is the prospectus published at the time of issue. You might phone the issuing company to get a prospectus by mail or get the prospectus from the SEC's site at www.sec.gov/edgar/quickedgar.htm.

Four other useful websites are www.quantumonline.com, a financial-services site that provides comprehensive lists of available preferred shares; www.yahoo.com, which provides information on Preferred dividends, current yields, and payment dates; and www.Moodys.com and www.fitchratings.com, which provide information on Preferred credit ratings.

>>SPECIAL FEATURES AND TIPS

Be careful of the kind of Preferred that you buy. Some Preferred shares automatically convert to common stock of the issuer after a number of years. Such Preferred stock is to be avoided because there may be an automatic conversion at a time when the price is unfavorable to you.

Under certain conditions, such as tax law changes or securities law changes, the issuer may redeem the Preferred. You must check the prospectus to find out about special redemptions, calls, or sinking funds.

Some Preferred issues are traded on an exchange and may be very liquid. However, other issues are not listed and may be very thinly traded, creating a liquidity risk if you wish to sell.

When analysts review Preferred issues, one of their main tests is to determine the company's ability to meet fixed-dividend payments, the so-called *coverage ratio.* The coverage ratio measures the degree to which a company's cash flow covers its interest and dividend payments. A ratio of two to one or better is considered comfortable.

Be especially careful of the possibility of an early call if you purchase the Preferred at an amount in excess of its par or call price. For example, assume that the par value of the Preferred is $25 per share, and you buy the Preferred for $30 per share. If the Preferred is called after one year for its par value of $25 per share, you will have lost $5 per share, a significant reduction of your principal. You would be subject to a similar risk if the Preferred has a sinking fund and as a result the Preferred is redeemed.

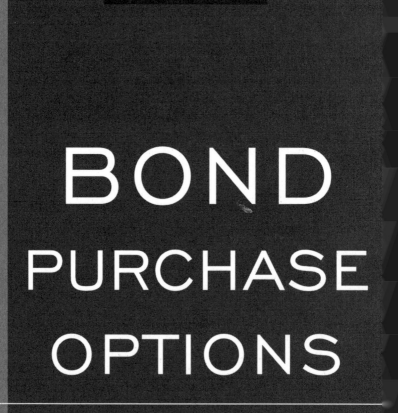

PART
THREE

BOND
PURCHASE
OPTIONS

HAVING LEARNED ABOUT bond basics and reviewed the vast number of bond choices, you now need to make decisions on how to invest your funds in bonds. Basically, you have two choices: You can purchase individual bonds or buy them packaged together as funds.

When you purchase individual bonds, you get to select the specific characteristics of the bonds that you wish to own. "How to buy them?" you ask. You can purchase Treasury debt and savings bonds directly on the Web or from Federal Reserve branch banks. Or you can check out sources of information on the Internet for municipal and corporate bonds before talking to brokers. We describe the ins and outs of buying bonds through the Internet, purchasing them newly issued or previously owned, and tucking them away in your bank vault or leaving them in a brokerage account. The choice is yours. When they come due, redeem them for their face value. Pay once to buy them and enjoy them until they reach maturity. We suggest websites to look at and ways to deal with brokers so you can get the best bang for the buck.

Alternatively, you can purchase bonds that are packaged together in a variety of forms. Funds provide safety through diversity in riskier market segments, but never come due. Open-ended mutual funds are the most generic type, with a variety of closed-end funds carving out market niches. There are a lot of bond funds out there, and their price quotations fill columns of small type in newspapers across the country. Many are hard to find because they are listed among fund families that include stock funds as well. And once you find a bond fund, it is often difficult to understand exactly what it consists of. Our book clears up the information fog surrounding these financial instruments and describes the composition of more than twenty different types of funds.

We explain the advantages of funds, when to use them, how to evaluate them, and how to size up their fees. Find out how the concept of yield for funds differs from yield-to-maturity used for individual bonds. Learn about duration, total return, and other measures of the payout from funds. We explain all this and more in the funds chapter.

Learn how to find great bond funds by using mutual fund selectors, and use calculators provided by websites to compare returns on different funds. Read about all the different choices in bond funds, and discover their advantages and disadvantages. Find out where to locate offering statements and more. You can profit in the bond markets, and we provide you with the tools and information you need to do so.

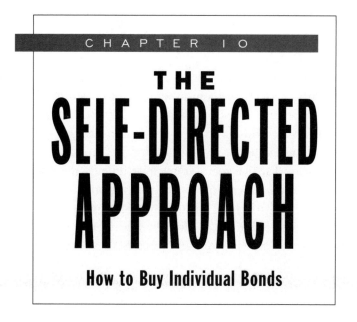

CHAPTER 10

THE
SELF-DIRECTED
APPROACH

How to Buy Individual Bonds

THE MOST COMPELLING REASON to buy individual bonds

is that bonds come due at a defined time. Unlike bond

mutual funds of any kind and stocks in particular, indi-

vidual bonds pay their face value in cash at maturity. This

distinguishing characteristic is a key ingredient in many

aspects of financial planning. Need a large chunk of cash

for a tuition payment on December 15? Buy a bond that

matures on December 1. Planning to retire? Buy a continuing series of bonds that come due when needed. The list is almost endless.

A frequent question is how do you decide between buying bonds and bond funds. There are a number of issues to consider. Diversification is a key one. Advisers suggest that if you have $50,000 to invest, you can purchase a sufficient range of high-quality securities to adequately diversify credit quality. We feel that if you can hold your bonds for five years, you are better off purchasing individual bonds. If you need liquidity or really want a lot of diversity, then it is better to purchase a fund. Also, some types of securities are simply better held through funds, including Ginnie Maes, junk bonds, and certain types of foreign bonds. Keep in mind that funds usually hold either stocks or bonds, and virtues attributed to funds are actually the result of the nature of the securities that are in the portfolio, as we show in Chapter 11.

Although the case for buying individual bonds is a simple one to make, trying to do so is a bit more complicated. This chapter gives you guidelines for evaluating online websites and for locating a bond broker.

Buying Online

THE FEDERAL GOVERNMENT offers the only unfettered bond purchasing avenue open to you as an individual investor. Begun in August 1986 by the U.S. Bureau of the Public Debt, TreasuryDirect is a book-entry securities system that allows you to maintain accounts directly with the U.S. Treasury. You can purchase all newly issued Treasury bills, notes, and bonds at auction by using this system without paying a commission. Complete the forms and arrange for a source of payment. If you use snail mail, you send in the face amount of the bonds you wish to purchase. If the bonds come at a discount, the difference is returned to you. The bonds are held in your TreasuryDirect account unless you direct them to be delivered to your broker by—you guessed it—filling out a transfer form.

With the advent of the Internet, TreasuryDirect at www.treasury direct.gov has become even more accessible and friendly. You can open your TreasuryDirect account online by filling in an account form on the spot. When your bonds come due, you can automatically reinvest your principal if you have given written instructions to do so. Interest flows to the account you designate. When you order bonds online, cash will be withdrawn from your bank or brokerage account to pay for them.

With the successful implementation of TreasuryDirect and the advent of day-trading stock buyers, it was widely assumed that buying bonds online would also evolve into a simple matter of a single click. As it turns out, that assumption was wrong. Individual retail clients don't have free access to purchase bonds online. Individuals can still only purchase certain Treasuries without a broker. Thus, while the Web allows you to check sites and view bond prices and offerings, in most cases you still have to use a broker to finalize your trade.

PRICING INFORMATION

PRICE TRANSPARENCY in the bond markets gained momentum from the House of Representatives Bond Price Competition Improvement Act of 1999 (H.R.1400). Responding to this new law, the Bond Market Association (BMA) established the site www.investinginbonds.com, which we have mentioned many times before. This site provides prices on bonds that have traded more than four times the previous day. Keep in mind that for bonds to do this, there must be quite a large supply of them available. This limits the number of postings since most bonds do not trade that frequently. The BMA site also allows you to track the history of specific bond issues to see how they performed and how their prices compare to similar securities. The database will not allow you to check for daily price swings in the broad marketplace.

The Municipal Securities Rulemaking Board (MSRB), itself established by Congress in 1976, has stipulated that bond purchasers have the right to receive "all material" information about a security available to brokerage firms before making the purchase. A material event might be notice of a pending downgrade resulting from economic weakness in a source of revenue that might materially affect the return. This kind of information does not fit into the formats currently used on websites dedicated to bond offerings. For example, only a few sites give access to an offering statement.

Even should websites become more sophisticated, the problem still remains that the obligatory material to be posted on them is not easily understood. Bonds, as must be evident by this point in our book, are complicated. In a hypothetical example, let's say that you purchased Smallville USA G/O muni bonds, of which 80 percent are escrowed to their April 1, 2013, maturity, and the remainder are not. Furthermore, the bonds have a 30-day call with a sinking fund beginning in 2006. Would you know how to interpret this information? Since you are reading our book, we hope the answer is yes. For most people, however, the answer is a resounding no. And what is really distressing is that many financial advisers cannot correctly interpret this information because they don't know much about bonds, either.

The MSRB further stipulates that brokers must recommend bonds to you that are "suitable" to your needs. There is some question as to whether or not posting bonds on the Internet is, for all intents and purposes, an offering to sell, thus sidestepping the suitability issue. Though it is argued by some that stock buyers have successfully mastered buying stock online from financial professionals, it is still the MSRB's position that trading in the electronic marketplace be limited to those who can make informed investment decisions without the services of a broker. You cannot declare yourself "informed" and say that you are willing to take on the risks. The website needs to verify that you will meet your obligations as its host company defines them: that you understand what you buy and are able to pay for the bonds. With each transaction, they must also verify that you chose "suitable" bonds.

"Wait a minute!" some of you might interrupt. "It is possible to buy bonds online. I just bought some last week." Well, yes, you may think you have, but what you actually did was to tell a clearing broker to buy your chosen bonds for you. This is an expensive process, because you now have two middlemen instead of one—the broker and the website managers. The websites charge fees similar to those of discount brokers. More traditional bond brokers charge only a spread. In addition, the websites must verify that you chose "suitable" bonds; if they are deemed unsuitable, the trade has to be unwound—somehow.

In the event that the MSRB reverses its position and allows you to trade online without dealing with a middleman, you should know that most of the trading sites do not own the bonds that they trade, and if you have access, that the bonds are screened and priced for retail. There are a number of online trading platforms— www.ebondtrade.com and www.TheMuniCenter.com allow individuals to look at their inventory and sign up to buy. Three other trading platforms currently cater to participating brokers but may have direct access to individuals in the future, so check out www. Valubond.com, www.bonddeskgroup.com, and www.Tradeweb.com to see if they are available to you. All of these sites post data from research firms and offerings from multiple dealers.

In addition to these sites with trading platforms, individual brokers are beginning to show their inventory online as well. The only way you will know if you are getting a good deal is to shop around.

Visiting a website offering bonds, however, can help you clarify your thinking. Alas, some of these sites tend to have fleeting lives due to lack of financial backing. As this book was being written, for example, www.munidirect.com announced it was no longer in business.

Here are some resources that we expect might be around for a while because they are rooted in existing brokerage businesses. Try www.buybonds.com, which is the site of Stone and Youngberg in San Francisco, California, a regional underwriter and dealer that was established in 1931. They list California offerings and give market commentary. Prospectuses are available for new offerings. Also look at www.stoeverglass.com, a national municipal bond dealer founded in 1964. For more broker listings look in the Appendix.

CAVEATS

WHILE SITES THAT POST offerings for sale may be helpful with regard to pricing, they may also be quite misleading at any given moment. The offering levels will not automatically change with the fluctuation of interest rates. Just like the offering sheets that were mailed out weekly, the posted prices of the bonds might be out of date. When you click to purchase the bond, the bond might not be there anymore, or the price might have changed. In fact, the broker might be just testing the water to see what kinds of offers are made for the bonds. Only when a trading desk is "live and executable" will the click result in a direct purchase.

Even dealers have problems with bond purchases on the Internet. If there is an offering of 100 bonds, and someone sells 50 bonds on the telephone in the office, there are now only 50 bonds left. Before the broker can update the screen, someone else is clicking on the 100-bond offering online. The selling broker is now "short 50 bonds." They can either cancel the trade in the office, try to find the bonds somewhere else, or tell the wire service: "I am such an idiot! I have only 50 bonds to sell." Customers and the wire service are not happy when the broker tells them that they have to break the trade. They can do that only so often.

Here are some questions you might want to ask before you become involved in online trading. What happens if there is a fail (the term used when a broker on the other side of the trade doesn't deliver)? What happens if the bonds that are delivered are not what you thought were described, or include an undisclosed call? If there is a material event you were not aware of because you lack access to the information sources that brokers have, do you have any recourse to return the bonds? In other words, to whom do you turn if you have a problem?

Choosing a Broker

EVEN THOUGH being unable to trade online is a disappointment for the active trader, there are certain comforts in talking to a person about your investments. Not so surprisingly, professional traders often find value in talking to one another as well. If they put in a trade electronically, they may follow that up with a phone call to discuss specific issues presented by the purchase. Relationships between brokers are especially important when they need to work out problems with a trade.

Given that the opportunities for unlicensed investors to trade bonds on an Internet exchange are quite limited, it then behooves bond buyers to select a broker to do so. "It vexes me to choose another guide," Emily Brontë once wrote. While it might vex you, it could translate into extra money and profits if you do it right.

How do you find a good bond brokerage firm? You can check with friends and family to find out if they have a firm they like. You can check the Yellow Pages of your local phone book or a website that has yellow pages like www.metacrawler.com under Investments and Mutual Funds or Stock & Bond Brokers. Firms advertise on The Bond Market Association website at www.bondmarkets.com; click on "Members," so you can get a flavor for what they do. Ask if the brokerage firm is a member of the Securities Investor Protection Corporation (SIPC). This member-supported insurance company provides limited customer protection in case of bankruptcy—though it does not protect against trading losses. The brokerage firm may also have additional insurance adding protection above the levels provided by SIPC.

It is probably not a surprise to hear that all brokerage firms are not alike. As in every other field, there are specialists, in this case, those who deal in certain kinds of bonds. While any broker can purchase bonds on your behalf, not all can execute the purchase or sale at the same price. Remember, most bonds trade in an over-the-counter market.

CRITERIA TO CONSIDER

SEEK A BROKERAGE FIRM that trades the kinds of bonds you want to buy and is willing to accommodate your investing style. You need to shop around in order to determine which firm has the kind of inventory you require. Some brokerage firms make the retail municipal market their specialty, though they may also offer other kinds of securities. They may have a specific regional orientation, specialize in national market bonds, or specialize in lower-quality bonds. Retail firms deal in smaller lots of bonds, and their salespeople are usually quite knowledgeable. The broker may tell you that they handle all kinds of securities, but once you see the firm's offerings you will know whether they provide the kinds of bonds you want along with good service and prices. They may not be able to offer you new issues if they do not participate in the selling syndicate.

Once you've gathered together a list of potential candidates, set your thinking into relationship mode. A brokerage firm may be outstanding, but it is a flesh and blood person with whom you will be dealing. To find a good individual broker, speak to the sales manager and ask for a recommendation. Then ask about the broker's experience with and amount of time allocated to bond trades. This is important, because when choosing a broker, you are seeking to establish a mutually profitable, long-term relationship. And because this relationship is founded on money—your principal and their income—it's worth taking some effort to make sure it is a solid one.

The first step in establishing such a relationship is gathering information. This will let you know if you can develop a rapport with the broker or whether there is a complete absence of chemistry between the two of you. Tell the broker what your goals are and ask how he or she thinks you might best achieve them. Do this well before you are prepared to make an investment so you can consider the recommendations. Ask what kinds of investments other clients have been purchasing. How does the broker evaluate those investments? Does the broker see a place for those investments for you? You do not wish to be hurried into taking actions that do not support your goals.

Find a broker whose basic philosophy aligns with yours or one who at least respects your perspective. The broker should inform you when bonds come due, or when there are substantial amounts of cash in your account. The broker should keep you up-to-date on marketplace swings and have patience to answer your questions. Remember, there is no such thing as a dumb question. You should not feel that your questions are out of place. The suggested securities should support your investment objectives.

It is a mistake to assume that just because you purchase stocks from a particular broker it is also wise to purchase your bonds from the same person. Many stockbrokers do not know about or have little interest in bonds. Stock buyers who use discount stockbrokers believe that they can also purchase bonds at a discount from the same source as well. Unfortunately, there are no discount bond brokers. Bond brokers generally act as principal in a sale, which means that they buy the bonds for their own account and then sell them for a profit. Contrast this with the purchase of stock, in which the broker acts as an agent, bringing together the buyer and seller for a disclosed fee, called a commission.

If you are convinced that you want to purchase individual bonds, be wary of any broker who tries to shift you into stocks or who strongly suggests packaged investments like mutual funds, unit investment trusts, and exchange-traded funds. This kind of recommendation indicates that the broker is not really interested in bonds, either from a lack of expertise or a belief that bonds don't generate enough money to warrant attention. However, as we have said elsewhere in this book, mutual funds do make sense if you are buying certain securities such as junk bonds or Ginnie Mae mortgage securities.

Final steps in a thorough due diligence might be to ask for a description of the broker's typical client and then ask to talk to some of the broker's longer-term clients. The SEC provides a toll-free hot line operated by the National Association of Securities Dealers (NASD) for a background check of the broker or sales representative (800-289-9999).

The broker can screen bonds to meet your specifications. If you are in a high tax state, for example, you may want to see bonds only from that state. You might have a particular maturity or rating in mind. Similarly, you would customize your search on the Web by selecting the criteria that matches the kind of bond that you seek. The broker will help you think through your options and then will show you the offerings that might match.

BROKERAGE INDUSTRY PRACTICES TO CONSIDER

THE DETERIORATION IN PROFITS among major brokerage firms in the early 2000s has led to a change in the way brokerage firms sell bonds to individuals. Some firms now penalize brokers for trading individual bonds by either charging them a fee or not compensating them for certain types of trades. Instead, brokers are encouraged to have their customers move their assets into fee-based accounts. One such account is called a *wrap account*. It is managed by your broker for an annual fee that is equal to a fixed percentage of assets and is unaffected by the number of trading transactions. Alternatively, your broker might suggest what is commonly called a *managed account* if you have at least $500,000 in assets. This is an account managed by an outside adviser. If you are a buy-and-hold investor doing limited transactions, these accounts are not a plus for you. The incentive for the broker is that he or she personally earns more. The reality is that the firm management has substantially reduced a broker's incentive to sell you bonds on a per transaction basis. Despite all the yachts the brokers are supposed to have, many of them still need income to pay off their mortgages.

Ask for a copy of the firm's commission and compensation schedule if you are curious about how your broker is affected by firm policy. As one broker said of fee-based accounts, "One of my clients said to me that they have been dealing with me for years on a transaction basis, and they see no reason why they should increase their expenses and pay me a fee. I can't even talk to them about it."

This emphasis on fee-only accounts is in part the result of the success of the National Association of Personal Financial Advisors (NAPFA). That organization's advertising pointed out the conflict of interest that commission-based advisers have. The ads ask: Do the advisers do what is in the best interest of the client or do they give advice that generates the most personal revenue? The media gave great press coverage to NAPFA, and the public responded by seeking those advisers.

The big investment houses were caught on the wrong side of the issue and so moved to co-opt the fee-only position by creating the wrap account. However, fee-only service means providing for the client what is in the client's best interest by charging a fee for advice, and letting the client decide what is best.

The brokerage firms prefer that new clients pay a fixed annual fee instead of paying per transaction for bond purchases. The minimum account size is usually $100,000. The annual payment may be collected at the beginning of the year or quarterly. There are two types of accounts: one in which the in-house broker makes the investment decisions independently or in conjunction with the investor, and so-called *discretionary managed accounts* run with out-side money managers making all the decisions. While a fee account might make sense for the active trader, as noted previously, it extracts a heavy price for the person who is going to purchase a few medium-term bonds and let their funds accumulate.

If you think a managed account would be a good idea because you do not have the time to do the work, you might ask what happens if it doesn't work out. For example, some brokerage houses impose exit fees on their in-house accounts, and these often include a closing fee that will not be more than the annual fee *plus* 1 percent of various eligible assets. In addition, certain fees on mutual funds or closed-end funds will not be waived.

Evaluating Bond Prices

IT IS IMPORTANT to keep in mind that trading bonds is not like trading stocks. Stocks can be bought at uniform prices and are traded through exchanges. Most bonds trade over the counter and are priced by individual brokers. For example, since the vast number of municipal bonds trade infrequently, you will probably never find three or more dealers offering the same bonds. This can make it difficult to compare prices, not only for municipals, but also for other market sectors as well.

NATURE OF THE MARKETPLACE

THE BOND MARKET is a dealer-to-dealer market, one in which firms hire traders to deal in specific types of bonds. The brokerage firm might have Treasury, corporate, and municipal bond desks. The desk is a euphemism for a group of traders, sitting in a room in front of computer monitors, who specialize and trade in a particular portfolio sector of bonds. The broker, often referred to as the account manager, discusses the bonds with you and is backed by the trader, who does the actual buying and selling of the bonds. The trader is always consulted, and must agree, when the account manager wants to give you a price break.

When the broker owns the bonds being sold to you, there can be some flexibility in the price, depending on the price the trader paid and the current market direction. For example, if a broker owns thirty-five bonds, and you only want twenty-five ($25,000), he might give you a price break if you bought all thirty-five instead of leaving him with an odd lot of ten. If he owned twenty-five bonds, they might be sold AON (all or nothing). If you were shown equally interesting bonds from different dealers, one might be willing to give you a break on the price. Remember that brokers want to sell you bonds, but they need to make a living, too. They won't work for nothing—even if you are a nice person.

If a trade is *done away,* meaning that the broker has to purchase the bonds from another brokerage firm, then you will pay two spreads in the transaction instead of one. Discount brokerage firms tack on a fee in addition to the spread because they purchase all their bonds from other firms.

The bond marketplace is divided into wholesale or institutional markets and retail markets. In the wholesale market, corporate, agency, and Treasury bonds trade in million-dollar blocks, with $100 million blocks not infrequent. Municipal bonds trade in $100,000 blocks by comparison. The prices you see in the newspaper are based on these large trades.

In an odd twist, bigger is not necessarily better when it comes to buying bonds. In buying small odd lots of an issue, individual buyers often get a better price than institutional traders buying large blocks. This is true in the municipal bond markets and is often the case with corporate bonds. You can do better purchasing off-the-run Treasuries, the older issues that trade less frequently.

Bonds of similar quality and maturity will trade in the same range as each other. If you don't like the yield on the triple-A insured bonds, then maybe you'll prefer lower-quality bonds with higher yields. Ask yourself if the added risk is worth the return. For a simple example, assume two bonds are selling at par, one rated triple-A and the other triple-B. While one has a higher yield, its interest payments are only $25 more per year or $250 for the ten-year holding period. Is that worth the risk and any subsequent loss of sleep?

NEW ISSUE ORDER AND CONFIRMATION DETAILS

YOU CAN TELL how any market is doing by watching the spreads. Are they widening or shrinking? While there is much greater yield in junk than in higher-rated bonds, the downside risk of losing your principal is also much greater.

When you put in an order to buy bonds of a new issue, called *an expression of interest,* you legally commit to buy the bonds if they are issued as described. Should interest rates rise between your order date and the bond's issue date, you are still expected to accept them. If the bond offering is changed in any way, then the broker will come back to you to describe the terms of the deal. If you like the new terms, then you buy the bonds. If not, you are no longer obligated to purchase them.

Once you have made your bond selection, you will receive a confirmation in the mail. Although each broker confirmation is slightly different, they all contain the same information. The bond description includes the amount purchased, trade and settlement dates, the unit price, accrued interest, total cost, and whether it is callable or not. Treasury bonds settle the next day, whereas corporate and municipal bonds currently settle three days after the trade, though the broker may be able to arrange for extra days to settlement if you ask. All bonds are assigned a CUSIP number, the equivalent of a Social Security number for bonds. Your account number printed at the top of the slip should be put on your check if the cash is not already in your account.

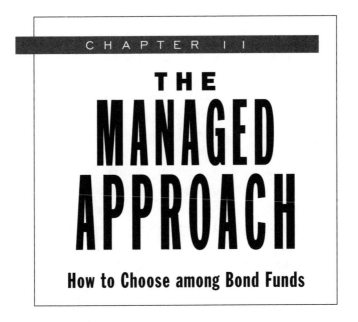

CHAPTER 11

THE MANAGED APPROACH

How to Choose among Bond Funds

LET'S FACE IT, the easiest—and in some cases the most profitable—way to invest in bonds is to buy a bond mutual fund. Financial firms have catered to this strategy by creating almost 3,000 such funds and packaging them with a variety of shapes, structures, and content.

While many view competition as a good thing (actually, we do, too), it is not in this case. The tremendous number of funds competing for your attention and dollars has created a severe case of obfuscation. Until recently, this situation was further compounded by the fact that only 65 percent of a bond fund had to consist of bonds described in the title of the fund. That changed when the SEC mandated that 80 percent of the securities in a fund must be within the parameters set by the fund name as of July 31, 2002. That still leaves 20 percent of fund assets to be invested either in cash for redemptions or in more lucrative and risky securities in an attempt to goose up yields. In other words, if it says it's a Treasury bond fund it must be a Treasury bond fund—mostly.

What remains unchanged is that trying to classify and categorize bond funds is a daunting task. We have chosen to review first the characteristics that all funds have in common.

No matter what the size or purpose, every bond fund has a per share Net Asset Value (NAV). This is the measure by which funds are valued on a daily basis. It is derived by dividing the sum of the values, including any liabilities, of all the bonds in a portfolio by the number of shares outstanding. All funds also provide a figure known as *total return*. This consists of a fund's cash distributions and change in share price during a specified period.

Unlike bonds, which have specific due dates, bond funds are described, as required by the SEC, in terms of their approximate maturity. Thus, all funds have dollar-weighted averages that reflect their stated maturities. Money market funds that are almost cash equivalents have maturities of one year or less. Funds with maturities of less than three years are defined as short term. While there is no SEC definition of the term *limited,* the word is usually applied to funds with maturities that fall between short and intermediate, generally less than five years. Intermediate funds are those with average maturities of three to ten years, and long-term funds are all those with maturities of ten or more years. The majority of bond funds are long term.

A general rule is that the longer the maturity, the higher the yield and the greater the fund's price fluctuation. This is not to say that short-term rates don't fluctuate. We saw the Federal Reserve Board cut short-term rates eleven times between 1999 and 2002, and the Fed can raise them again just as easily. The difference is that the bonds in short-term funds come due quickly, and new ones are bought at the prevailing rates. If new money is flooding into a fund it helps a fund mirror the going rate for bonds, so the yield adjusts rather quickly on the upside or downside.

Because bonds in a fund do not all mature at the same time, and bonds in many funds are replaced when they no longer are within the fund's investment parameters, the concept of yield-to-maturity is not applicable. Instead the SEC has mandated a 7-day yield calculation specifically for money funds in addition to a 30-day yield calculation required for all funds, including money market funds. The SEC-mandated yields are standardized calculations that are the same for all funds. They allow you to compare return after fees and expenses. These yields are not comparable to the yields on individual bonds.

In addition, an SEC rule that took effect in February 2002 requires all mutual funds, bonds and stock alike, to calculate their returns on an after-tax basis. Since there are so many factors that go into an after-tax calculation, the SEC has mandated a uniform approach that uses the highest tax bracket (38.6 percent in 2002). The SEC rule also requires that any loads be subtracted from the after-tax return. This calculation is a useful tool for comparing one fund with another. It appears in each fund's prospectus and advertising material that touts tax efficiency.

The advertised yield on a bond fund can and will change over time. The yield you expect to get will not necessarily be sustained. You can get some indication of how much money your fund will earn over the course of a year by looking at the 12-month distribution yield. It shows how much in dividends were actually paid out. This return is comparable to a current yield on bonds and includes a payout of both principal and interest. There are likely to be disparities between the 30-day and 12-month yield calculation because of the time difference and the nature of the calculation.

Bond funds tend to offer the following advantages:

◆ **Regular monthly income** with interest and principal payments made as dividend distributions. Individual bonds usually offer semiannual payments, though some pay monthly.

◆ **Reinvestment opportunities** with that income. Be aware, however, that this advantage is minimized if the fund charges for the reinvestment.

◆ **Diversification,** which is a key aspect in any kind of investing. Should one bond in a fund sink, the others will supposedly smooth out any disaster ripples. As was mentioned in the previous chapter, it is recommended that you invest a minimum of $50,000 for a five-year holding period in order to obtain adequate diversification through buying individual bonds; you can invest much smaller amounts and need not have such a long holding period to obtain adequate diversification through a fund.

◆ **Daily liquidity.** A simple phone call translates into an instant sale; indeed, some funds offer free check writing on the accounts.

◆ **Bookkeeping services.** Funds keep track of all your purchases and redemptions for reporting to the Internal Revenue Service.

◆ **Professional management.** Many, it should be noted, do not view this last feature as an advantage but rather as an unnecessary expense.

ON THE OTHER SIDE of the proverbial coin, bond funds generally feature the following disadvantages:

◆ **Lack of fixed maturity date.** An individual bond always provides a redemption date when you will receive all your money back, but a bond fund never does; in other words, bonds come due, bond funds don't.

◆ **Lack of income guarantee.** With an individual bond, the payment schedule is fixed, whereas payments from the various bonds in a fund can vary.

◆ **Susceptibility to capital gains tax.** You have to pay capital gains tax even when you have not sold or if you bought the fund just before it paid dividends. Funds generate capital gains when they sell bonds to raise cash for redemptions or trade securities. Funds that have a high turnover rate, a measure of annual portfolio change, are said to be tax inefficient when they generate capital gains. Funds do not pass through tax losses.

◆ **Susceptibility to market risk.** Even conservative Treasury bond funds are subject to market risk. For example, *Business Week* warns:

"If the yield on a 10-year Treasury jumps by a half a percentage point from 5 percent now, it will lose about 10 percent of its market value."[1] That means that even the bond fund holding the safest securities could still experience a market decline.

Checking the Costs, Hidden and Unhidden

MANAGEMENT AND OTHER FEES are another constant among all bond funds. After all, these funds are created for management's benefit and not necessarily for yours. Therefore, we feel it important for investors to review this feature of bond funds thoroughly.

The largest and most blatant cost is what is referred to as the *load*. In effect, this is the sales commission earned by the person who sells you the fund. You lose money right from the start because the load is deducted from the amount of money you initially invest. Write-ups about *front-end loads,* as they are called, have led fund companies sometimes to allocate the loads over a number of years or to tack them on at the end.

Fierce competition between funds has reduced load amounts over the years. Whereas once they were frequently as high as 8 percent, 4–5 percent figures are more typical now. Funds that have such sales commissions are known as *load funds.*

Other funds, while hoping to reap commission riches and still be competitive, have introduced smaller loads, with assessments ranging from 1.5 percent to 3.5 percent of the initial investment. These funds are known as *low-load funds.*

And then there are the funds that are without commission charges known as *no-load funds.* Because there are no commissions involved with their sale, these funds must be bought. That is, you must seek them out rather than expecting a salesperson to find you. Fortunately, they are easy to find because they advertise extensively.

Other costs, decidedly camouflaged, include back-end loads (yup—some funds sock you a charge for getting rid of them); annual management fees to cover administrative expenses; advertising fees on the no-load and load funds (these are officially designated as 12b-1 fees); plus all the transaction fees that the fund's firm pays when it buys and sells the bonds in the portfolio. And there's more: Funds may have loads on reinvested dividends, exchange fees if you want to transfer from one fund to another, frequent transaction charges, and shareholder accounting costs.

These fees add up. Vanguard, the giant mutual funds organization and pioneer in no-load funds, capitalized on this in one of its ads. The headline stated: "This is the story of the investor who lost $31,701 and didn't even know it." The copy went on to show how management fees ate up that much in the potential income from an initial $25,000 investment over a twenty-year period.

Although Vanguard proclaims that all its fees are low by industry standards, this is not true of all no-load funds. When brokers sell funds and they do not have either front- or back-end loads, they may have a type of very high annual fee called a 12b-1 fee. On the other hand, a fund sold by a broker from a no-load fund family might have a small load attached to it to compensate the broker for making the sale.

Both load and no-load funds are beginning to group buyers by the amount of their purchases. They do this by creating classes of shares for the same offering, generally labeling them by letters of the alphabet. As you might expect, larger depositors pay lower fees. This information is all spelled out in a fund's prospectus. The *Wall Street Journal*'s website at www.wallstreetjournal.com contains prospectuses of many fund companies, as do some of the other sites mentioned below. This offering statement details the charges levied by your fund.

Some funds have instituted retirement shares for 401(k)s and IRAs that over the long term have the highest fees of all, which are designated by a different letter. Other fund families skip the alphabet soup and have specially designated funds for high-net-worth individuals that have the lowest cost. For example, Vanguard has its Admiral Funds, T. Rowe Price has Summit Funds, and Fidelity has Spartan Funds for substantial depositors.

High fees associated with the purchase of funds are there to compensate the broker for the time spent with you. Since bonds of the same quality and options trade in a narrow range, high fees hobble the fund manager in the race to produce good performance results. To compensate, these funds are more likely to swell the yield by purchasing non-rated, longer-term, and lower-rated bonds.

When you reach for the highest-yielding, best-performing mutual fund, stop for a moment and consider this: A manager took risks to achieve it. Next year the fund could tank even if the strategy remains the same, because of changing economic conditions. Strategies that reach for yield are a necessity for funds with substantial fees.

Obviously, we are biased in favor of funds with the lowest costs. We were therefore quite pleased to read about work undertaken by Morningstar, the fund tracking and rating company. As reported in November 2001, funds with the lowest fees performed the best overall:

> In areas ranging from ultrashort bond funds to the multisector and intermediate-term bond categories, we found that the lowest-cost quartile of funds posted total returns over the year through October 31 that were better than those of the high-expense offerings.[2]

Furthermore, Morningstar found that the higher-cost funds took on added risk in order to boost the yield and compensate for the added fund costs. The article concludes with the following: "If you pay less, you're likely to get better returns and lower risk. That's not a bad combination."[3]

In order to aid investors, the SEC introduced a free online service in 1999 to help investors calculate mutual fund fees described in the fund prospectus. Find it at www.sec.gov/investor/tools /mfcc/mfcc-int.htm. Using this calculator helps you to focus on and understand the fee structures of the funds. For a fun alternative, try *SmartMoney*'s "Fund Fee Analyzer" at www.smart money.com.

Another great tool is available at Andrew Tobias's site at www.personalfund.com. This site asks you to choose a fund family and then the particular fund that interests you. All you have to input is your own tax information, your ordinary income and capital gains tax rate, how long you plan to hold the fund, and your expected return. The site provides you with some information about the investment, its tax consequences, and some less-expensive alternatives. It's really neat!

Classifying the Funds

WE HAVE DECIDED to first classify bond funds by their exit strategy or how you cash them in. Viewed this way, there are two broad categories, and they are known as *closed-end* and *open-end funds*. A closed-end bond fund consists of a fixed number of shares in an asset pool of fixed-income securities. Once the pool is created, ownership shares in the pool are either redeemed by the issuer or traded as stock. When you wish to redeem or sell a share, you are subject to the vagaries of the marketplace and how much it deems your shares are worth. This figure could be higher or lower than the stock's underlying net asset value.

An open-end bond fund also consists of an asset pool of fixed-income securities. In this case, the number of ownership shares is not finite. Rather, the fund is inaugurated with an initial number of shares, and this number is divided by the total value of the asset pool to come up with the net asset value figure. Because the pool is open, anyone can buy additional shares. They are charged the existing net asset value, plus any loads, and then the fund manager uses that money to go out and buy more assets. In this type of bond fund, you buy a pro rata share of the fund's value. When you wish to exit, or cash out, you are given the net asset value of your shares, minus any fees, at the end of the trading day that you exit.

We have next grouped bond funds along a continuum using the fund industry's terminology. In so doing, we've designated four types, with the order going from the most closed to the most open. These are: Unit Investment Trusts (UITs), Closed-End Funds, Exchange Traded Funds, and Open-End Mutual Funds.

UNIT INVESTMENT TRUSTS

ALSO KNOWN AS DEFINED PORTFOLIOS, unit investment trusts (UITs) are the purest form of the closed-end fund concept. Once a trust is created and sold, it is considered closed with regard to any management guidance or the creation of further shares. Bond portfolios in UITs consist of ten or more securities that are packaged together and sold as a fixed number of shares. The portfolio usually consists of some high-coupon bonds balanced by long-term zeros. Once these bonds are selected, the portfolio never changes. At a specified date, the originator of the trust redeems the shares. Before that date, the shares can be costly to sell. Check Part B of the prospectus to find out early redemption provisions.

UITs carry high front-end loads or back-end loads—sales charges up to 8.5 percent are permissible, though they are usually between 4 and 5.5 percent. The effect of the load is to reduce the actual amount of funds that you have to invest by the cost of the load. If you consider purchasing them, ask: What kind of return would it take to recover my load expenses as well as to make a good profit?

UITs came into vogue in the 1950s, when muni mutual funds were not permitted to pass through income tax-free, while UITs were. It was not until 1976 that the tax laws changed and allowed open-ended mutual funds to pass on income tax free. Although they no longer serve the alternative, money-saving purpose for which they were conceived, UITs persist as a form because their high loads have made them a very lucrative broker product. They are touted as an easy way to obtain diversification without having to pay any management fees. The load fees are always in very small type and are never touted.

CLOSED-END FUNDS

CLOSED-END BOND FUNDS also have a fixed number of shares, but they differ from UITs in every other aspect. Closed-end funds are managed, and the managers have great latitude in their investment practices. Although 80 percent of the bonds in the portfolio must match the description of the fund, the managers may use derivatives to make interest rate plays, use repurchase agreements, buy zero-coupon bonds, and invest in floating and variable rate debt. The managers can and do leverage the bond portfolios by creating auction-rate preferred stock (ARP). The management uses the proceeds from the stock to buy additional long-term bonds, giving the portfolios extra oomph; in the process, it also gives the share price of the funds greater volatility.

Closed-end bond funds do not have specified redemption dates and are traded on exchanges much as stocks are. There are two values to watch when dealing with closed-end funds: the net asset value (NAV) of each share and the amount of money investors are willing to pay for that net asset value. Often investors are not willing to pay the full net asset value, and thus the shares trade at a discount to that value.

The general rule of thumb is that a closed-end bond fund is an attractive buy when its discount to NAV is significantly greater than its average discount over the previous five years. The thinking is that the share price of the fund will rise as the discount narrows to its normal range. Thumbs come in many sizes, and so do the discounts that may never disappear even when the NAV is much higher.

Closed-end bond funds selling at a discount to their NAV are popular when interest rates are declining. At such times, the yield on the bonds in the portfolio is attractive, because it is higher than the most recent reduction in rates. This yield advantage is further enhanced, according to some people, by the fact that you can buy the bonds at a discount to their NAV. During 2001, when the Federal Reserve reduced interest rates eleven times, investors clamored for the yields on closed-end bond funds, so much so that several of the funds were selling at more than 130 percent of their NAV. Other firms, sizing up the profit potential in the situation, scrambled to introduce new closed-end funds. For example, Nuveen Investments, the most prolific introducer of closed-end muni funds, brought forth twenty new ones in 2001, raising over $4 billion in the process.

With the flattening of or rebound in interest rates, closed-end funds lose some of their luster. Being highly leveraged, funds bought during low interest rate periods will suffer greater losses than unleveraged funds when yields rise.

Management, as well as market condition, counts when it comes to the performance of individual closed-end bond funds, and the result is a tremendous variation in returns. In 2001, for example, the one-year NAV return among high-yield closed-end bond funds varied from +13.2 percent to −33.1 percent. Even among the more conservative closed-end, national muni funds, the returns varied from a high of +8.1 percent to a low of −0.9 percent.

EXCHANGE-TRADED BOND FUNDS

EXCHANGE-TRADED FUNDS (ETFs) with bond portfolios are a new concept and, as this book was being written, an intriguing one. These funds combine attributes of closed-end and open-end funds. They are, for example, traded on stock exchanges like closed-end funds. They are pegged to indexes, such as 10-year Treasuries or the Lehman Bond Index, which means that there is minimal management activity. The funds, however, can issue new shares at net asset value, much as open-end funds do.

There are four advantages commonly assigned to these funds: (1) There are no hidden surprises, as they are pegged to specified indexes; (2) you can sell them any time the exchanges are open, as opposed to mutual funds in which you receive the net asset value at the end of the trading day; (3) because they are passive portfolios following an index, there are minimal management fees; and (4) the funds are supposed to be tax efficient. Through complicated tax regulations, they are able to avoid making yearly capital gains distributions while all other categories of index funds face that obligation.

These funds also have their disadvantages. They can sell at a discount to their net asset value, but the discounts on these funds are much less than those on typical closed-end funds. You have to pay a management fee when you own these funds, as well as a commission to either buy or sell them. These charges add up and could well wipe out any tax advantages in an ETF when compared with a no-load index mutual fund. Finally, these funds are relatively untested. We do not yet know how they will fare in all market conditions.

OPEN-END MUTUAL FUNDS

OPEN-END BOND MUTUAL FUNDS are just that. Their number of outstanding shares changes constantly as investors buy or redeem them. Their contents also fluctuate as managers buy or redeem the bonds to readjust the maturities of the bonds, take advantage of favorable market conditions, meet redemptions, or invest new funds.

Unlike closed-end funds, open-end mutual funds are not traded. They are bought either directly from the fund family or from a broker. Their net asset value at the end of the trading day is always the basis on which they are bought or redeemed.

The greatest variety of funds is offered in this format. Information about them is widely published and easily obtained in the media and on the Internet. Prices are quoted daily. Newsletters track funds, giving buy/sell recommendations. Most funds discourage active trading, though, because it requires a portfolio readjustment if cash needs to be raised to pay for the redeemed shares.

Of all types of funds, open-ended mutual funds have the most variable fee schedule depending upon whether they are sold by a broker who charges a load or bought directly from the fund company.

Understanding the Portfolio Types

CONTINUING ON WITH OUR categorization of bond funds, we now look at them from the point of view of their taxable status and, within that status, the different portfolio types. The latter is particularly important. When comparing the returns on bond funds, it is necessary to examine the portfolios to understand why the returns are different. As you will read, types of bond portfolios may be presented in more than one format, and we have indicated this under the various descriptions. The fund types are presented in alphabetical order.

TAX-EXEMPT FUNDS

THERE ARE FEWER VARIETIES of tax-exempt funds than there are taxable funds. We describe five here. Just as you do for individual munis, compare the after-tax return on a taxable bond fund with a tax-exempt fund to determine which would give you a better return.

It is also essential to check out the yields on the state-specific funds compared with the national funds. Although you may think that you should buy a fund with the name of your state on it, there are times when a national muni fund would be more advantageous. Funds may purchase bonds subject to the alternative minimum tax in order to boost yields. If you are subject to this tax, you might want to check into the fund's policy.

Municipal Bond Funds: Cash Management Accounts

These are money market fund look-alikes. They are also called *cash reserves, ready assets,* and *enhanced cash funds.* They are all ultra-short bond funds that usually maintain a fund share value of $1.[4]

These funds tend to offer higher yields and can routinely use a variety of financial instruments described in the prospectus, including derivatives. They may also have higher fees that can wipe out any yield advantage the funds may have. They are available through brokers or directly from independent mutual funds. Visit www.imoneynet.com for information about these funds and money market mutual funds, or ask your broker.

Municipal Bond Funds: High Yield

As described in Chapter 7, the credit quality of municipal bonds varies tremendously. Those that are at the lower end of the spectrum are forced to offer a higher yield to attract investors. Some financial institutions buy these up and package them as high-yield municipal bonds funds. These funds suffered great setbacks in 1999 and 2000 as a result of the credit crunch following the bankruptcy of Orange County, California. Investors in a Heartland Advisors fund, for example, saw the fund's value decline by more than 70 percent—in one day.[5] These losses were the result of illiquidity in the high-yield market that limited the ability of the pricing services to adequately value the bonds. The fund manager decided to retain higher values than were justified. The Heartland management repriced the funds when wind of the problem reached them.

Although Heartland got caught in the crunch, other high-yield funds suffered as well. When the savings and loans stopped lending due to their own credit crisis, municipalities opened the spigots to let Industrial Development Bonds flow. Generally backed by the revenue generated from the projects, many failed to reach their revenue targets. While municipal bonds are generally considered a credit snooze, Industrial Development Bonds were racking up defaults.

In short, high-yield municipal bond funds are every bit as risky as corporate high-yield bond funds. Buyers of these funds must be ever vigilant. The funds are available as open-end mutual funds and as closed-end funds.

Municipal Bond Funds: Money Market Funds

These funds offer all the convenience of traditional money market funds plus the fact that their income is tax exempt. The trade-off, of course, is a smaller yield than that offered by traditional funds. The tax-exempts are divided into national and state-specific funds. National funds generally provide higher yields than state-specific funds as well as greater diversity. However, someone in a high tax state might choose a fund holding securities yielding income that is tax free on the local, state, and federal level.

Containing short-term notes outstanding for a period of six months to one year, the bonds in the fund are named for the source of the funding that will repay them. These funds also buy tax-free commercial paper issued by municipalities and variable-rate debt to satisfy the demand for product.

In a state like Florida, where there is an intangibles tax, funds in the money market are taxed. Even though the investment is "like cash," for tax purposes it is considered an investment.

Money market mutual funds are sold only through brokers or independent mutual funds. Visit www.imoneynet.com to compare rates.

Municipal Bond Funds: National

These funds come in two varieties: investment grade and high yield (junk). The title of the fund will tell you which variety you are looking at. Included in these funds are bonds from all states.

Investment-grade funds, like their corporate cousins, come in short, intermediate, and long varieties. Some bond funds only contain insured bonds, which pay a lower yield due to the added protection. Because of the broad diversity of these funds, it is often felt that the extra protection is not necessary.

If your state charges some tax on out-of-state bonds, the fund management will provide you with an end-of-the-year statement that will outline what percentage of bonds it holds from your state. If 10 percent of the bonds were from your state, for example, you would not pay any tax on that income. The prospectus will tell you how the assets in the fund are allocated.

Both investment-grade funds and high-yield funds are available as UITs, closed-end funds, and open-end mutual funds.

Municipal Bond Funds: State Specific

If you have to pay high in-state taxes on bonds issued by other states, then this is the fund for you. These funds provide double or triple tax-free exemptions, depending on your residence. The funds may be more volatile than national market funds if state-specific credit quality issues arise. Always compare the returns on state-specific funds with the national counterpart. Buy the national funds whenever returns permit.

These state funds always contain the name of the state in the title. They are available in UIT, closed-end, and open-end mutual fund formats.

TAXABLE FUNDS

BILLIONS AND BILLIONS of dollars were pumped into taxable bond funds in 2001 as investors fled the falling stock market. These investors were seeking an easy way to capture the safety and promised return of bonds. Many investors discovered, as readers of this book now know, that there are great differences among bonds and, consequently, among bond funds as well. While investors in broad-based bond funds racked up profitable returns in 2001, those rushing into lower credit quality high-yield bond funds actually lost money when all was said and done.

The moral of bond fund performance in 2001 is that the funds run the gamut of the risk spectrum. The fund categories are described below, again arranged in alphabetical order. We considered putting the safest and most conservative first, and the riskiest and potentially most lucrative last, but that would have been misleading. While some kinds of bonds in funds are intrinsically safer than others, there is always the 20 percent of a fund's assets that can be invested at the manager's discretion. That may make a safe-appearing bond fund not so safe.

Adjustable-Rate Mortgage Funds (ARMs)

Consisting of mortgages that are mostly guaranteed by a federal agency, these funds invest in highly leveraged short-term securities that have backfired in the past, creating losses instead of gains, thus disappointing investors. Derivatives are allowed in these funds. Due to their less than stellar performance, this category has been placed under the rubric *Ultrashort*. They are available as open-end mutual funds or as closed-end funds.

Cash Management Accounts

These are money market fund look-alikes and are available through a broker, under the wrapper of a variable annuity, or through a mutual fund. They are also called *cash reserves, ready assets,* or *enhanced cash funds.* They are all ultrashort bond funds that usually maintain a fund share value of $1.[6]

These funds tend to offer higher yields because they hold commercial paper, which is riskier than Treasuries and can routinely use a variety of financial instruments described in the prospectus, including derivatives. They may also feature higher fees that can wipe out any yield advantage these funds may have over conventional money market funds. They are found among mutual funds. Visit www.imoneynet.com for information about these funds as well as money market mutual funds, or ask your broker.

Convertible Bond Funds

Convertible bond funds act more like stocks than bonds and are a steamy addition to any portfolio. Read all about their underlying components in Chapter 8 and take particular note of the fact that the majority of convertible bonds are below investment grade. These funds perform best when the stock market is on a roll and interest rates are rising. They are for players looking for total return, as convertibles pay more than stock dividends but less than bonds. If you are looking for income, it is best to look elsewhere.

Compared to losing stock market returns, convertible bond funds posted gains between 1999 and 2001. If you are looking for gains to top stocks, check out convertibles when stock market volatility is subdued. Investing in the lowest-grade bonds is not always a walk in the park. In February 2002, for example, Lipper and Company's convertible hedge fund slashed its value by 40 percent, or $215 million. This dramatic one-time repricing reflects a fund manager's desperate attempt to cover losses in the hope that better times were imminent. These funds are available as open-end funds.

Corporate Bond Funds: High Yield (Junk)

Funds having this title will vary greatly in their holdings and, thus, in their returns as well. They can contain almost any kind of investments in widely different proportions, as long as the information is disclosed in the prospectus. The turnover of a portfolio can be as low as 20 percent or as high as 80 percent. The fund can be dedicated to providing high income or total return, but not to both simultaneously. Probably more so than for any other fund category, it is important to know the investment philosophy of the sponsoring firm. The Vanguard High-Yield Corporate Fund, for example, consists principally of cash-paying bonds that carry credit ratings of B or better, which means that some of the bonds in the portfolio are investment grade. This mix lowers the offering yield, but reduces exposure to bond defaults and losses of capital.

Other high-yield funds could contain predominately C-rated bonds—a situation that could send shivers of despair through some and dreams of lucrative glory through others. Try to fathom why the fund you are considering offers a higher yield.

The perceived wisdom on "the Street" is that the best time to buy these funds is after there has been a shakeout in the corporate market with lots of defaults. The thinking behind this is that when the recession is over, it is likely that the survivors will be able to regroup and sustain themselves until the next downturn and credit squeeze.

Since this is a book for both good and bad times, we must remind you that it is before a recession is actually announced that these funds can get dicey. Between 1999 and 2000, for example, there were $11 billion worth of redemptions in junk bond funds, leaving the valuation of the underlying bond portfolios in question. It was reported:

One analyst reckons that some managers are overstating the value of their bonds by ten percentage points or more. That is partly because the market has become so thin that they are hard to price, but also, presumably, because their true values are so frightening.[7]

There are both closed- and open-end varieties of corporate high-yield bond funds.

Corporate Bond Funds: Investment Grade

Containing bonds in the top four rating categories, these funds are grouped into those with short, medium, and long maturities. It is important to consider these maturity distinctions; long-term corporates are extremely sensitive to changes in interest yields.

In recent years, investment-grade corporate bonds have been very popular with overseas investors; in 2001 these investors purchased almost half of all new corporate bonds. Should these bonds fall out of favor with foreign investors, there could be a value decline in funds holding these bonds. Before buying such a fund, ask if junk bonds are included in the mix to spruce up the yield. These funds are good to park in your retirement accounts because you can defer paying taxes on their income.

Investment-grade corporate bonds are available as either closed-end funds or open-end funds.

Foreign Bond Funds

International bond funds invest only in foreign bonds. Global bond funds hold U.S. corporate bonds in addition to the bonds of foreign countries. There are also funds that hold bonds of emerging markets or sectors of those markets. Multisector and balanced funds may contain a mix of foreign and American securities. These funds have higher fees and greater risk than U.S. bond funds. Currency fluctuations present a unique risk to this bond sector no matter what the maturity structure. Ask yourself, are you prepared to bet against the U.S. dollar? Some people do, but timing is everything. The funds are available in closed-end and open-end fund formats.

Government Bond Funds

This is a catchall category. These funds can contain a variety of securities. Some are plain-vanilla funds having a mixture of Treasuries and agency securities and mortgages. Some of the mortgage debt might not be issued through government agencies. Others may allow the trading of futures and options, which increases potential profit and multiplies the risk. Some funds are managed for total return and include the separate trading of Treasury zero-coupon bonds (STRIPS). Look in the prospectus to find out what is in the fund portfolio and to Chapters 3–6 in this book to understand what you are purchasing. This is not a one-size-fits-all category, despite its benign title. They are available in closed-end and open-end fund formats.

GNMA Funds

The most popular and well-known fund in this category is the GNMA, or Ginnie Mae, fund. Your money is invested in mortgage-backed securities guaranteed by the U.S. government. These are very liquid, high quality, and actively traded securities. Here is an example where bigger is better, and Vanguard takes the prize. The largest funds have enough diversity usually to cushion market fluctuations from principal prepayments while providing very attractive risk-adjusted returns. When mortgages are being refinanced at a rapid rate due to declining interest rates, this fund does not perform as well as funds with noncallable bonds. However, this kind of fund handles moderate ups and downs extremely well, especially if the fund is very large. Size matters here because mortgage securities are always being called and new ones purchased to replace them. This is the only fund that we personally own, and we recommend that your GNMA purchases be through a fund because of the unpredictability of the calls and pricing opaqueness. They are available through open-end mutual funds.

Index Funds

Like stock index funds, bond funds that are indexed invest in a broad array of bonds that represent a sampling of the bond index rather than all the issues in the index. Currently, the index of choice is the Lehman Brothers Aggregate Index for investment-grade bonds. Thus, while the Lehman Brothers aggregate contains over 5,000 issues, a fund may hold only a fraction of those. Fund managers have considerable flexibility in what they choose, and bonds may be traded more than you would expect. Between 1996 and 2001, the Vanguard Total Bond Index had annual turnover rates ranging from 36 percent to 57 percent in an attempt to mimic the underlying characteristics of the index.[8]

Bonds incorporated in the index must come from sizable issues—$100 million for government bonds and $50 million for all others. Government and corporate bonds make up 70 percent of the index, but mortgage-backed and asset-backed securities and Yankee bonds are also included. When a bond's maturity falls below one year, it is dropped from the index and from these portfolios. Although the bonds are not exactly the same in all portfolios as in the index, management attempts to match the duration and yield profile of the index so that the fund fluctuation will be comparable.

Index funds come in short, intermediate, long, and total market formats. As a policy, they tend to steer away from low-grade bonds.

Those who believe in indexing make a powerful case for bond index funds. Vanguard, a leading proponent of indexing, compiled the following data:

Managed Fund versus Index Fund Performance, 1981–2000

	Stocks*	Bonds**
Managed funds outperforming index funds	36%	22%
Managed funds underperforming index funds	64%	78%

*Wilshire 5000 Stock Index   **Lehman Aggregate Bond Index

Until recently index bond funds were offered only in the open-end format. The introduction of Exchange-Traded Bond funds has changed this situation. The ETFs also mirror indexes and are purported to have the additional advantage of not passing through capital gains. It is too soon to say how the two types of vehicles compare. Information about index funds is posted on the Internet at www.indexfunds.com.

Inflation-Protected Securities Fund

These are relative newcomers to the mutual fund family, with asset pools primarily consisting of TIPS issued by the Treasury. Although these funds are thought of as conservative investments for individuals fearful of inflation, they have delivered very handsome returns. In the period from spring 2000 to spring 2001, for example, both the PIMCO Real Return Bond Fund and the Vanguard Inflation-Protected Securities Fund handily beat the sagging S&P 500 Index by providing returns above 10 percent. These are considered excellent candidates for tax-sheltered retirement accounts because they provide current income as well as built-in protection so that inflation will not harm the principal.

This is a type of bond that is advantageous to own through a fund. When owned individually, some of the return is added to the principal amount but is not realized until the bond matures. Nevertheless, if you own the bond outside of a tax-advantaged retirement account, you will have to pay tax on the phantom income you receive annually. However, when purchased through a fund, you receive not only the base amount but the accumulated income as well.[9] Bond managers pass on this benefit to you by selling the fraction of the face value of their bond holdings corresponding to the inflation accrual, a step that represents only an iota of the fund's net asset value.

Inflation-protected bonds are available in open-end format.

Loan Participation Fund

This type of fund consists primarily of repackaged bank loans and contains risky credits made to finance highly leveraged buyouts, mergers, and acquisitions. When the economy is troubled, the liquidity of these funds evaporates.

Similar funds are sold with names such as "floating rate" or "prime rate" in their titles. Because the loans are short term, these funds are often sold as higher-yielding alternatives to money market funds. In the closed-end format, they do not feature the flexibility of money market funds because the shares can be redeemed from the company only for a thirty-day time period at the end of a quarter.

A flagging economy increases the risk that you will lose money invested in them. Banks are now delighted to have a way to shift the risk of widespread loan defaults to you. Substantial loads further cut down the attraction of these funds.

Bank loan funds frequently return principal when the loans are prepaid, triggering some capital gains that are passed on to the shareholder. They have the same pricing difficulties as high-yield bonds.

Mutual fund companies offering these funds include Fidelity and Eaton Vance. To maintain liquidity, the funds must keep a substantial sum in cash and liquid securities. Originally appearing in the closed-end format in 1988, they are now also offered as open-end funds.

Money Market Funds

Sometimes viewed as an alternative to certificates of deposit and savings accounts, money market funds invest in high-grade, short-term securities. By law they are required to invest 95 percent of the fund in highest-quality debt obligations with maturities of thirteen months or less. The average weighted maturity or duration must be ninety days or less. They can invest no more than 1 percent in any bond issuer that is of less than stellar quality.

The yield on money market funds fluctuates with the rise and fall of interest rates. Bonds mature constantly, and new ones are purchased. In that way, the funds quickly mirror any changes in short-term rates controlled by the Federal Reserve.

Maintaining a fund share value of $1 is considered sacrosanct, although fund managers have occasionally absorbed losses in order to do so. In 1994 one institutional fund "broke the buck" and was subsequently liquidated for ninety-four cents NAV. There is no guarantee that the $1 price will be maintained. In 2001 a number of firms reduced the fees on their money market funds so the NAV would not fall below the magic number. Visit www.imoneynet.com for information about these funds and cash management reserves.

Stable Value Funds

We love these funds when they are packed with highly rated assets. As this book was written, they were only offered as options within retirement plans such as 401(k)s or defined benefits. If you have an opportunity, ask your employer to consider including these funds in your company's employee retirement plan options.

Stable value funds are composed primarily of Guaranteed Investment Contracts (GICs) and are sweetened with the addition of government bonds, high-quality asset-backed securities, and corporate bonds. Banks or insurance companies provide a "wrapper," or insurance policy, that cloaks the assets and locks in principal and interest payments. As with any other investment, the quality of these funds will vary depending upon the asset mix. More diversified funds will have a return like that of a short-term bond fund, while less diversified portfolios will have a return more like an intermediate bond fund.

GICs ran into trouble in the 1990s when Executive Life and Mutual Benefit Life failed. More product transparency and diversity makes current funds safer. Look for a minimum of a double-A rating. Penalties established either by the fund or by the retirement account regulations may be imposed for early withdrawal. To find these funds visit www.stablevalue.org.

Strategic or Multisector Bond Funds

Players seeking high total returns in the high-yield, foreign, and U.S. bond markets gravitate to this type of fund. Relatively new to the game, the portfolio managers can shift their assets to the sectors they view as most rewarding. It is very difficult to evaluate these funds since there is no benchmark against which to measure them. However, they are considered to be very high risk. They are available as closed-end and open-end funds.

Target Funds: Zero Coupon

These funds hold bonds that pay no interest, although every year you must report the imputed interest; i.e., the interest they would have paid if they were paying interest. The title of the fund states a targeted maturity, but what is referred to is really a targeted duration. The entire bond portfolio does not come due at the same time; however, bonds that do not mature with the majority of the securities are sold at the fund maturity target. Mostly composed of Treasury and agency bond strips, the funds pose no default risk. Although they may be purchased to buy and hold, more often they are bought to make an interest rate play. In a declining interest rate market these bonds appreciate rapidly. Longer-term funds are extremely volatile. For example, a 1 percent decline in interest rates on a portfolio of 30-year bonds will return 30 percent, while a corresponding increase in interest rates will provide a substantial decline in fund value. Adding these funds to a portfolio is not for the faint of heart.

Since these funds have a targeted termination date, they have a specific redemption price. They can be selling at a discount to the NAV, yet at the same time sell at a premium to the termination value. For example, in 2002 BlackRock NY Insured Muni 2008 was valued at $15.30. "It was trading at a 2.2% premium to its target termination value of $15…. BLN (BlackRock NY) also faces a large amount of call risk through 2005, with 57 percent of the portfolio callable."[10] As the bonds approach their call date, the NAV will decline gradually, and precipitously fall if the bonds are called. That will result in a further decline in the price of the shares. Find them among closed-end funds.

Treasury Bond Funds

Plain-vanilla Treasury bonds fill these funds in short, medium, and long maturities. Paying the lowest yields, their claim to fame is safety and state tax exemption. We cannot understand why anyone would buy these funds when they could simply obtain the securities, in minimum amounts of $1,000, for no transaction or management fees through TreasuryDirect, or through your broker for a one-time fee (see Chapter 10 for details).

Treasury bond funds are available in closed-end fund and open-end formats.

Ultrashort Bond Funds

These funds invest in floating rate securities, whose interest rates are periodically reset. The definition of what is ultrashort varies from one-year to five-year maturities. Likewise, the mix of securities and the use of derivatives differ from one portfolio to another. Their purpose may be high current income only, or there might be mention of preservation of capital and liquidity. They may be called *variable rate, short term, capital preservation,* or have *ultra short* in the name.

Ultrashort bond funds have high expense ratios. They do best in a down market and may not earn enough to cover their expenses in an up market. Since they are not money market funds, there is no commitment to maintain an even share price, although some funds in this category do so.

Open-end mutual funds are the place to look for them.

Choosing a Bond Fund

THE INFORMATION RESOURCES on the Internet are a great boon to investors seeking to narrow down their fund choices. Before undertaking a search, however, it is important to determine what kind of investor you are or want to be. Do you want to engage in the thrills of trading, always being one profitable step—you hope—ahead of the market, or do you want to simply buy and hold and get on with the rest of your life? We call the former an *active investor* and the latter a *passive investor.* An active investor seeks out total return funds, or plans on investing in no-load funds. The passive investor should also seek out no-loads.

The next question to review is your tax status. If you want to shelter your income, you definitely want to have munis in your portfolio.

If a fund holds taxable bonds, its distributions are taxable, even if they are reinvested, unless the funds are held in a tax-sheltered retirement account. Income dividends from municipal bond funds may be state tax exempt based on the laws of your state affecting muni income.

With regard to choosing the specific type of fund, you need to determine your level of risk tolerance and then match that with the categories we have just finished describing. Remember that you need to determine the level of credit risk you are willing to assume and the amount of interest rate risk.

Finally, you should also review whether you need income for a short period, an income stream for many years, or just the knowledge that you'll be reaping income in the future.

Most of these choices are among the criteria you can use at websites to narrow your fund selection. Let's say, for illustrative purposes only, that you would like to receive a safe, steady stream of taxable income that is slightly higher than that of a broad market bond index. After rereading the above descriptions, you settle on a long-term, investment-grade corporate bond fund.

Your next step is to go on the Web and type www.yahoo.com, for example, or to your local library to find Morningstar reports. On Yahoo! click on finance, then mutual funds, then mutual fund screener. You can then click on a number of settings to narrow your search. The more specific you are, the less likely you will be satisfactorily rewarded. We recommend choosing between taxable and tax free and focusing on fees. See what comes up. Then go back and experiment by narrowing your search criteria. We recommend that you always click on no load. We also strongly recommend that you buy only highly rated funds with low expense ratios. These, however, are not always easy to find.

In our illustrative example, we followed the instructions and set these parameters for our search:

Type: Bond, long term
Morningstar rating: 5 stars
Load: None
Expense ratio: Less than 0.5 percent
Minimum investment: Less than $1,000

We then clicked on the "Find Funds" button and, to our dismay, learned that not one fund fit our requirements. We then started to change the parameters here and there. Finally, when we reduced the rating to four stars, increased the minimum investment to less than $2,500, and increased the expense ratio to less than 0.7 percent, we located three funds that met our criteria. For each one of these we could obtain a current quote, a chart, a profile, a performance review, a listing of the holdings, and a comparison with all others in its category. You could also choose to review some prospectuses.

This site presents a wealth of information to help you make a knowledgeable decision about which bond fund you want to buy. Other helpful information sources that could augment your decision are the Morningstar website, www.Morningstar.com; the magazine and news sites of *Forbes,* www.Forbes.com; *Business Week* at www.BusinessWeek.com; www.CNN.com; *SmartMoney* at www .smartmoney.com; and www.cnbc.com. Look for the mutual fund screener or prospectuses.

Why should you visit more than one site? Some have really annoying advertising that you cannot look at for more than a few minutes, so you might want to vary what kind of headache you get. Another reason is that the websites do not profile the same funds—or profile them in exactly the same way. *Forbes*'s site, for example, tells how the funds perform in up and down interest rate markets. This is very useful information to impress upon your mind so there won't be any surprises. Some sites have a bond calculator, chat rooms, informative articles, and a variety of other interesting features.

We have mentioned Morningstar a number of times. Morningstar is a company that analyzes funds and provides comprehensive information in an easily accessible format. In fact, many online sites purchase their information from Morningstar, although this data is not as complete as that found in their own website. Formerly available only in libraries, Morningstar now offers its services online for an affordable price (presently $109 annually), with a free, thirty-day trial period.

What the online site gives you that the printed library version does not, is easy access from anywhere and the ability to sort the information based on your individual preferences. The first sort is based on the Morningstar star ranking, modified in July 2001. To be rated at all, a fund must be in existence for three years. In the new system, funds are rated against other funds in the same category. Within the category, there will be as many five-star as one-star funds because they will be arrayed along a bell curve. The ratings are adjusted for fund "loads" or sales charges. No guarantees, though, that a precipitous event might not catch them off guard, or that what performed well in the past will continue to do so. However, Morningstar has also changed its risk measure to reward consistent performance rather than fiery flashes of brilliant returns.

In the free version, the list of funds does not comprehensively include all funds, and exchange-traded closed-end funds and open-end mutual funds are mixed together. Morningstar's Quicktake report overviews the basic information about a fund with links to deeper analysis. It is easy to be overwhelmed by the sheer amount of information presented. However, if you keep your perspective, you will find your way. What is important are the fund fees, the kinds of bonds included, the duration of the fund assets, credit quality, and the table of annual returns.

In addition to providing comprehensive information, Morningstar online has some smart tools, including Portfolio Analyzer, Cost Analyzer, Fund Compare, Fund Quickrank, Fund Selector, Asset Allocator, and a lot of other interesting aids to help you understand your investment decisions. You are able to compare your fund to other funds in the same category.

WHOEVER SAID FUND PICKING was quick and easy? It can, however, be both fun and profitable.

BOND

INVESTMENT

STRATEGIES

IN THIS PART, the last section of our book, we provide an overview of how bonds fit into your investment portfolio and present specific strategies on how to make the most of your bond investments.

Throughout our many years as financial advisers, we have followed a basic set of rules that have stood the test of time and have served our clients and us well. We call them the Richelson Investment Rules. As an introduction to Part IV, we would like to share these rules with you. They are conservative in that they are designed to both protect and enhance the value of your investments.

Rule 1. *Precisely define all your objectives.* List your financial objectives, life objectives, and values as specifically as you can. These objectives determine the type of investments you will choose; e.g., short term versus long term, risky versus safe.

Rule 2. *If you can't afford the risk, don't play.* Define the risks you're willing to take in order to realize your financial objectives. The potential return from an investment is always proportional to its risk.

Rule 3. *Don't lose money!* This is not said in jest. People only talk about their winners, whether at the racetrack or in the stock market. You will come out way ahead if you never lose money, compared to investors who win some and lose some.

Rule 4. *Evaluate the return on all investments on a risk-adjusted after-tax basis.* Our investment philosophy is that an investment should generate the largest after-tax economic return with the least risk of loss of capital and the least aggravation. To compare apples to apples, always look at each investment on a risk-adjusted after-tax basis. *Risk adjusted* means that in comparing one investment to another you determine what is the possibility of the loss of your capital. There are no good investments solely for tax purposes.

Rule 5. *Understand the investment.* Don't invest in anything unless you completely understand its economic and tax aspects. A warning flag should be raised when you register MEGO (My Eyes Glaze Over). Promoters of investment products love to tell you about the front-end tax benefits of an investment and the gains that will surely be yours. However, they often don't tell you what the downside case looks like, how difficult it might be to sell the investment product, who will buy it, what the spreads might be, and whether there are adverse tax consequences when an investment terminates.

Rule 6. *Understand the investment's liquidity.* Be in control of the investment. Liquidity and flexibility are as important as yield, particularly if you need to have access to your money or you decide that the investment looks like it will be heading down.

Rule 7. *Check for the seller's conflicts of interest.* Always look for the seller's potential conflicts of interest and try to determine whether this may affect the description you're given. Brokers, for example, often get larger commissions on stocks than on bonds.

With these rules as background, we now review asset allocation and detailed strategies on how to increase your returns from bonds.

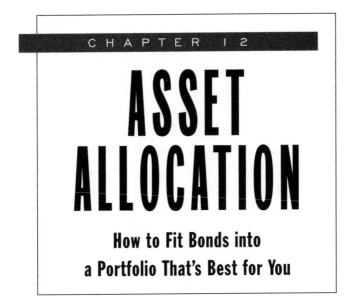

CHAPTER 12

ASSET ALLOCATION

How to Fit Bonds into a Portfolio That's Best for You

BONDS, LIKE RODNEY DANGERFIELD, often get no respect.

Their advantages, particularly when compared to stocks,

are woefully underappreciated. We believe that bonds

are among the premier investments available today and

wholeheartedly agree with Andrew Mellon's prescient late

1920s observation that "gentlemen prefer bonds." Being

a husband and wife team, we feel that ladies should, too.

We also feel that while Mellon's statement was memorable, it was a bit too pithy. As those of you who have read every word up to this point know, bonds are an extremely diverse financial category. They come in all denominations and maturities—from ultrasafe Treasury bills to risky junk bonds and unfathomable CMOs—and they serve a variety of income needs and purposes. You don't just buy "a bond" just as you don't just buy "a car." In both cases, there are innumerable choices, and you need to understand the specific aspects of your intended purchase, what you are going to use it for, and how long you intend to keep it.

We have found that investors tend to buy bonds with two very different strategies in mind. One strategy is to trade bonds in the hope of making big speculative returns. The other strategy is to invest in very conservative bonds to preserve principal and receive a steady stream of income. Neither one is correct if it doesn't take into account the overall financial picture of the investor. That's what asset allocation is all about.

Allocating Your Assets

ASSET ALLOCATION IS the process of dividing your financial assets among various categories. Although real estate (your home) and life insurance are essential assets, we do not consider them part of an investment portfolio and do not discuss them in this book. Rather, we concentrate on the division of dollars between stocks, bonds, and cash and what proportion should be in each.

The subject of asset allocation is actually a very old one. The Talmud, written by Jewish scholars from 1200 B.C. to 500 A.D., gave the following advice: Let every man divide his money into three parts: invest a third in land and a third in business, and a third let him keep in reserve.

The subject of asset allocation is also an extremely important one. We have found no more powerful statement on its importance than that written by Vanguard founder John Bogle: "The most fundamental decision of investing is the allocation of your assets: How much should you own in stock? How much should you own in bonds? How much should you own in cash reserves? ...That decision [has been shown to account] for an astonishing 94% of the differences in total returns achieved by institutionally managed pension funds .... There is no reason to believe that the same relationship does not also hold true for individual investors."[1]

While some financial planners believe that a smaller percent of investment returns are due to the asset allocation decision, the lowest estimate we have come across is 40 percent of a portfolio's performance. That's still a hefty number.

Let's face it. Sitting down and reviewing your personal needs and financial objectives is time consuming. Perhaps it will be a more attractive process if you think of it in terms of providing a big payoff. At least 40 percent of your future returns will be due to how you assess your objectives and make your asset allocation.

Once you have set your objectives you then need to decide what mix of assets will best meet those objectives. Examine the full range of investments and evaluate each category for both its risks and its rewards. Next, align these assets with your financial needs. If you need income and can't afford to lose money, bonds will be a major player in your investment portfolio.

Many financial advisers believe that investors should allocate 65 percent to stocks and 35 percent to bonds and cash equivalents. This view does recognize the need for diversification; i.e., that one should always follow the old saying about never putting all of your eggs into one basket. However, the 65/35 view does not reflect the individual needs and circumstances of investors. Suppose, for example, that you need to make a down payment on your dream home in two years. If your stocks decline in value over the two-year period, you may be forced to sell your stocks at a significant loss when you need the cash. In this example, your needs dictate investments in assets that can be readily converted to cash and won't decline in value over a two-year period.

Thus, when advising our clients, we first ask them to review their objectives and financial needs. With these established, we then ask them to evaluate their risk level or the amount of loss they can accept without seriously endangering their lifestyle. This is sometimes known as their *risk capacity*. Finally, we see how tax planning may benefit them, allocating funds to tax-sheltered accounts whenever possible.

Individuals nearing retirement and needing income without loss of principal might very well say they want their investment portfolio allocated 80 percent to bonds paying current income and 20 percent to dividend-paying stocks. A new, recently employed college graduate who has just learned she has inherited $100,000 from a beloved uncle might want to invest very aggressively and allocate that money 90 percent to nondividend paying stocks and 10 percent to bonds. However, both individuals—the soon-to-be retiree and the recent graduate—need to think through their asset allocations further.

The first step in the crucial process of asset allocation is defining the life objectives and values that reflect who you are now and the lifestyle that you would like to enjoy in the future. Once you define your objectives and your values, the key question in all of financial planning is *what investments will best support your objectives and values with the least amount of risk?* In essence, the answer to this question is the short answer to all financial planning. Note that the key question is *not* what will perform well next year or in the next ten years. No one knows the answer to that question. We advise clients to invest in what best supports their objectives and values with the least amount of risk, rather than try to find the next "hot" investment area that will double their money in a year or two.

Your present and future financial objectives, life objectives, and values depend on many factors that are specific to you and your family. Let's briefly look at some of them.

1 How much ready cash and safe investments will you need to provide for the transitions in your life such as job loss, the desire for a job or career change, retirement, or downshifting (trading money for time)?

Should the twenty-something career ingenue, for example, find herself joining her many unemployed peers, she might regret her 90 percent allocation to stocks. Furthermore, should she have put the remaining 10 percent of her inheritance into junk bonds, she might very well find that they have tanked along with her job. Although she might have thought she was protecting herself with her 10 percent allocation in bonds, she had not considered that the bonds she invested in were not a ready cash equivalent. In short, she had made no provision for an unexpected emergency.

In a true example, one of our clients left a large corporate employer to become an independent consultant. At the time he was setting up his new business, his investment portfolio was completely in stocks, with most in the high-tech sector. We advised him to sell all of the stocks. When he asked whether we were making a market call that stocks were going to decline substantially in value we said no. The reason for our advice was that he was creating a new business, and it was not clear how long it would take to launch and how much cash he would need to fund his new venture. Thus, if his new venture needed cash, it could not financially survive a serious stock market decline. The next day he sold all his stock and kept his money in cash equivalents and other default-free securities without market risk. As it turned out, we unknowingly had made the correct market call, because over the next nine months the stock market actually declined in value. While the market went down, however, our client's business went up, and it is now self-generating. Since he can now afford to lose principal, he is prudently investing some of his portfolio in stocks.

The old perceived wisdom was that one should have a year's worth of income available in assets that can be readily cashed. Today, some financial advisers have reduced their ready cash recommendation down to a three-month supply, especially for those with medical and disability insurance. We advise keeping a minimum of six months' living expenses in cash equivalents and short-term securities for emergencies. This is for you to decide, but decide you must before going on to the remainder of your asset allocation.

2 What is your risk tolerance and capacity for loss? Once you have set aside or attained your ready cash reserve, review the remainder of your assets to see how much risk you can take on in order to get a higher return. Your asset allocation can be used as a risk-control strategy. Modern portfolio theory holds that diversification of assets reduces the overall risk of a portfolio. This means that adding bonds to an all-stock portfolio actually reduces the risk in the portfolio without reducing the expected return. In fact, the return may actually be increased.

3 What is your investment horizon? For example, do you have significant family requirements to satisfy in the future such as college tuition, support of family members, or saving for a new home?

Depending on the time horizon, stocks may or may not be a sensible investment. To comfortably invest in stocks you should be able to stay with them for at least ten years, a time period that has traditionally averaged out the good and the bad years. Stocks are not suitable investments for short-term goals such as a rainy-day fund, saving for a home, or college tuition that comes due within the near future. Neither are long-term bonds, because these are also quite volatile in times of large interest rate swings.

Safe but not necessarily current income investments are called for here. Zero-coupons bonds are often a good investment category for providing cash at a specified date.

4 Will you need more reliable income as you get older and have fewer years to make earned income? If so, consider shifting your asset allocation toward bonds. For example, John Bogle—long a stock advocate—cut his personal asset allocation from about 75 percent equities to 35 percent equities after his retirement.[2]

5 What is your tax bracket? Should you be investing to reduce your taxes? If so, consider tax-exempt municipal bonds (remember, as explained in Chapter 7, not all munis are tax-exempt). Also consider U.S. savings bonds and fixed deferred annuities for a tax deferral.

6 If you have earned income that is high one year and low the next, do you need a stream of income from your assets to smooth out the cash flow ups and downs? Dividends from stocks have proven an unreliable source of income in recent years. Investment-grade bonds, however, do provide predictable income streams.

It's important to remember that asset allocation is not a one-time affair. As your needs and lifestyle change, so, too, should the allocation of your assets.

Comparing Stocks and Bonds

DESPITE OUR UNABASHED admiration of bonds, we also believe that stocks are a key component of an investment portfolio. We do not, however, feel that stocks should always be the major component. Indeed, we have found that an astute selection of bonds often outperforms stock indices. We tell our clients that to the extent that their asset allocation is to be in stocks, they should adopt a passive investment strategy and use broad-based index funds such as the Russell 3000 to reduce the risks and fees of investing in stocks.

That stocks have become such a disproportionate financial asset category for so many households is due, we believe, to the false assumption that stocks consistently provide better returns than bonds. In comparing the performance of stocks and bonds, the S&P 500 Index is generally used as the representative of all stocks. This index is a volatile average, disproportionately affected by large growth stocks. On the other hand, Treasury bonds and bills are generally used as the representative of all bonds. Treasury bills are cash equivalents, the safest investments in the United States, and thus generally yield less than any other bond. Many other bonds that are safe (although not completely without risk) provide higher returns than Treasury bills and bonds. This creates, in our opinion, a very distorted picture favoring stocks and one that adversely affects asset allocation.

Furthermore, the comparison of the return on stocks and bonds does not include trading costs, income taxes, and, in the case of mutual funds, management fees. William Bernstein examined the latter costs and reported the following in the April 2001 *Financial Planning:*[3]

◆ The average actively managed large-cap fund has annual fees and expenses of about 2 percent.

◆ The average small-cap and foreign fund has annual fees and expenses of about 4 percent.

◆ The average microcap and emerging market fund has annual fees and expenses of almost 10 percent.

◆ Federal and state income taxes will reduce returns further. If a fund trades a great deal, some of the reportable gains will be treated as short-term capital gains that may be taxed at the highest marginal tax rate.

◆ After paying fees, expenses, and taxes, the returns on stocks in the real world are more likely to be 6–7 percent rather than the widely believed figure of 10 or 11 percent.

Another important factor in evaluating the performance of stocks is the drop in the dividend rate. The average dividend yield for the Standard & Poor's 500 Index was 1.35 percent in 2001, compared with 3.3 percent ten years earlier. The impact of this decline was described in the January 4, 2002, *Wall Street Journal* as follows:

> ...the 10.7 percent average annual gain that the Standard & Poor's 500 Index has historically enjoyed would be cut to 6.3 percent without dividends.... To gauge the impact, with dividends and compounding, $100 invested in the S&P 500 Index in 1926 would be worth $253,000 today.... Back out dividends and that return shrinks to just $10,000.[4]

We also know that the widely held assumption that stocks have delivered an 11 percent return for decades is not what it seems to be. The figure comes from a broad study of stocks that was conducted by Ibbotson & Associates that covered the 1926–1996 period. It takes into account a very long holding period. Returns are very different if shorter periods are used. For example, in the years 1965–1982, the Dow started out at about 1,000 at the beginning and ended pretty much at the same place at its end.

Not only that, long-term returns on bond mutual funds beat those on stock funds for certain periods without the adjustments suggested above. According to an article by Beth Stanton of Bloomberg News, for the five years ended September 25, 2001, "...the average bond fund gained 5.7 percent a year, according to New York-based fund tracker Lipper. Over the same period, the average stock fund has returned just 4.6 percent a year.... [Prior to that time] the last time long-term returns for bond funds beat stocks was for the five years ended September 1992...."[5]

As Nobel physics laureate Nils Bohr observed, "Prediction is very difficult, especially if it's about the future." Predicting the financial future is so difficult because the basic questions are too complex to solve with any degree of consistency or certainty. The culture of the financial world is like other cultures of the world. It is about intangible, ambiguous, unstable, and often-contradictory stories that people tell each other as they try to make sense of the actions of the marketplace. Since we don't know what the future holds, we believe your investment strategy should consist of aligning your investments behind your goals rather than trying to guess what will outperform what in the coming year.

What we do know with certainty and what we most like about highly rated short- and intermediate-term bonds is that there are no surprises when you buy them and the return is predictable if you hold them until they come due. For example, Treasuries and U.S. savings bonds will never default, and you will never lose money if you hold them until they come due. The same is generally true for agency, high-grade municipal bonds, CDs, and fixed annuities. Your principal will be returned at a predetermined time, and you will receive the stated income. In contrast, stock returns are volatile and not predictable, and the dividend component is often inconsequential. In addition, the temptation to reallocate your money into different "hot" investments and "hot" sections every year can be costly and unproductive.

Selecting Bonds That Meet Your Needs

WITH THE ABOVE IN MIND, it is now time to allocate your assets. You will, of course, have a readily available cash component and then divide your remaining dollars by your specific needs and stage in life, taking into account your risk capacity and tax status.

For simplicity's sake, we have categorized the risk spectrum of investments as follows:
◆ Those that are rock-solid and often deemed conservative
◆ Those that are somewhat riskier and often known as balanced or middle of the road
◆ Those that are speculative

Divide your investment portfolio by these risk grades. There is no one right proportion; just what is right for you and your needs.

You may choose to be conservative with some of your funds, middle of the road with others, and aggressive with the balance. You will probably have different expectations and risk levels for different pots of your money. Not only that, but also your feelings about risk may change over time as your life unfolds and your goals and market conditions change. We are not cookie-cutter people but rather have complex personal and investment needs compounded by living in a very multifaceted world that is changing at an accelerating pace.

Let's say, for illustrative purposes only, that you want to have one-third of your fixed-income assets in conservative instruments, one-third in speculative, and the remainder in middle-of-the-road investments. As must be evident by now, the next step is not a matter of blindly assigning bonds to each category; you must select specific kinds of bonds.

CONSERVATIVE INVESTMENTS

THE PERCENTAGE OF your assets that you allocate to rock-solid investments will consist of cash equivalents, default-free securities, and those securities without significant market risk because they come due within five years. Securities that fit into the rock-solid category, all described earlier in this book, are as follows:

◆ Cash equivalents—money market mutual funds and Treasury bills
◆ Bank CDs that have FDIC insurance and come due within five years, but not broker CDs, unless you can hold them until they come due
◆ Treasury notes, STRIPS, and TIPS which come due within five years
◆ EE, I, and HH U.S. Savings Bonds
◆ Agency debt securities coming due within five years
◆ Highly rated municipal and corporate debt securities that are rated either AA or AAA and come due within five years

Depending on your tax status, you would further winnow down this list. For example, if you are seeking tax-free income, you would concentrate on highly rated tax-exempt munis. If you were looking to defer tax payments, you would choose Series EE and I U.S. Savings Bonds. You may want to stay away from STRIPS and TIPS because you pay current taxes on interest income that you don't receive until maturity unless they were held in a tax-sheltered retirement account. If you live in a high tax state, you might find Treasuries attractive because they are free of state and local income tax while most other taxable securities are not.

If you do not have a substantial portfolio or if you have smaller amounts of cash, buy EE and I Savings Bonds. Also consider short-term corporate bond index funds and short-term Treasury funds. An inflation protected bond fund will provide safety and income.

With the above securities in mind, we suggest that you allocate the fixed-income portion of your conservative investments as follows.

Conservative Fixed-Income Asset Allocation

Cash equivalents: 10 percent
Short-term bonds: 40 percent
Intermediate-term bonds: 50 percent
Long-term bonds: 0 percent

Bonds in this conservative portfolio provide the ultimate in security. There is little possibility of a default, and market risk has been minimized. That does not mean that this portfolio is without risk. We wouldn't want your life to be lacking in excitement, now would we?

Investment advisers will tell you that your portfolio may be eroded by inflation, that silent financial thief. By investing in some intermediate-term securities you will mitigate that risk somewhat and add some market risk. However, if you are like our mothers, you don't care about the specter of inflation. They like their money short term and within reach. If you are like our client who is a real estate contractor, he might find this portfolio just fine because he has other money working in high-risk investments. For him, this would be his safe money, his port in the storm.

BALANCED INVESTMENTS

IN SEEKING A somewhat higher return, you might wish to allocate some of your portfolio to riskier investments. These investments are generally safe but are either somewhat lower rated than the rock-solid investments and/or have market risk because of their longer maturities. You may wish to include stocks in this part of your asset portfolio. If so, evaluate the riskiness of these before selecting the bond component. If you choose nondividend paying stocks or those with high price/earnings ratios, you should probably balance the portfolio with the bonds just described above. If, however, you choose dividend paying stocks that are not overvalued or the Russell 3000 Index that we recommend, you may wish to complete this part of your portfolio with one or more of the following bond securities.

◆ Treasury notes, Treasury bonds, STRIPS, and TIPS with a maturity between five and fifteen years

◆ Bank CDs that have FDIC insurance and come due in more than five years but less than fifteen years

◆ Agency debt securities with a maturity between five and fifteen years

◆ Agency mortgage securities with an expected maturity between five and fifteen years, but not mortgage securities without credit enhancements such as lower tranche CMOs

◆ Municipal and corporate debt securities that are investment grade, but not AA or AAA, with a maturity between five and fifteen years

Middle-of-the-road bonds include corporate and muni bonds rated single-A or better. For the intermediate term, buy bonds that will come due within five and fifteen years. For the long term, buy bonds that will come due between fifteen and twenty-five years.

If you do not have a substantial portfolio or the money is held in a retirement account, buy an intermediate- or long-term corporate bond fund with bond ratings clustered in the higher end of the scale to diversify your risk. We particularly like GNMA funds and intermediate-term bond index funds. Check the duration of the funds you are considering and stay in the five- to seven-year range or shorter for intermediate-term bond funds. The longer the maturity, the more interest rate risk you assume.

If your tax bracket warrants, purchase intermediate- and long-term munis instead of taxable bonds. You can expand your horizon to include a wide choice of issuers without adding much risk. There is no cause for concern if they are not insured bonds if they are rated single-A or better and are in safer market sectors.

If your portfolio is not large enough to provide diversification, purchase intermediate- or long-term tax-exempt muni bond funds. Longer-term munis add more return and more interest rate risk to your portfolio. Consider bond funds that hold state-specific funds if you live in a high tax state. Although these maturities are long, the duration of munis and muni bond funds is always quite a bit shorter because they are callable, thus changing the risk mix.

With the above securities in mind, we suggest you allocate the fixed-income portion of your balanced portfolio as follows:

Middle-of-the-Road Fixed-Income Asset Allocation

Cash equivalents: 10 percent
Short-term bonds: 10 percent
Intermediate-term bonds: 40 percent
Long-term bonds: 40 percent

The middle-of-the-road investments that we suggest provide a higher yield than the conservative investments without significantly more default risk. There is an increase in market risk if the bonds must be sold, whether you purchase individual bonds or a bond fund. Who might adopt some of these choices? A young family looking for growth but not willing to assume a significant amount of risk might purchase these securities as well as other investors seeking safety and income. The young family might purchase more zero-coupon bonds in the mix if interest rates were at the higher end of the interest rate continuum.

SPECULATIVE INVESTMENTS

THERE IS ALSO A PLACE for aggressive and risky bond investments. They can be used to increase the overall return on your portfolio to meet your needs and financial objectives. They can also be used for pure speculation for a defined part of your portfolio because you like to speculate. The key is to understand the nature and degree of risk that you are taking and to make sure that it is appropriate to your situation.

You will find both stocks and some categories of bonds in the more speculative part of your asset allocation scheme. And take heed of Richelson Investment Rule 3: *Don't lose money.* You should consider speculative investments only when you understand the nature of the investment and have the capacity to deal with a possible loss.

Remember, there is a direct correlation between risk and reward. While you have a chance to make a lot of money in this category, you also have the chance to lose a lot of money. Certainly, nondividend-paying stocks belong in here. If you can't resist buying these, we suggest once again that you balance this part of your portfolio with the rock-solid investments we described above. On the other hand, if you want to take a flyer with some high-yield bonds, we also suggest you balance these with rock-solid securities. And, if you just want to spice up your overall portfolio, we suggest that this part of your allocation consist of some dividend-paying stocks and the following fixed-income securities. Even though what we consider speculative investments might not seem very risky to some, we have an aversion to losing money. These securities are as follows:

◆ Long-term Treasury bonds, STRIPS, TIPS, and agency debt securities that come due in more than fifteen years. While these investments will never default, they have significant market risk.

◆ Long-term mortgage securities or nonagency mortgage securities without credit enhancements and CMOs whose estimated life is more than fifteen years. These may be speculative or safe. You must investigate to find out. Use the market price as a guide.

◆ Non-rated or poorly rated corporate and municipal bonds that come due in more than fifteen years. Poorly rated bonds have credit risk, and, since they are long term, they have significant market risk as well.

◆ All junk bonds.

◆ All common and many forms of preferred stock.

For those in a high tax bracket, the best returns are often found on the longest-term munis and munis with very short calls. However, each has a different kind of market risk. We do not recommend 30-year muni bonds in times of very low interest rates because of their severe market risk. High-yield muni funds are available, as are leveraged closed-end muni funds, both kicking the risk level of munis up a few notches.

High-yield (junk) bond funds are a way to boost your total return in good times. However, in bleak economic periods they become extremely dicey. Timing is everything.

There are mutual funds called "government bond" or "mortgage bond" funds. While these sound safe enough, they might be risky if they contain a significant amount of nonagency mortgage securities including CMOs and high leverage. Investigate the mix of investments to see what the funds contain to make a determination if it suits your needs and risk level. Foreign bond funds, including global, multi-sector, and balanced bond funds are potentially high return and definitely high risk. Long-term target bond funds containing zero-coupon bonds may also be part of this portfolio and have considerable market risk despite the fact that they contain Treasuries, as well as long-term corporate bonds.

With the above in mind, we suggest the following allocation among speculative, fixed-income investments.

Speculative Fixed-Income Asset Allocation

Cash equivalents: 0 percent
Short-term bonds: 10 percent
Intermediate-term bonds: 20 percent
Long-term bonds: 70 percent

Even among aggressive investments the risks are not the same. Long-term munis and muni funds have less risk than similar high-yield corporate portfolios and funds holding foreign bonds. Corporate bonds are generally more risky than munis. Long-term zero-coupon bonds have very high interest rate risk even if the default risk is minimal. Buying zero-coupon Treasuries in a closed-end fund creates risks of its own. A leveraged bond fund will also increase the potential return and the actual risk.

All professional bond traders speculate with bonds and so do many individual investors. One way to carry out this broad strategy is to place a bet on the direction of interest rates. For example, if you believe that interest rates will decline, you buy long-term bonds; they might be very conservative Treasury bonds or corporate bonds. If you are right, you can make a bundle. To increase the size of your bet you might buy the bonds on margin and thus use leverage to increase your return. When you buy on margin, your broker lends you part of the purchase price. For Treasury bonds, the margin might be up to 96 percent of the purchase price. In this case, you will lose all of your money if interest rates go up, instead of down, and the price of your Treasuries declines by more than 4 percent!

Reevaluating Your Portfolio

AN ASSET ALLOCATION EXERCISE is not a once-in-a-lifetime event. It must be done periodically to reflect the changes in your lifestyle and income as well as changes in the economy. When you are younger, you should review your asset allocations with each major change in your life, such as getting married or becoming a parent. As you get older, you need to review your asset allocations with regard to the needs of your dependents. Finally, as retirement looms it is imperative that you review what income you will need and how best you can achieve that objective.

It sounds like work, and it is work. Remember, however, that at least 40 percent of the gains you receive will be directly due to the time and effort you put into reviewing and allocating your assets.

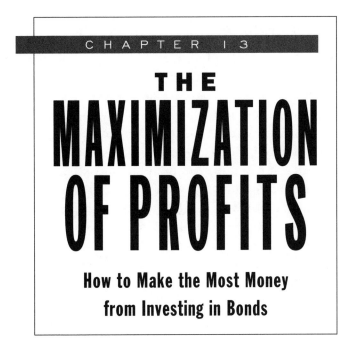

CHAPTER 13

THE
MAXIMIZATION
OF PROFITS

How to Make the Most Money
from Investing in Bonds

LET'S GET DOWN to the nitty-gritty: making money from bonds. We review a variety of techniques and strategies that will help you know when to buy and sell bonds, how to take advantage of tax benefits, how to minimize the risks to your capital, and how to increase your returns. In short, here are ways to use practically and profitably all the previous information presented in this book.

Knowing When to Buy and Sell

THERE ARE TWO TYPES of bond buyers: those who engage in a buy-and-hold strategy and those who try to time the market. We view the former as investors and the latter as speculators. By their very description, those in the first group buy bonds and, in the absence of personal financial or strategic reasons to sell, hold them until they come due. Market timers, on the other hand, seek to anticipate interest-rate movements and then capitalize on short-term market swings by a strategy of in-and-out trading.

There is little evidence that the top pros can consistently guess the winner of next year's Super Bowl, much less the direction of interest rates. If the world has yet to produce an individual who can accurately and consistently predict the future, what is the prospect that you or your broker can? Even if, through sheer random luck, you do properly guess the direction of interest rates, you still must overcome the dual costs of trading spreads and taxes on the gain.

We particularly like a buy-and-hold strategy because you only need to make one right decision—when to buy. The variations in a bond's price while you hold it are not very important because you will be paid both your scheduled interest and the face value of the bond at its due date. By comparison, when you trade bonds you must make two right decisions to be successful: when to buy and when to sell. We recommend to our clients that they avoid market timing and leave this activity to traders who move big positions and watch the trading action all day every day. Making one right decision is hard; making two is even harder.

Therefore, unless you hold long-term bonds, the ups and downs of a bond's price should not matter to you if you can hold the bond until it comes due at face value. However, there are certain times when it may be financially necessary or strategically advantageous for you to buy or sell bonds. Although it's not easy to spot buying opportunities in the bond market, there is a tool—known as the yield curve—that is widely used to discover such opportunities.

A **yield curve** is the name given to a chart that plots the interest rates being paid by bonds of the same credit quality but different maturities. In the chart, the interest rate is found on the vertical axis and the maturity on the horizontal axis. Short-term rates reflect investors' perception of near-term events. When they fall, they reflect investors' desire to stay liquid and safe. Long-term rates reflect investors' view of the more distant future. Rising longer-term rates reflect a fear of uncertainty and inflationary pressures.

The experts can agree on neither which way interest rates will go next nor on what the shape of the yield curve means for interest rates in the future. Although this is disappointing, you will still get significant information from studying the yield curve because it can tell you where to be careful and where an advantage may lie at a particular point in time.

The yield curve has three classic shapes: normal, flat, and inverted. Each, as depicted in the actual examples below, tells a different story.

◆ **Normal yield curve.** In a tranquil world, all yield curves would look like this. Bonds with the shortest maturities (those on the bottom left) would have the lowest yield (also on the bottom left) because there is less risk associated with holding them. As the years to maturity stretch out, this creates more uncertainty and additional risk. The greater risk of long-term bonds comes from their greater volatility, inflation risk, and default risk. Bondholders are

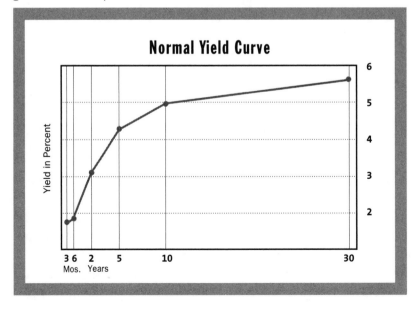

paid for this extra risk in the form of higher interest rates. The additional return on longer-term bonds is called the *risk premium* and is shown in the upper right part of the chart.

◆ **Flat yield curve.** If there is a flat yield curve, you receive more or less the same interest rate whether you buy a short-, intermediate-, or long-term bond. In this case we generally advise our clients to stay in the intermediate range due to greater market uncertainty about long-term bonds. It is not unusual for there to be a normal yield curve for, say, the first ten years and then a flatter yield curve from year 10 to year 30. In this case it usually makes sense to buy bonds with maturities only as far out on the yield curve as is comfortable until it flattens, because after this point you are not being paid for the risk of the longer-term bonds.

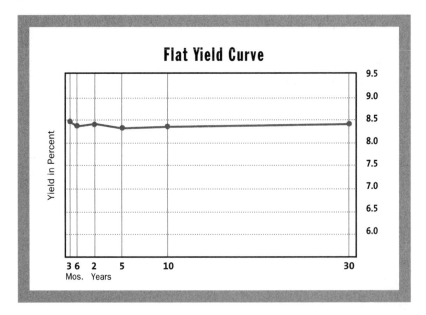

◆ **Inverted yield curve.** If there is an inverted yield curve, bonds with a short maturity have a higher yield than long-term bonds. An inverted yield curve is infrequent and sometimes indicates that a significant economic change is coming, such as a recession. Bond-buying decisions are more difficult under these conditions. If you buy longer-term bonds, you are not being paid for the risk. You can get the highest yield by taking what appears to be the safest path,

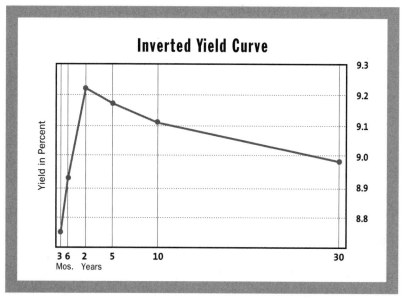

SOURCE: BLOOMBERG

buying short-term bonds. However, this strategy might have an unfortunate outcome because the inverted yield curve does not usually last for long. Short-term yields may rapidly decline, leaving you averaging down to ever-lower yields. You also miss the opportunity to lock in higher yields available in longer maturities. For example, in the early 1980s all interest rates were sky high, and the yield curve was steeply inverted. During this period many very conservative CD buyers bought six-month CDs and kept rolling them over. Unfortunately for them, they missed a huge buying opportunity to lock in long-term Treasury bonds yielding 15 percent.

FOR AN EXCELLENT PRESENTATION and discussion of the yield curve, visit *SmartMoney*'s website at www.smartmoney.com. Follow the path to "Bonds" and then to "The Living Yield Curve." You can see for yourself how the yield curve has changed from 1978 to the present.

STRATEGIES FOR DECIDING WHEN TO SELL

WHILE WE DO NOT RECOMMEND market timing, there are many times that it is appropriate to restructure your bond portfolio and sell bonds before they come due. Using the following strategies should help you decide when to take action.

◆ *Watch your federal tax bracket level.* A change in your federal tax bracket might lead you to sell municipal bonds and purchase taxable bonds, or vice versa. For example, your federal tax bracket might decrease as a result of your retirement, large business losses, substantial charitable contributions, or other deductions, or increase due to a great business opportunity or an inheritance.

◆ *Check tax rates when you move from one political jurisdiction to another.* A change in your residence from one high tax state to another high tax state or from a low tax state to a high tax state can trigger a need for portfolio reallocation. In each of these cases, you might sell the municipal bonds in one state and buy bonds in the other. For example, if you move from New York to California, you might want to sell your New York municipal bonds and buy California municipal bonds to take advantage of the tax exemption for in-state bonds.

◆ *Follow changes in the tax code.* Some municipal bonds, for example, are subject to the alternative minimum tax (AMT). There was some discussion in the fall of 2001 about abolishing this tax; any tinkering with it could affect the desirability of owning or selling these bonds, for better or for worse.

◆ *Profit from price gains.* Consider selling if you have a gain on your bonds and you have a specific use for the money elsewhere.

STRATEGIES FOR FINDING BARGAIN BONDS

WHEN THE GENERAL LEVEL of interest rates goes up or down, most bond sectors usually follow. However, a bond sector may become relatively cheap compared to others as a result of the supply and demand for that sector.

◆ *Study the Treasury bond yield curve.* Determine the most desirable maturity range based upon your needs. Suppose you were considering purchasing a bond with a five-year maturity. You might find that purchasing a bond in a longer or shorter maturity would better support your particular situation. Also, compare the yields on outstanding Treasury bills, notes, and bonds in the same maturity. The off-the-run securities might yield a little extra.

Maybe you wanted to purchase a longer-term bond. The large projected federal government surplus and the government buyback of 30-year Treasuries resulted in a sharp decrease in the yield of long-term Treasuries in 2000. However, when the projected surplus significantly diminished in 2001, the yield increased because the potential supply of Treasuries going forward seemed ready to increase.

◆ *Compare the Treasury yields to tax-exempt muni yields.* Even if you are in a lower tax bracket, municipal bonds might make sense for you if their yields approach those of Treasuries. There's a lot of historical data supporting the premise that on average the yields on tax-free municipal bonds are 80–90 percent of Treasury bonds for similarly dated maturities. Thus, if yields on tax-free municipal bonds are greater than 90 percent of Treasuries, as they were for a time in 1986 and 2000, the municipals are considered a good buy because they yield almost as much as Treasuries and the income is tax free. In this situation even the taxpayers in the lowest tax bracket will benefit from munis.

◆ *When buying corporate bonds, compare the returns of subsectors in the same maturities.* All corporate bonds do not move in unison. By comparing the yields of automobiles to rail companies, for example, you will understand that there is a yield differential for similarly rated bonds in different market sectors.

Junk bonds became relatively cheap in 1989, 1990, and 2001 because of actual defaults and the threat of more of the same caused by recessions in those years. Junk bonds became a buy after the yields had increased significantly and the threat of default had subsided.

◆ *Look for hammered credits that look promising.* Washington, D.C. and New York City ratings were upgraded, signaling that these bonds were becoming safer. It helps if the bonds are insured, just in case your best guess turns out to be a mistake.

STRATEGIES FOR STAYING AWAY FROM OVERVALUED BONDS

JUST AS THERE ARE periodic bond-buying opportunities, there are also bond-avoidance situations, times when one or more sectors may be relatively expensive.

◆ *Compare the Treasury yield curve to the yield curve of other taxable market sectors.* Professional bond traders always speak of the yield above Treasuries as a way to describe how a bond is priced. If you are not getting a satisfactory risk premium above the Treasury yield, don't take the risk. The Treasury bond yield curve is published daily in the *Wall Street Journal.* Also, check out www.rate curve.com or www.bloomberg.com for interesting online displays that list the yields and spreads between maturities of Treasuries.

The large supply of investment-grade corporate bonds issued in 2001 caused an increase in their yield so that the spread between Treasuries and corporates widened, presenting what appeared to be a buying opportunity, although Bill Gross of PIMCO Funds had sounded an alarm. By 2002, we found out that he was on target because prices deteriorated due to accounting and management scandals.

◆ *Watch out for junk bonds.* When the yield spread between Treasuries and junk bonds moves to within 200 basis points (2 percent), this is an indication that junk bonds are comparatively expensive unless they are an improving credit.

◆ *Compare maturities.* If the yield curve is relatively flat, there is little or no risk premium being offered for buying longer-term bonds. As a general rule you want to be in short- or medium-term maturities if you are not getting enough interest to warrant longer-term bonds.

◆ *Compare asset classes among corporate bonds.* Some sectors should be cheaper due to market news, but they may not have been repriced yet to reflect the increased risk. When a sector is being flailed, prices drop substantially.

◆ *Ask questions about corporate bond yield spreads over Treasuries.* The yield spreads indicate the market's perception of corporate strength, and they fluctuate based on rumor and market news. If a yield looks too good to be true, it probably is.

STRATEGIES WHEN INTEREST RATES ARE HIGH OR RISING

WE ALWAYS LOVE IT when interest rates are rising because it creates wonderful opportunities for investing money at higher rates and increasing our income. Remember, when the commentators say it is a bad time for bonds because rates are rising and prices are falling, you should say, let the bad times roll.

◆ *Quickly invest your cash.* If you hold cash or cash equivalents, you can now invest the cash at a more favorable rate of return than when rates were lower. This can only be good news.

◆ *Consider cashing in your bank CDs.* This strategy holds true for only a bank CD purchased from a bank and not for one obtained from a broker.

If you hold a CD purchased directly from a bank, take advantage of the fact that the principal of the CD never goes down. If interest rates have risen significantly, you might cash in your bank CD, pay the penalty, and then reinvest your cash in a higher-yielding and just as safe investment such as an intermediate-term Treasury, agency security, or even another five-year CD. To discourage this strategy some banks charge one year's interest or more. In fact the penalty might be higher than the interest that you earned and thus will reduce your principal. Check with your bank on the withdrawal penalties before you invest.

◆ *Cash in savings bonds that have been held for six or more months.* If you hold EE or I Savings Bonds, you can cash them in after you hold them for six months. If you hold them for less than five years, you will pay a penalty equal to three months' interest, but if you hold them for more than five years there is no penalty. The key point here is that you never lose any of the amount you invested or the accrued interest with a savings bond (except possibly the three-month penalty). Thus, if interest rates have risen significantly you can cash in your savings bonds and earn even more income by reinvesting in safe but higher-yielding fixed-income investments.

◆ *Buy new issues.* When rates are rising, you might consider buying new issues because new issues are price leaders. The brokers are hoping they will not have to take a loss on their existing inventory and thus do not mark down their price readily. New issues are priced at the current market value. However, when most investors rush to buy new issues, the better buys may be elsewhere. That's the market at work.

◆ *Inflation-protected bonds such as TIPS and I Savings Bonds sold individually or through a fund appear to be a good hedge when rates are rising.* If rising interest rates are a result of inflation, your TIPS and I Savings Bonds will generally increase in value.

◆ *Swap your bonds.* There are many opportunities to swap your bonds, although it is better to sell twenty-five bonds or more to get a better price. Three kinds of swaps are suggested below:

◆ *Swap short-term bonds for intermediate- or long-term bonds to lock in higher returns.* If the maturity date on a bond is two years or less, sell and buy an intermediate- to longer-term bond to lock in higher returns. You may either take a gain or sell at a small loss. While selling at a loss might not initially seem like a great idea, keep in mind that your loss will be small because the bonds that you are selling will come due within two years and are thus priced close to their face value.

◆ *Do a tax swap and take a tax loss.* This is a trading strategy that is applied to one-up the tax collector. It involves selling low-interest bonds that you own to generate a tax loss and simultaneously buying new bonds to lock in the same or a higher return. In the 1970s when interest rates were constantly rising, tax swaps were considered every year. In fact, the last quarter of the year was called the tax-swapping season.

◆ *Upgrade your credit quality.* Swaps can be done to upgrade the credit quality of your portfolio by swapping a weaker credit for a stronger one at a time when the spread between better credits and weaker credits has narrowed.

STRATEGIES WHEN INTEREST RATES ARE LOW OR FALLING

AS WE SAID, we love it when interest rates are rising. However, there is also money to be made when rates are falling, as long as you think strategically. Here are our suggestions.

◆ *Don't stay in cash.* When interest rates are low, you may believe that it will be best to keep your money in a low-yielding money market fund and wait for interest rates to rise. While this strategy may work out well, many other times staying in cash may prove costly because the longer you wait for rates to go up, the higher the rates must go to compensate you for waiting and earning lower rates. For example, if money market rates are 2 percent and 5-year bond rates are 4 percent, if rates stay the same, you have lost 2 percent for the period involved. Even if rates do move up later, they must move up enough not only to make up for the lost interest, but also to make up for the risk that the rates may not rise. Staying in cash is a type of market timing and is unlikely to work out favorably over the long term.

◆ *Take a capital gain.* When interest rates are low or are falling, consider selling some of your bonds to take a capital gain. The only time you should use this strategy is if you intend to invest the proceeds in another asset class such as equities or real estate or have a need for cash for a personal expenditure such as buying or improving your home. There is no advantage in taking a capital gain and then investing in similar bonds. This will just increase your tax bill, and your interest rate bet may backfire.

◆ *Buy EE Savings Bonds and convert to HH Bonds after six months.* You can use this strategy in place of a money market account if interest rates remain low. In 2001 the HH Bond rate was 4 percent, considerably higher than the rate on a money market account. When interest rates go up, you can redeem your HH Bonds without the risk of loss of principal.

◆ *Investigate the previously owned bond market.* When interest rates are falling, you might consider buying bonds in the secondary market rather than new issues. New issues, being price leaders, tend to have lower yields at these times.

◆ *Consider constructing a barbell portfolio.* Many financial advisers advocate using what is called a barbell structure for a portfolio if you want to concentrate a significant part of your bond portfolio in long-term bonds. In this structure, you split your portfolio between long- and short-term bonds (each constituting one part of the barbell). In doing so, you capture the higher returns of 20- to 30-year long-term bonds and their gains if interest rates decline, while having ready access to the cash in short-term bonds that have maturities of two years or less. The combination of long-term and short-term bonds provides an intermediate-term average maturity and portfolio duration. When interest rates are low, investors flock to intermediate-term bonds, pushing the yields of these bonds down. In this environment you might increase the yield of your bond portfolio by using a barbell structure because the prices of short-

and long-term bonds may provide better prices and thus more favorable yields to a buy-and-hold investor.

If you are a trader, a barbell will provide gains for you if long-term yields decline and you can sell your long-term bonds at a gain. If the long-term interest rates go up, the substantial short-term bond position would cushion the decline in the value of your portfolio. However, keep in mind that if you guess wrong, you may take substantial losses.

◆ *Buy bond funds with longer-term maturities.* When interest rates are falling, longer-term bond funds will give you the highest total return. For the adventurous, consider target maturity funds and long-term corporate bond funds. For the more conservative, consider long-term Treasury or municipal bond funds.

Investing for Tax Advantages

ALWAYS VIEW PURCHASES of bonds and other investments on an after-tax return basis. To do so, you must first determine your highest federal income tax bracket. You then compare the return you would get on an investment that is taxable with the return on one that is not. The result is called the *taxable equivalent yield.* Using the following simple formula makes this comparison:

Taxable bond rate x (1 − your top tax bracket) = Tax-free bond rate

For example, assume that the taxable bond rate is 7 percent and your top tax bracket is 28 percent. The computation would be made as follows:

.07 x (1 − .28) = (.07 x 0.72) = .0504 or 5.04 percent

In this example, a taxable yield of 7 percent is equivalent to a tax-free yield of 5.04 percent if you are in the 28 percent tax bracket. Thus, if you can get more than 5.04 percent on a tax-free bond, the tax-free bond would give you a higher after-tax return than a 7 percent taxable bond.

Brokerage firms and bond funds provide up-to-date tables that show tax equivalent yields so that you do not have to make any computations. Check out the bond calculator at www.investingin bonds.com, for example.

This is as good a place as any to review the tax implications of the fixed-income investments discussed in this book. Keep these distinctions in mind when you compare yields and risks and decide on your asset mix.

♦ *Income exempt from federal income tax.* Interest from tax-exempt municipal bonds and dividends from tax-exempt municipal bond funds, but not interest from taxable municipal bonds and, for some taxpayers, from bonds subject to the AMT.

♦ *Income exempt from state income tax, but not federal income tax.* Interest from Treasury bonds, notes, bills, STRIPS, TIPS, and certain agency debt securities and dividends from bond funds that hold these securities.

♦ *Income deferred from current federal and state income tax, but ultimately subject to tax.* Interest from EE and I Savings Bonds until they are redeemed or converted to HH Savings Bonds. However, interest from EE and I Savings Bonds may be tax-free if used for education by qualifying taxpayers. Fixed deferred annuities are tax deferred until payout begins and then fully taxable.

♦ *Income subject to federal and state income tax immediately.* Interest from HH Savings Bonds, some agency debt, all mortgage securities, taxable municipal bonds, bonds subject to the AMT for some taxpayers, corporate bonds, convertible bonds, CDs, immediate fixed annuities, and dividends from corporate bond funds, GNMA funds, preferred-stock funds, and money market funds (except when they hold municipal bonds and Treasury securities).

STRATEGIES FOR PLACING BONDS IN TAX-EFFECTIVE ACCOUNTS

ONE SUBJECT OFTEN RAISED by our clients is how to place bonds in their accounts to minimize taxes most effectively. Which should be placed in a taxable account and which should be placed in a tax-sheltered pension account such as an IRA or 401(k)?

♦ *Place taxable bonds and bond funds that are frequently traded in tax-sheltered retirement accounts.* The advantage of this strategy is that the gains are not subject to current tax. The disadvantage is that both short- and long-term capital gains generated in these accounts are treated as ordinary income when they are distributed. In addition, there is no tax benefit for losses in such an account.

◆ *Place bonds that are not frequently traded in taxable accounts.* The results produce long-term capital gains treatment on the gains and the benefit of a tax loss if there are losses.

◆ *Place all tax-exempt municipal bonds in taxable accounts.* These should *never* be placed in tax-sheltered retirement accounts because distributions from these accounts are always treated as ordinary income even if they result from tax-exempt municipal bonds.

◆ *Hold Strips and TIPS in tax-sheltered retirement accounts.* Interest from these securities results in imputed or phantom income that is currently subject to tax if held in taxable accounts, but creates no current tax liability if the securities are held in tax-sheltered accounts.

◆ *Place EE and I Savings Bonds in taxable accounts.* The tax deferral is wasted in a tax-sheltered retirement account, even assuming that you can get a trustee to hold them.

◆ *Put longer-term taxable bonds and bond funds into tax-sheltered retirement accounts.* Use taxable bond funds for liquidity and easy access to funds. There are penalties on early withdrawals before age 59½ from a retirement account.

◆ *Use stable value mutual funds as a safe way to boost your return in tax-sheltered retirement accounts.* Note, however, that some such funds are more conservative than others.

STRATEGIES FOR HIGH-TAX-BRACKET INDIVIDUALS

HIGH-TAX-BRACKET INDIVIDUALS should take particular note of these following two strategies.

◆ *Buy tax-free munis.* Tax-free municipal bonds are the best and last great tax shelter. While individuals with high tax brackets benefit most from an investment in municipal bonds, anyone in the 25 percent tax bracket or higher (combining your federal, state, and local income taxes) generally can benefit from an investment in these bonds on an after-tax basis. In 2002 a single taxpayer reached the 27 percent federal tax bracket when his or her taxable income exceeded $27,950. In 2002 married taxpayers reached the 27 percent federal tax bracket when their taxable income exceeded $46,700.

◆ *Watch out for muni AMT bonds.* Certain municipal bonds are called *AMT bonds* because the interest income from such bonds is subject to the federal alternative minimum tax for certain individuals.

STRATEGIES FOR MINORS AND OTHER LOW-TAX-BRACKET INDIVIDUALS

GENERALLY THE SAME bonds that are good for minors and other low-tax-bracket individuals are also good for tax-sheltered retirement accounts, because both cases deal with income that is either not subject to tax or taxed at a low rate.

◆ *Consider STRIPS, TIPS, and Treasuries.* They are safe. The adverse tax consequences of STRIPS and TIPS (due to their phantom income) will not result in a significant amount of tax if the minor has little or no other taxable income.

◆ *Check out muni AMT bonds.* If you are not subject to the AMT, buying AMT bonds may be an opportunity for you. They often provide 20–30 basis points more yield than non-AMT bonds, frequently without any sacrifice of credit quality. However, keep in mind that AMT bonds may be difficult to sell at a good price. In addition, even if you are not subject to the AMT today, you might be subject to the AMT in the future. Some muni funds may hold a higher proportion of these bonds to boost their yield.

◆ *Examine the benefits of EE and I Savings Bonds.* As described in Chapter 4, the income from such bonds might be tax free if used for educational purposes.

◆ *Buy higher-yielding corporate bonds in $1,000 minimum size.* If the child is fourteen years or older the bonds are taxed at the child's income tax rate.

STRATEGIES FOR KEEPING TAXES LOW AFTER RETIREMENT

MANY INDIVIDUALS WILL be in a lower tax bracket after they retire from their full-time job and their earned income terminates along with their job. Should this be your case, review your bond portfolio carefully. You may be in a position to take advantage of your new lower tax bracket and increase your after-tax income.

◆ *Exchange EE and I Savings Bonds for HH Savings Bonds.* As explained in Chapter 4, the exchange will be tax free and, as a consequence, the tax on all of your accumulated EE and I Bond income would continue to be deferred. Going forward the income that is paid to you from the HH Bonds will be taxed at your now lower tax rate. This is great tax planning. You receive a tax deferral when you are in a high tax bracket and then pay tax at a lower tax rate when you actually receive the interest income.

◆ *Sell your tax-free municipal bonds.* If you are no longer in a high-enough tax bracket, you may do better on an after-tax basis by selling your muni bonds and buying higher-yielding taxable securities. This may also be the time to buy a fixed immediate annuity. If you are still in a high tax bracket, consider living in a state with a favorable attitude toward municipal bonds.

◆ *Buy TIPS and GNMA mutual funds for safety and income.* GNMA funds produce predictable income in most interest rate scenarios. When interest rates drop sharply, the diversification inherent in these funds alleviates value declines caused by early redemptions of the underlying mortgages. TIPS funds are an inflation hedge that provides income.

Investing by Risk Tolerance

INVESTORS MUST WALK THE LINE between fear and greed. We want to have as much as we can and often feel envious when our peers are doing better with their investments than we are. The reality is that the return on an investment is generally proportional to the degree of its risk. Your peers, for the most part, have simply taken on more risk when their returns are better than yours. There is no free lunch. However, there is this book, and the following information provides guidelines on how to reduce risk while still getting a good return.

Since you have read this far, you have probably already assessed your need for income, the level of risk that you are willing to assume with your bond investments, and your capacity to actually sustain losses. Now consider the following questions:

If your bond portfolio declined in value would you panic and sell your bonds? If so, you probably have a low risk tolerance and failed to keep in mind that your bonds will come due at their face value. In order to be at peace with your bond investments, you should consider only short- and intermediate-term bonds that you can hold until they come due. If you can hold bonds until they come due you will have no reason to panic or sell your bonds prematurely.

Would you engage in an interest rate play by buying 30-year bonds with an eye toward selling for a significant gain if interest rates decline? Would you buy a bond with a 12 percent yield and take the risk of losing a significant amount of your capital? If so, you are a speculator and should have a high capacity for loss.

Is your portfolio heavily weighted in equities and illiquid investments such as real estate? If so, a conservative bond portfolio will provide a safe foundation enabling you to take on more risk with other investments and business ventures.

STRATEGIES FOR REDUCING THE RISK OF DEFAULT

WHEN INVESTORS THINK of risk, the main risk that many consider is default risk—when an issuer goes bankrupt and they lose their investment. A default might be caused by bad times in an industry or problems that are specific to the issuer. Here's how to stay away from such risk.

◆ *Buy only bonds rated single-A or better and determine when the bond was last rated by the rating agency.* In general, ratings by the major rating agencies are often good predictors of the likelihood of a default. However, if the rating was done years ago, it may not reflect the current financial position of the issuer. Ask your broker not only for the rating of the bond, but also for the date the bond was last rated and by which rating agencies—then hope for the best, because we all know that the rating agencies sometimes make big mistakes, such as in the rating of Enron.

◆ *Purchase bonds that are insured by a highly rated insurer or have some other credit enhancement that you can understand.* Bond insurers are only as good as their asset base and can get overextended. If a credit agency downgrades a bond insurer, all the bonds that it insures will be downgraded as well. Thus, if you buy a portfolio of insured municipal bonds, vary your holdings so that different municipal insurance companies are represented in order to provide diversity.

◆ *Diversify, diversify, diversify.* Diversification is a good way to minimize the risk to your portfolio. Diversify your holdings by issuer and, where applicable, by geographic region and market sector. If you don't have the minimum $50,000 we consider adequate to buy a sufficiently diversified bond portfolio, buy bond funds. There are many to choose from, including corporate bond index funds, junk bond funds, and mortgage bond funds, particularly GNMA funds. Bond funds consisting of bonds issued by less-developed countries or denominated in a foreign currency are "high risk/high reward" investments. These bonds are exceptionally risky and could be subject to losses due to currency fluctuations as well as country defaults, as evidenced by the defaults in Russia and Argentina.

◆ *Include different geographic regions in your municipal bond portfolio, even if you are in a high tax state.* While you may pay something extra in taxes, this protects you from the economic impact of regional downturns.

◆ *Diversify your corporate holdings by purchasing bonds from different market sectors.* This way you can obtain the higher yield offered on corporate bonds while protecting yourself from the impact of an economic decline affecting one sector. One corporate bond fund would provide you with enough diversity.

◆ *Purchase bonds that are simple to describe and understand.* While stories about stocks might help you to find an undervalued stock, stories about bonds are usually bad news. If the features of the bond are complex, remember that they were constructed for the benefit of the issuer, not you. Simple is good.

◆ *Think twice about an investment in a sector, market, or region that is getting bad press.* Take some time to consider if the extra yield is worth the extra risk. You should spend more time picking out a bond than a shirt. Purchase bonds in thriving areas and growing sectors of the economy.

STRATEGIES FOR REDUCING MARKET RISK

WITH THE EXCEPTION of money market funds, CDs, and savings bonds, all bonds are subject to market risk, whether they are Treasury bonds or junk bonds. The principal cause of a price decline caused by market risk is generally a rise in interest rates.

◆ *Use a bond ladder to reduce market risk and reinvestment risk.* A bond ladder is a powerful risk-reduction technique that will smooth out the interest rate that you earn and thus reduce reinvestment risk. Laddering a portfolio means that you buy and hold fairly equal face amounts of bonds that will come due over a period of years. The period might range from five to twenty years. When the first bond comes due, it is replaced with a bond of an equal amount at the longer end of the maturity ladder. For example, you want to invest $100,000 in a bond ladder over a ten-year period beginning with the year 2005. In this case you would buy $10,000 of bonds coming due in each year starting with 2005 and ending in 2014. When the first $10,000 bond came due in 2005, you would buy a $10,000 bond coming due in 2015. If you have a particular expense such as college tuition, you can modify your ladder to target particular years so that the required tuition money would be available for each year. This is called *income matching*.

A laddered portfolio has several advantages. It averages the rates of interest that you earn over a period of years. A ladder provides more overall return in a rising interest rate market than a single bond. It provides less market risk than investing only in longer-term bonds. It provides flexibility by giving you access to your funds (because some bonds will come due each year) without the cost of selling a longer-term bond. It allows you to buy some longer-term bonds without undue market risk. Laddering is a strategy for individual investors who know that they can't predict where interest rates are going. It produces a steady, predictable stream of interest income that pays more than a strategy based on short-term investments only.

When constructing a ladder, take into account all your investments, including money market funds, bank CDs, and savings bonds. Once you have your ladder, don't worry about the current value of your bonds in good or bad times, unless you are looking for signs of quality deterioration. Unless you are going to sell, market fluctuations don't matter. In a so-call bear market for bonds (when the price of bonds is going down), you can reinvest at higher rates. In a bull market (when the price of bonds is going up), you can take capital gains. A hypothetical 12 percent coupon rate for a Treasury bond purchased in September 1981 and held until October 1993 would have returned 20 percent per annum compared to a 10 percent quoted return in the stock market.

◆ *Purchase bonds that you can hold to their due date.* If you buy short- and intermediate-term bonds, your market risk will be significantly reduced, since it is more likely that you can hold them until they come due. If there is inflation and interest rates go up, this is good news because when your bond comes due you can reinvest at a higher rate.

◆ *Buy individual bonds rather than bond funds.* Remember that bond funds never come due. If interest rates go up and stay up for many years, which they have done in the past, you might have the equivalent of a permanent loss. Individual bonds come due at their face value. However, we do recommend bond funds for junk bonds, TIPS, and mortgage securities. If you are adventurous, you might use funds to invest in foreign bonds, convertible bonds, and other off-the-beaten-path investments.

STRATEGIES FOR REDUCING LIQUIDITY RISK

THIS IS THE RISK that you may not be able to sell your bonds quickly at an attractive price if you can't hold until they come due. Listed below are strategies on how to reduce the liquidity risk.

◆ *Buy bonds in minimum blocks of $25,000.* If not, consider open-end bond funds for great liquidity.

◆ *Purchase bonds that will come due when you need the cash.* This reduces transaction fees and provides security knowing the money will be there when you need it.

◆ *Select bonds with good credit ratings.* Look for ratings from well-known issuers or bonds supported by insurance or other credit enhancements that are in stable market sectors, both regional and industrial.

◆ *Sell the bonds you own that are close to face value.*

◆ *Select bonds that have wide market appeal.*

STRATEGIES FOR REDUCING EARLY CALL RISK

A CALL IS GENERALLY not favorable to an investor, because issuers call bonds when interest rates have declined. A call results in a reinvestment risk, because the money returned from a called bond may have to be reinvested at a lower interest rate.

◆ *Before you buy a bond, ask your broker for a statement of all calls, not just the fixed calls.* Request a copy of the bond description from one of the information agencies such as Bloomberg or J. J. Kenny. They have a listing of all the calls.

◆ *Buy bonds that are not callable for at least seven years.*

◆ *Buy bonds selling at a discount.* Low-coupon discount bonds are less likely to be called. However, if they are called it may result in a gain to you because the bond must be called at its face value or at a premium over its face unless it is a zero-coupon bond.

◆ *Request a listing of a fund's holdings.* Before you buy a fund, request a complete listing of its holdings to see if they consist primarily of premium bonds. If they do and the bonds are called away, it will reduce the fund's net asset value.

STRATEGIES FOR SAFE INVESTING

IN BAD TIMES not only do interest rates often go down, but also the spread between the interest rates payable by solid issuers and weak issuers widens to reflect the higher chance of default of the weak issuers. The opposite happens in good times. The spread between solid issuers and weak issuers lessens, and you are not paid for the risk that you take by buying the weaker issues.

◆ *When spreads lessen across the rating spectrum, buy the good credits.* Don't reach for extra yield in good times when you are not being paid enough to take the risk. But, when spreads widen out between low- and high-grade credits, purchase lower credits, if you feel safe in your judgment. If not, keep your assets in higher-rated bonds.

◆ *Buy pre-refunded munis.* These are the safest financial instruments in the municipal bond area because they are backed by assets placed into an escrow account. Ask what the prerefunded assets are, especially if the bonds have not been rerated.

◆ *Purchase Treasuries and agencies instead of corporates.* You don't need to diversify when you purchase Treasuries, so a Treasury fund is overkill unless you want the check-writing privileges. Some agency funds may contain leverage and derivatives and thus may not be as safe as you think. Pure GNMA funds are safe and worthy of your consideration.

Investing for Income Needs

BONDS ARE ALL ABOUT generating income to satisfy your financial needs. In this section we consider strategies that you might use to satisfy short- and long-term goals and, finally, strategies we have developed over the years to generate additional income.

STRATEGIES FOR SHORT-TERM GOALS

YOU SHOULD INVEST at least some money in short-term securities in order to create a readily available source of funds that will take care of you if you lose your job or have some other emergency needs. Your overall goal would seek to create a significant income flow while protecting your principal. In addition, you may want to save for other short-term goals such as education expenses or the down payment on a house, car, or boat. The following strategies will help you accomplish these objectives.

◆ *Buy bonds that come due when you need the money.* That way you can minimize the amount of money that you need to keep in short-term investments. Longer-term investments generally yield more than shorter-term ones.

◆ *Buy Treasury bills, Treasury notes, and STRIPS.* You can buy them to match your maturity needs. You would hold them until they come due or roll them over at maturity into other Treasuries. If you use TreasuryDirect to buy them, you don't have to pay any transaction costs.

◆ *Buy money market funds and CDs.* Whether interest rates go up or down while you are saving, your principal will be protected. However, distinguish between cash management accounts, money market mutual funds, and tax-exempt money market accounts. (See Chapter 11 for descriptions of each.)

◆ *Buy short-term bonds.* Consider agency debt, highly rated corporate bonds and retail notes, and municipal bonds that all come due within five years. If you can hold them until they come due in five years or less, there would be no market risk and no loss of principal unless there is a default. These short-term securities are also available in a variety of mutual funds. There are short-term corporate and muni bond funds. For the more adventurous, there are riskier funds such as loan participation funds, municipal preferred stock, and ultrashort bond funds.

◆ *Check out the advantages of EE or I Savings Bonds.* Although you can't cash them for six months, your principal is completely protected and the interest earned is tax deferred until you cash them.

◆ *Buy callable bonds.* If you can accept that they might or might not be called, you will receive a higher yield-to-call and to maturity. Only purchase them if the calls and the maturity work with the rest of your portfolio. Do not overload your portfolio with bonds all maturing or callable in the same years.

◆ *Use bank money market accounts for small sums of money.* They provide limited checking privileges but yield more than a traditional checking account.

◆ *Use money market funds tied to your checking account.* Most or all of your cash will earn interest if you do.

◆ *Use a stand-alone money market mutual fund for excess short-term funds if they yield more than funds tied to your checking account.*

◆ *Use cash management accounts for added yield and somewhat more risk.* Invest with a strong sponsor for added safety.

◆ *Buy death put bonds if you are anticipating a death in your family.* These are corporate retail notes that you can sell back to the issuer if the bond owner dies. This will enable you to fund final expenses and estate taxes.

STRATEGIES FOR LONG-TERM GOALS

SOMETIMES YOUR STRATEGY will be to invest for the long term in order to create a fund for retirement and for significant family needs such as paying for education expenses in ten to fifteen or more years. In this case, consider using the following kinds of bonds to accomplish these objectives.

◆ *Buy intermediate- or long-term Treasury bonds, STRIPS, and certain agency debt for safety and to eliminate state taxes on your savings.* These bonds are among the safest you can buy. The Treasuries are exempt from state income tax, as may be some of the agencies.

◆ *Buy certain federal mortgage securities through funds.* Ginnie Mae funds provide safe investments with good returns that will not default. Long-term Treasuries and funds are also a possibility.

◆ *Buy EE Savings Bonds to let your savings grow tax deferred.* EE and HH Savings Bonds can be held for thirty and twenty years, respectively, without market risk or the risk of loss of any principal. EE Savings Bonds also provide a tax deferral, and, if they can be used for education, a tax-exempt return for certain qualifying individuals.

◆ *Use I Savings Bonds and intermediate- and long-term TIPS as hedges against inflation.*

◆ *Check out intermediate- and long-term highly rated corporates and highly rated municipal bonds.* Corporates and taxable municipal bonds will generally provide a higher rate of return than Treasuries and agencies. Tax-free municipal bonds may provide a higher return on an after-tax basis. If the highly rated corporate and municipal bonds are bought carefully and properly diversified, they should prove to be good investments for the long term. They can also be purchased through bond index funds, targeted maturity funds, and municipal bond funds. If you're willing to take on extra risk for extra return, consider convertible bond funds, foreign bond funds, and junk bond funds.

STRATEGIES FOR INCREASING YOUR INCOME FROM BONDS

CERTAIN BONDS AND SECURITIES will enable you to increase the return from your bond portfolio if you are prepared to take on additional risk. Here are some suggestions:

◆ *Consider fixed immediate annuities.* These might be good investments if used as an income replacement for earned income when you retire.

◆ *Buy highly rated taxable bonds.* If you are retired and in a low-enough tax bracket, consider selling your tax-free municipal bonds and buying higher-yielding corporate bonds and retail notes, corporate bond funds, and bond index funds. Keep in mind that highly rated corporate bonds are riskier than similarly rated muni bonds.

◆ *Buy junk bonds funds.* Only consider junk bonds if you can earn substantially more as compared to safer taxable bonds to compensate you for the added risk. The amount of additional return will depend upon how dicey the market is. Although you may buy them in good times, you need to be compensated for the losses you may experience in bad times. Remember that junk bonds trade more like stocks than bonds. Two well-regarded junk bond funds are Vanguard High-Yield Corporate and T. Rowe Price High Yield. The Vanguard fund is conservative and as a consequence the yield is not as high as those of some other junk bond funds.

◆ *Buy long-term bonds.* Although we have cautioned you against buying long-term bonds, they have their advantages. They generally yield more than shorter-term bonds, and they appreciate more in declining interest rate markets. If a higher current return is important to you and you can afford to risk some of your principal, consider buying long-term bonds in the following cases:

—There is a steep yield curve so that long-term bonds yield considerably more than short- and intermediate-term bonds, and you have more than a ten-year period during which you can hold these bonds.

—Long-term bonds yield considerably more than intermediate-term bonds, but you do not have a ten-year holding period. However, you are prepared to take a market risk because of the high current return and the possibility of a significant capital gain. In other words, you are knowingly speculating on the direction of interest rates.

—Long-term bonds yield considerably more than intermediate-term bonds, and you have a substantial portfolio of bonds that are short term and intermediate term, so that you can hold the long-term bond forever as part of your permanent portfolio. In this case adding long-term bonds to your bond ladder to get the extra yield is not a risky strategy, and we recommend it. You may also want to buy long-term bonds if you have a substantial portfolio and are concerned with reinvestment risk.

◆ *Use premium bonds to get more current income.* Why would you pay $1,200 for a bond that comes due at its face value of $1,000? As one investor said, "I didn't build my capital by paying premiums for anything!" The impression is that you are paying more than you should. This reluctance on the part of some investors provides you with an opportunity to get the following possible benefits from premium bonds: a higher yield-to-maturity than a par or discount bond; a higher cash flow; and a cushion in the face of declining interest rates.

◆ *Use discount bonds including zero-coupon bonds to grow your portfolio.* Consider buying discount bonds (including zero-coupon bonds), such as Treasuries, STRIPS, and zero-coupon municipal bonds, if your income is high and you want discount bonds to act as a savings and growth portfolio. They are also available through target maturity funds. Consider buying discount bonds in the following cases:

—They are yielding more than par and premium bonds on an after-tax basis. Take into consideration that the discount may be subject to tax over its life if this is a taxable bond. The discount may be subject to tax when the bond comes due if this is a tax-free municipal bond.

—You are concerned that currently high interest rates will decline significantly in the future. In this case the appreciation of the discount bond as it approaches its face value will help maintain the bond's yield-to-maturity. If you buy a zero-coupon bond, you will get the stated yield-to-maturity because there is no income from the bond that you need to reinvest. In addition, if interest rates do decline, discount bonds will appreciate in value more than par or premium bonds.

—Because of its lower coupon, there is less chance of a discount bond being called than a par or a premium bond.

◆ *Reread this book.* It's all here—descriptions of specific bonds, information on how to find a bond broker, details on many different funds, and numerous strategies on how to make and save money. Enjoy and profit from the efforts of our labors to make you wealthier and wiser.

USEFUL WEBSITES

www.annuity.com A plethora of information about annuities, including a simple calculator and a variety of fixed annuity offerings.

www.annuity.net Find a focus on fixed annuities, a simple calculator, and a variety of fixed-annuity offerings.

www.annuityadvantage.com A simple discussion of the ins and outs of annuities.

www.bankrate.com Search for all kinds of interest rates for loans and deposits offered by the nation's banks.

www.bauerfinancial.com A simple, easy-to-use site for CD rates and bank ratings.

www.bloomberg.com A multipurpose site that provides current Treasury bond and TIPS yields, mutual fund prospectuses, selectors, a calculator, and more.

www.bonddeskgroup.com For broker/dealers only.

www.bondmarkets.com Mainly a trade group home site. Find market updates, interesting statistical information, and links to other websites.

www.bondpage.com A wealth of offerings for a variety of securities, for individuals and professionals.

www.bondtalk.com A source for current news, composite bond rates, yield curves, economic data, market indicators, market calendars, and Federal Reserve information.

www.bondvillage.com Bond calculators, lists of references, articles, plus more for the subscriber.

www.businessweek.com Uncluttered and user friendly, with a variety of financial calculators, including those for stocks, bonds, and mutual funds.

www.buybonds.com Find California bond offerings, weekly newsletters, and other bond information.

www.cefa.com A website devoted to closed-end funds.

www.cnbc.com Look up a fund family, do research on a particular fund, use a fund screener, view charts, and much more. You can also reach this site by using the URL http://moneycentral.msn.com, then click on "Investing."

www.CNN.com Click on "Business" then "Markets and Stock" if you want to check bond rates and read bond news, or "Mutual Funds" for fund information, plus extras. You can also use http://money.cnn.com to access this site.

www.directnotes.com Source of weekly corporate retail note rates from some high-quality issuers. The notes can be purchased through one of the affiliated brokers.

www.dpcdata.com Access brief material event notices by CUSIP, state, or through a more specific request.

www.ebondtrade.com Individuals and institutions can purchase municipal bonds. Find Fitch reports and extensive market news.

www.emuni.com Standard & Poor's, J. J. Kenny, and E-Muni established this site containing prospectuses of new and recently issued bonds for viewing.

www.fanniemae.com The latest news about Fannie Mae and information about new offerings.

www.fccouncil.com Website of the Farm Credit System, a federal agency.

www.fhlb.com Website of the Federal Home Loan Bank, a federal agency.

www.finance.state.ut.us The state of Utah posts the most recent prospectuses online, as well as annual reports under "State Bonds."

www.fitchratings.com Read rating actions on the Fitch home page.

www.forbes.com Articles and information about personal finance, plus a fund screener and top fund picks.

www.freddiemac.com Information about Freddie Mac's program to issue debt, new mortgage issues, and the good works of the company to further affordable housing.

www.ginniemae.gov Gain a general education about these pass-through securities and view prospectuses.

www.imoneynet.com A good source of information about money market rates.

www.insure.com Information about all kinds of insurance, including annuities, and a tool to evaluate the tax consequences of policy changes.

www.internotes.com View current offerings of corporate retail notes and prospectuses of selected corporations.

www.investinginbonds.com Reports of bonds traded four or more times on the previous day and trading histories of individual bonds. Decide whether to purchase taxable or tax-exempt securities using their updated tax calculator, plus a wealth of information.

www.irs.gov The Internal Revenue Service assists with your taxing questions.

www.kiplinger.com Oodles of information and tools that are clearly organized and user friendly.

www.metacrawler.com A search engine that has a very good phone directory.

www.moodys.com Search for bond ratings by CUSIP or name of issuer.

www.morningstar.com A premier site for mutual fund information of every sort, with many tools.

www.personalfund.com Composed of one interesting tool that evaluates fund costs and the effect of taxes on your mutual fund choice.

www.publicdebt.treas.gov The home page for the Bureau of Public Debt, it is a gateway to buying Treasury and savings bonds online.

www.quantumonline.com Search for information about corporations and their securities online.

www.ratecurve.com See the spread between Treasuries of different maturities and market information.

www.salliemae.com Website provides student loans and other loans.

www.savingsbonds.gov All you need to purchase savings bonds, including a savings bond calculator, and an introduction to savings bonds for older children.

www.sec.gov/edgar/quickedgar.htm The entryway to EDGAR for corporate and fund document searches at the Securities and Exchange Commission.

www.sec.gov/investor/pubs/certific.htm Guidelines established by the SEC for purchasing certificates of deposit and a phone number to call if you unwittingly purchased a CD with which you are dissatisfied.

www.sec.gov/investor/tools/mfcc/mfcc-int.htm The SEC's tool for evaluating fund fees.

www.smartmoney.com Lots of eye-candy is available from this magazine site including a yield calculator, a moving yield curve, fund cost calculator, and more.

www.stablevalue.org Dedicated to educating the public about stable value funds, check out the glossary to review terms that show how these funds can be made risky.

www.standardandpoors.com Some interesting articles are posted about bond ratings.

www.stoeverglass.com Open to individuals and professionals, choose muni bonds by clicking on a map of the United States, plus other bond selections.

www.TheMuniCenter.com Provides live two-sided trading, price negotiation, and sophisticated analytical tools.

www.tradeweb.com A broker/dealer site for bond trading.

www.treasurydirect.gov Go directly here to purchase Treasury bills, notes, and bonds at the Federal Reserve auctions.

www.tva.com Website of the Tennessee Valley Authority, a federal agency.

www.valubond.com A broker/dealer site for bond purchases.

www.wallstreetjournal.com Mostly for subscribers, though under "Free Content" there are prospectuses and annual reports for viewing.

www.yahoo.com Go to "Finance" then "Funds" for prospectuses, a fund finder, Morningstar editorials, and more at this megasite.

NOTES

CHAPTER 1: THE EVOLUTION OF A BOND

1. Henry Campbell Black. *Black's Law Dictionary* (St. Paul, MN: West Publishing Company, 1951), p. 224–225.

2. Black, p. 211.

3. Black, p. 1210.

4. Black, p. 1266.

5. Sidney Homer and Richard Sylla. *A History of Interest Rates* (New Brunswick, NJ: Rutgers University Press, 1991), p. 88.

6. Cynthia Crossen, *The Rich and How They Got That Way* (New York: Dow Jones and Company, 2000), p. 98.

7. Homer, p. 81.

8. Black, p. 1157.

9. Homer, p. 154–155.

10. Myers, p. 18.

11. Principal is the capital sum of a debt or obligation, as opposed to interest.

12. Steven Dickson, "Civil War, Railroads and 'Road Bonds': Bond Repudiation in the Days of Yore," *The Bond Buyer Centennial Edition* (New York: The Bond Buyer, 1991), p. 36.

13. Dickson, p. 30.

14. Homer, p. 333.

15. Homer, p. 346.

16. Homer, p. 356.

17. Matthew Kreps, "Ups and Downs of Municipal Bonds: Volume and Yield in the Past Century," *The Bond Buyer 100 Anniversary Edition: A Salute to the Municipal Bond Industry* (New York: The Bond Buyer, 1991), p. 18.

18. Homer, p. 367.

19. Edward Chancellor, *The Devil Take the Hindmost: A History of Financial Speculation* (New York: Farrar, Straus & Giroux, 1999), p. 278.

20. William Greider, *Secrets of the Temple: How the Federal Reserve Runs the Country* (New York: Touchtone Press, 1987), p. 552.

21. Read Michael Lewis's *Liar's Poker* (New York: Penguin USA, 1990) for a hilarious and caustic appraisal of the inception of the securitized markets.

CHAPTER 2: THE LIFE OF A BOND

1. James A. Klotz, "A Short-Term Outlook Leads to Long-Term Misery," www.fmsbonds.com, November 27, 2001, Commentary.

2. Riva D. Atlas, "Enron Spurs Debt Agencies to Consider Some Changes," *The New York Times,* January 22, 2002, p. C6.

3. www.AARP.com.

CHAPTER 3: U.S. TREASURY SECURITIES

1. *NAPFA Advisor,* January 2001, p. 28.

2. Frances Denmark, "Safe Harbor," *Bloomberg Wealth Manager,* December 2000/January 2001, p. 88, p. 96.

CHAPTER 4: U.S. SAVINGS BONDS

1. "U.S. Savings Bonds: Something Old, Something New," www.aarp.org /confacts/money/bond.html.

2. RIA, *2002 Federal Tax Handbook,* ¶1342 (2002).

CHAPTER 7: MUNICIPAL BONDS

1. Ryan McKaig, "Desperation Rears Head in New York," *The Bond Buyer,* October 12, 2001, pp. 1, 39.

2. "Moody's Downgrades JFK Terminal Debt," *The Bond Buyer,* October 8, 2001, p. 37.

3. Deborah Finestone, "California Gets 58 Negative Outlooks: Every County Cited by Moody's," *The Bond Buyer,* October 10, 2001, pp. 1, 34.

4. Shelly Sigo. "Florida Issuer Details Cash-Flow Trouble Of $158m Deal," Thomson Financial (www.TM3.com), December 14, 2001.

5. Matthew Vadum, "Most States Should Withstand Recession: S&P Analyst," *The Bond Buyer,* October 30, 2001, p. 1.

6. Robert Lamb and Stephen P. Rappaport, *Municipal Bonds* (New York: McGraw Hill, 1987), p. 85.

7. Lynn Hume, "NFMA Releases Final GO Disclosure Guidelines for Issuers," *The Bond Buyer,* December 7, 2001, np.

8. Wayne Peacock, "Charter Schools—Threat?" *The Bond Buyer,* May 30, 2001, p. 1.

9. Elizabeth Albanese, "Fitch Calls Its Charter School Ratings More 'Attentive' Than Others," *The Bond Buyer,* May 31, 2001, p. 3.

10. Standard & Poor's, *A Complete Look at Monetary Defaults in the 1990's* (New York: Standard & Poor's), p. 11.

11. Standard & Poor's, p. 22.

12. Lamb, p. 91.

13. Elizabeth Albanese, "Arkansas to Sell $60 Million Tobacco Deal Next Week," *The Bond Buyer,* August 30, 2001, p. 4.

CHAPTER 8: CORPORATE AND JUNK BONDS

1. Jeff Somer, "And Then There Were 9: A Shrinking Credit Club," *The New York Times,* July 29, 2001, p. C1.

2. Deborah Solomon, "Under Rising Pressure AT&T's CEO Tries to Hold On to an Icon," *The Wall Street Journal,* November 16, 2001, p. A6 (A1).

3. Christopher B. Steward, "International Bond Markets and Instruments," *The Handbook of Fixed Income Securities* (New York: McGraw Hill, 2000), p. 369.

4. Frank J. Fabozzi, Richard S. Wilson, and Richard Todd, "Corporate Bonds," *The Handbook of Fixed Income Securities* (New York: McGraw Hill, 2000), p. 275.

5. "Corporate Bonds: Debt Delirium," *The Economist,* May 20, 2000, p. 90.

6. Fabozzi, p. 269.

7. Gregory Zuckerman, "AT&T Sells $10.09 Billion of Corporate Bonds As Investors Line Up, Lured by Enticing Yields," *The Wall Street Journal,* November 16, 2001, p. C13.

8. Don Kirk, "Concerns Over Hidden Debt Led to End of Hyundai Deal," *The New York Times,* January 19, 2001, p. C2.

9. Abby Schultz, "Some Municipal Bonds Leave a Corporate Taste," *The*

New York Times, February 10, 2002, p. BU 9.

1 0. Suzanne Kapner, "Global Slump Is Blurring Line at Bank Units for Junk Bonds," *The New York Times,* November 6, 2001, p.W1.

1 1. Phyllis Berman, "In Their Debt," *Forbes,* November 12, 2001, p.138.

1 2. Fabozzi, p. 281.

1 3. Jeremy Stein, "Convertible Bonds as Backdoor Equity Financing," www. financeprofessor.com/summaries/Stein1992ConvBond percent20paper.htm.

CHAPTER 9: BOND LOOK-ALIKES

1. See for example, Allison Bisbey Colter, "Fixed Annuities Stage Comeback", *The Wall Street Journal,* October 8, 2001, p. R31.

CHAPTER 10: THE SELF-DIRECTED APPROACH

1. Henry Sender, "How to Spot Signs of Companies' Distress," *The Wall Street Journal,* December 31, 2001, p. C1–2. Reporting comments of Henry Miller, vice chairman of Dresden Kleinwort Wasserstein, an investment-banking and advisory boutique.

CHAPTER 11: THE MANAGED APPROACH

1. Paul B. Farrell, "Bond Funds Offer 'Danger Zone' Shield," www.cbs.mar ketwatch.com, January 29, 2002.

2. Scott Cooley, "High-Cost Bond Funds Are for the Birds," *Morningstar FundInvestor,* November 30, 2001, www.advisor.Morningstar.com, posted December 26, 2001.

3. Cooley.

4. Aaron Lucchetti, "BP Workers Discover Money-Market Funds Can Carry More Risks Than Expected," *The Wall Street Journal,* December 17, 2001, pp. C1, C17.

5. Joe Mysak, "Events at Heartland Are Only the Beginning," www. Bloomberg.com, October 25, 2000.

6. Lucchetti.

7. "Corporate Bonds: Debt Delirium," *The Economist,* May 20, 2001, p. 90.

8. Albert J. Fredman, "Keeping Costs Low: Intelligent Indexing with Bonds," *American Association of Individual Investors,* January 1, 2001, p. 5.

9. Frances Denmark, "Safe Harbor," *Bloomberg Wealth Manager,* December 2000/January 2001, p. 88.

1 0. John Maier, "Closed-End Funds," *UBS Warburg Research Note,* June 7, 2001.

CHAPTER 12: ASSET ALLOCATION

1. John C. Bogle, *Bogle on Mutual Funds: New Perspectives for the Intelligent Investor* (New York: Dell Books, 1994), p. 235. The 94 percent number that Bogle refers to relies on a study performed by Gary P. Brinson, L. Randolph Hood, and Gilbert L. Beebower, entitled "Determinants of Portfolio Performance," *Financial Analysts Journal*, July–August 1986, pp. 39–44. This study was updated and confirmed with additional data by Gary P. Brinson, Brian D. Singer, and Gilbert L. Beebower, "Determinants of Portfolio Performance II: An Update," *Financial Analysts Journal*, May–June 1991, pp. 40–48.

2. William Bernstein, "Sucker's Bet," *Financial Planning*, April 2001, pp. 183-184.

3. Karen Talley, "After Their Steepest Drop in 50 Years, Dividends Gain Cachet With Investors," *The Wall Street Journal*, January 4, 2002, p. C14.

4. Elizabeth Stanton, "Bond Returns Beat Stocks Over Last Five Years: Mutual Funds," September 25, 2001, Bloomberg News, New York.

INDEX

About Bloomberg

Bloomberg L.P., founded in 1981, is a global information services, news, and media company. Headquartered in New York, the company has nine sales offices, two data centers, and 85 news bureaus worldwide.

Bloomberg, serving customers in 126 countries around the world, holds a unique position within the financial services industry by providing an unparalleled range of features in a single package known as the BLOOMBERG PROFESSIONAL™ service. By addressing the demand for investment performance and efficiency through an exceptional combination of information, analytic, electronic trading, and Straight Through Processing tools, Bloomberg has built a worldwide customer base of corporations, issuers, financial intermediaries, and institutional investors.

BLOOMBERG NEWS®, founded in 1990, provides stories and columns on business, general news, politics, and sports to leading newspapers and magazines throughout the world. BLOOMBERG TELEVISION®, a 24-hour business and financial news network, is produced and distributed globally in seven different languages. BLOOMBERG RADIO℠ is an international radio network anchored by flagship station BLOOMBERG® WBBR 1130 in New York.

In addition to the BLOOMBERG PRESS® line of books, Bloomberg publishes *BLOOMBERG MARKETS*™, *BLOOMBERG PERSONAL FINANCE*®, and *BLOOMBERG WEALTH MANAGER*®. To learn more about Bloomberg, call a sales representative at:

Frankfurt:	49-69-92041-200	São Paulo:	5511-3048-4500
Hong Kong:	85-2-2977-6600	Singapore:	65-212-1000
London:	44-20-7330-7500	Sydney:	61-2-9777-8601
New York:	1-212-318-2200	Tokyo:	81-3-3201-8950
San Francisco:	1-415-912-2980		

FOR IN-DEPTH MARKET INFORMATION and news, visit the Bloomberg website at **www.bloomberg.com,** which draws from the news and power of the BLOOMBERG PROFESSIONAL™ service and Bloomberg's host of media products to provide high-quality news and information in multiple languages on stocks, bonds, currencies, and commodities.

About the Authors

A nationally recognized bond adviser and financial author, **Hildy Richelson** advises clients nationwide about the art of buying fixed-income investments. President of the Scarsdale Investment Group, Ltd., she has coauthored four books and has written numerous articles. She has also been quoted as a bond expert in such publications as the *Wall Street Journal, Money* magazine, and the *Nation's Business.*

Hildy's husband and coauthor **Stan Richelson** is a fee-only financial planner, business adviser, attorney, and personal coach. Coauthor of four books, he has taught courses in investments at the New School for Social Research in New York City and has appeared with Hildy on a variety of radio financial talk shows.

Contact them with your questions and comments:
HildyRichelson@aol.com
StanRichelson@aol.com